Gary Gentile started his diving career in 1970. Since then he has made thousands of decompression dives, over 170 of them on the *Andrea Doria*. He was instrumental in merging mixed-gas diving technology with wreck-diving. In 1994 he participated in a mixed-gas diving expedition to the *Lusitania*, which lies at a depth of 300 feet.

Gary has specialized in wreck-diving and shipwreck research, concentrating his efforts on wrecks along the east coast, from Newfoundland to Key West, and in the Great Lakes. He has compiled an extensive library of books, photographs, drawings, plans, and original source materials on ships and shipwrecks.

Gary has written scores of magazine articles, and has published thousands of photographs in books, periodicals, newspapers, brochures, advertisements, corporate reports, museum displays, postcards, film, and television. He lectures extensively on wilderness and underwater topics, and conducts seminars on advanced wreck-diving techniques, high-tech diving equipment, and wreck photography. He is the author of more than two dozen books: primarily science fiction novels and non-fiction works on diving and nautical and shipwreck history. The Popular Dive Guide Series will eventually cover every major shipwreck along the eastern seaboard.

In 1989, after a five-year battle with the National Oceanic and Atmospheric Administration, Gary won a suit which forced the hostile government agency to issue him a permit to dive the USS *Monitor*, a protected National Marine Sanctuary. Media attention that was focused on Gary's triumphant victory resulted in nationwide coverage of his 1990 photographic expedition to the Civil War ironclad. Gary continues to fight for the right of access to all shipwreck sites.

Above: "Sinking the Stone Fleet in Charleston Harbor." (From *Harper's Weekly*.)
Below: "The Wrecks of the Great Rebellion in the Bay of Charleston - Divers Examining the Bottom of the Harbor." (From *Frank Leslie's Illustrated Newspaper*.)

THE POPULAR DIVE GUIDE SERIES

Shipwrecks of South Carolina and Georgia

by Gary Gentile

GARY GENTILE PRODUCTIONS
P.O. Box 57137
Philadelphia, PA 19111
2003

Gary Gentile Productions
P.O. Box 57137
Philadelphia, PA 19111

Additional copies of this book may be purchased from the same address by sending a check or money order in the amount of $20 U.S. for each copy (postage paid). For information about consulting services, artifact appraisals, workshops, presentations, and a list of available titles that can be ordered by credit card, visit the GGP website:

http://www.ggentile.com

Picture Credits
The front cover illustration of the *Evening Star* is from *Frank Leslie's Illustrated Newspaper*. The photograph of the author on page 1 was taken by Geoffrey Booth. All uncredited photographs were taken by the author. Every attempt has been made to contact the photographers or artists whose work appears in this book, if known, and to ascertain their names if unknown; in some cases, copies of pictures have been in public circulation for so long that the name of the photographer or artist has been lost, or the present whereabouts are impossible to trace. Any information in this regard forwarded to the author will be appreciated. Apologies are made to those whose work must under such circumstances go unrecognized.

The author wishes to acknowledge Pete Manchee for proofreading the galleys.

International Standard Book Number (ISBN) 1-883056-12-8

First Edition

Printed in Hong Kong

CONTENTS

INTRODUCTION

Long before I begin the actual task of writing a volume of my Popular Dive Guide Series, I compile a list of shipwrecks that were lost within the borders that define the geographical parameters of the book. Then I conduct extensive research on those wrecks by visiting archives, museums, and libraries - primarily in Washington, DC, but in other states as well. After doing this preliminary homework, I fine-tune my research efforts by visiting libraries in the locality - sources that might provide additional information that is not available outside of the State that I am covering. I dive the wrecks to conduct the surveys. I also ask about residents who may have particular knowledge of regional maritime history. Invariably, I am disappointed to learn that I have become the expert I sought - that I already know more about shipwrecks in the area than anyone living there.

South Carolina and Georgia present notable exceptions. Two individuals have done exceptional research on historic shipwrecks. The first is my long-time friend and dive buddy Pete Manchee. His shipwreck interests range the entire gamut from the early 1800's to World War Two. In addition to other forms of research, he has meticulously combed the microfilm records of the local newspapers, in the process of which he has unearthed facts that exist nowhere else. He was kind enough to share with me the efforts of his research. Additionally, he and I have spent many hours in speculating about the names of wrecks that have so far defied positive identification. In some cases he confirmed what I already suspected. In other cases he proposed names for wrecks that had not occurred to me. I owe him a great debt of gratitude.

The other person who has perhaps personified the justification for the existence of underwater archaeology is Lee Spence. He has spent a lifetime in the research, location, and salvage of historic shipwrecks, concentrating his efforts largely on the wrecks of the Civil War, and on those that predate the Civil War. He has written numerous books on the subject, but his magnum opus is the compilation of Spence's List: a chronological listing of maritime casualties that is complete with annotations of his primary sources. See the bibliography for a selected list of his titles.

It is important to mention some wrecks that are conspicuous by their absence. First and foremost are the *Hunley* and *Housatonic*. The *Hunley* was a Confederate submarine which, during the Civil War, was the first submarine ever to sink an enemy warship. So much has been written about this famous naval engagement that I could not do justice to the subject in a single chapter. Indeed, an entire book has been written about the *Hunley*. Furthermore, it is not my custom to write about shipwrecks that were salvaged - as the *Hunley* was in 2001. I direct the interested reader to the Suggested Reading list.

Another wreck about which much has been written - including several books - is the *Central America*. The remains of this paddle wheel steamer lie some 200 miles from shore, in 8,000 feet of water. The wreck was the object of a widely publicized robotic salvage operation, involving the recovery of some of the cargo of gold that the *Central America* was transporting when she foundered in a savage storm in 1857, with tremendous loss of life. Again I direct the interested reader to the Suggested Reading list.

The *Nashville* was a Southern-owned side wheel steamer that approached Charleston just as the opening shots of the Civil War were fired on Fort Sumter. As smoke wafted over the beleaguered fort, the *Nashville* charged past Union warships for protection in the harbor. The Confederate government then purchased the side wheeler from her owners, armed her, and outfitted her as a blockade runner. The *Nashville* successfully broke through the Union blockade and proceeded to England. After numerous adventures, the *Nashville* (renamed *Rattlesnake*) evaded capture by steaming up the Ogeechee River, south of Savannah. She was trapped there for several months until the Union ironclad *Montauk* destroyed her by gun fire, in 1863. A book on her history and archaeological salvage is given in the Suggested Reading list.

As usual, my research has revealed a few surprises and has dispelled some parochial myths. One such myth concerns the Norwegian vessel *Torungen*. In 1979, divers claimed that a wreck known locally as the Georgetown Wreck was the *Torungen*. This identification seems unlikely. According to Naval documents, the *Torungen* was on a passage from Halifax to Charleston when she was torpedoed by a German U-boat on February 22, 1942. "A lifeboat with the body of the chief engineer was picked up off Nova Scotia on March 2nd, but nothing more was heard of her crew." The distance from Georgetown to Nova Scotia is a thousand miles: a long way to drift in eight days. To be sure, dead men tell no tales, and a vessel that is lost with no survivors leaves little trace of its demise. In this case, however, there were observers on hand to verify the sinking: Korvettenkapitan Heinrich Lehmann-Willenbrook and the crew of the *U-96*. According to official records, "*U-96* identified the *Torungen* clearly." The position ascertained by the U-boat was 44° north latitude, 63.30° west longitude; this position is south of Halifax and east of Cape Sable (which lies at the southwestern tip of Nova Scotia). Additionally, the wartime records of the Eastern Sea Frontier do not list the *Torungen* as a casualty that occurred within its sphere of operations.

The belief that the *Torungen* may have gone down off the South Carolina coast could have originated from a wreck list compiled by the Hydrographic Office either during or shortly after World War Two. Confusion may have arisen from an erroneous report which stated that the *Torungen* was torpedoed on February 26 - four days after her actual date of loss - by which time the vessel could have proceeded a thousand miles toward her destination. From this information, the divers in 1979 may have concluded that the wreck that they "found and investigated" was indeed the *Torungen* - despite the fact that it was only 90 feet in length instead of 276. Today, the Georgetown Wreck is the centerpiece of the Georgetown Reef. (See Artificial Reef Wrecks, below.)

Another vessel that is shown on the charts as a wreck symbol is the *Daventry*, which ran aground on December 28, 1900. The position of this British steamship was plotted as 32° 41' 48" North, 79°49'12". Readers are cautioned not to look for this wreck. On January 2, 1901, it was reported that the *Daventry*, "from Hamburg via Shields, went ashore inside of the south jetty at Charleston, SC, Dec 28, but was afterward hauled off without lightering." It is anyone's guess why NOAA has kept the *Daventry* posted on modern charts despite the fact that she was salvaged.

Off the Georgia coast, two tankers were torpedoed with an hour of each other on April 8, 1942: the *Esso Baton Rouge* and the *Oklahoma*. Both vessels sank as a result. However, both vessels were raised, repaired, and returned to service. Local lore claims that these vessels still lie undiscovered on the bottom. This may be true, but their remains do not lie off the coast of Georgia. The *Esso Baton Rouge* was torpedoed and sunk again, on February 23, 1943, this time in the South Atlantic. The *Oklahoma* was also torpedoed and sunk again, on March 28, 1945, off the coast of South America.

One wreck for which researchers and wreck-hunters should maintain vigilance is the *Amanda Winants*. She was built as a steam tug in 1863, and measured 131 feet in length. These unimpressive statistics assume significance with the addition of the fact that at the time of her loss - in late September 1874 - she was owned by the Coast Wrecking Company and was employed as a salvage vessel. She had on board a complete wrecking outfit whose value was estimated at $25,000: the same value that was placed upon her hull. In addition to ropes, pumps, and derricks, this wrecking outfit contained several sets of hard-hat diver's dress, complete with brass helmets!

The *Amanda Winants* departed New York for Key West, Florida on September 23. Captain C.M. Quinn was in command. She put in at Norfolk, Virginia, departed that port on September 29 - and steamed straight into the teeth of a northbound hurricane. Neither she nor her crew of sixteen souls was ever seen again. Since the hurricane struck Georgetown on September 28, the assumption was made that she foundered in the storm in that vicinity. According to the Steamboat Inspection Service, "A boat, with life-preservers in it marked with the name of the steamer, was afterward picked up." The report did not state where, but newspapers speculated that the tug "went down somewhere between Cape Lookout and Frying Pan light-ship."

The *Amanda Winants* will be distinguishable by her walking beam engine and paddle wheels.

Civil War Wrecks

An entire book could be written just on shipwrecks of the Civil War. A great deal of naval activity occurred off the coasts of South Carolina and Georgia between 1861 and 1865. As a result, a large number of vessels of all descriptions were sunk by various and sundry means. Most of these vessels went down in shallow water not far from shore. Some, such as blockade runners, were run up on the beach in order to avoid capture. Others, the two stone fleets in particular, were scuttled outside of Charleston in order to prevent Union warships from entering the harbor. Still others were lost in naval engagements along the coast. Charleston harbor and Savannah harbor are littered with the remains of ships of all descriptions.

Despite the rich history of these casualties of Civil War, the present volume does not seek to cover each of these wrecks in detail. To do so would take too much space away from the many other events that occurred during two centuries of maritime commerce: events that constitute the primary thrust of this book. Besides, a great deal has already been written about the naval battles of the Civil War and the consequent losses. More than three dozen sunken vessels may be found in the Charleston area alone: in the rivers, in the harbor, and outside the harbor approaches. And this figure does not include the stone fleets. Once again I direct the interested reader to the Suggested Reading list for other reference materials. Lee Spence has been especially prolific in this regard.

The locations of these wrecks are not always known with precision, and even if known, the wrecks may not be detectable by ordinary means, despite the fact that loran or GPS coordinates exist for their locations and the wrecks are marked on navigation charts. For example, the ram *Georgia* is covered with two feet of mud. No spike will appear on a depth recorder, no colored blips on a fish finder. In this case, the Corps of Engineers determined that "vessels will ground out before hitting wreck, therefore this is a non-dangerous wreck." Symbols on the charts may be added or removed, as ongoing surveys advise.

Other Civil War wrecks present considerable relief. The Union monitor *Patapsco* "protrudes 8-10 feet above bottom." The blockade runner *Constance* was located by wire drag "with a least depth of 4 ft verified by leadline and divers." One of the stone fleet wrecks was found to have "a least depth of 9 feet at MLW [mean low water]. Obstruction verified by leadline and divers. Item determined to be a barge loaded with stone from the Civil War era." Both the *Georgiana* and the *Mary Bowers* presented 6 feet of relief in 1989, when Lee Spence was in the process of excavating them.

Although some sources declare that the *Keokuk* and *Weehawkin*, for example, show relief, other sources proclaim that they are completely buried. In actuality, these inshore wrecks come and go because the bottom is ever moving, sand bars are ever shifting. "Here today, gone tomorrow" is only a slight exaggeration.

Unidentified Wrecks

Appended in the back of the book is a section on wreck sites that are unidentified. The purpose of this section is twofold: to describe the sites for divers and anglers, and to present information that may lead to the wrecks' eventual identification. Some wrecks will be found in this section listed by their local names even though a tentative identification has been made. This is for readers who are unaware of these identities and who will therefore not be able to locate a description of the wreck. If a site has been identified (either positively or tentatively), a notation will direct the reader to the appropriate chapter where its history is related or its description is given.

Artificial Reef Wrecks

Accidents and the forces of nature still take their toll, but not with the regularity that has been shown in the past. Lately, a program of environmental enhancement has added to the number of wrecks that litter the seabed, as outdated vessels are scuttled to create artificial reefs on which marine flora and fauna can aggregate. These fishing havens are needed for communities whose offshore features are nothing but vast, undulating, underwater deserts.

Artificial reefs provide a substrate to which marine fouling organisms can adhere. Coral, sponges, barnacles, mollusks, sea anemones, and hydroids are filter feeders: they siphon living microplankton from the rich organic soup that flows with the current. Tiny baitfish live among this marine encrustation; juveniles of bigger fish hide there. Worms and crabs inhabit the substrate. These creatures form the bottom links in the food chain.

Large predators are attracted to shipwrecks and other reef materials by the sounds that are emitted as moving water is disturbed by the uneven surfaces. This is similar in principle to cavitation: the noise created by the collapse of tiny bubbles as a rotating propeller cleaves through the water. Fish hear this harmonic signature from far away, and home in on it. Once they locate the source, many fish decide to stay because of the food that is available and the protection that is offered by the convoluted structures. The wreck or reef has become a habitat.

These wrecks become gathering places for lobsters, weakfish, spotted seatrout, black sea bass (blackfish), sheepshead, snapper, porgies, grouper, cobia, both red and black drum, and a large assortment of many-hued tropicals that ride the Gulf Stream. One might see (or catch) pelagics such as barracuda, spadefish, triggerfish, pompano, jacks, mackerel, scamp, tomtate, tunny, porgy, and bluefish. Turtles and huge southern stingrays are frequent visitors. And on rare occasions one might even catch a glimpse of a dolphin or sailfish.

Both South Carolina and Georgia have aggressive programs for the creation of artificial reefs, and have had for many years. Most of these reefs are constructed of concrete in different forms: from the rubble of demolished wharfs, bridges, and roadways, to pre-cast structures in the shape of pipes, pallet balls, and tetrahedrons. Military tanks made of the finest steel armor are guaranteed to last a long time under water. Armored personnel carriers have been deployed strategically. But perhaps the greatest artificial reef materials are the hulls of outdated vessels. Not only do these sunken hulls provide the highest relief, but their sheer size ensures that fish will find a wide variety of suitable habitats.

Artificial reef wrecks may be the sites most visited by anglers and divers alike. For anglers, wrecks that have not progressed far along the path of deterioration to total compaction, offer a range of game fish from bottom dwellers to pelagic predators. For divers, intact hulls offer rare visions of shipwrecks the way the non-diving public believes that accidental wrecks appear - thanks to the fabulous visions presented by Hollywood. Plus, there is the added measure of excitement that derives from the exploration of the corridors and vast interior compartments. Divers should not overlook the exploratory value of these wrecks.

A special section at the back of the book provides some basic information about the large artificial reef wrecks, such as the type and size of the vessels. This will enable anglers and divers to determine which wrecks they would like to visit. Most barges and tugboats are included in the descriptive section, although small vessels such as landing craft are excluded. All artificial reef wrecks appear in the Loran/GPS list.

Divers should note that Georgia's near-shore wrecks are particularly prone to poor visibility, sometimes ranging from zero to several inches. This is due to the muddy run-off from coastal rivers. Those wrecks that are typically bad in this regard lie in 50 feet of water or less. The visibility increases at around the 60-foot depth. The visibility is best in summer - although this is not necessarily the best time for fish (either for catching or for observing). The prime fishing season is May, early June, and October - when the migrants are moving through the area and when the water temperature is lower. Visibility is adversely affected by storm events, because large particulate matter is lifted off the bottom and suspended in the water column.

Loran and GPS Coordinates

I have collected these "numbers" from a variety of sources, largely from boat captains and the artificial reef departments. A few have been passed on to me from other individuals. As the Romans used to say, "Caveat emptor" ("Let the buyer beware"). In this case, "Let the user beware." I can vouch for the majority of the numbers in the list, either because I have been on the site when the readings were taken, or because I trust the boat captain who was the primary source, or because I believe implicitly in the accuracy of coordinates that were published by government agencies.

I have suspicions about a few of the numbers: generally, those loran numbers that I collected many years ago and for which I do not have GPS numbers. However, some of the wrecks for which I have only loran numbers are artificial reefs (designated by the letters "AR" after the name of the wreck). This is due to the fact that when South Carolina's artificial reef department switched completely to GPS, loran numbers were not given for comparison in the updated lists. Thus, I was unable to correlate (on paper) which site given as a loran number referred to which site given as a GPS number.

Loran is slowly being phased out of use. At this point in the conversion from loran to GPS, many boat owners have receiving units for both systems on board. I suggest that the user employ a loran unit to locate the sites for which I do not give GPS numbers, then write the GPS number in the appropriate space.

The wrecks for which I give only GPS numbers are artificial reefs for which loran numbers were not recorded by South Carolina's artificial reef department.

Beware of store-bought charts that give precise coordinates for inaccurate locations. Just because a number is given to the third decimal place does not mean that the number is accurate; it means only that the number is precise. If the number was based upon the wrong position, the three-digit precision is worse than useless - it is misleading. One chart that I saw gave numbers for the *Virginius* that were a mile off. Once again, caveat emptor.

Fossil Hunting

Generally, the volumes of the Popular Dive Guide Series do not divert from their fundamental focus to discuss non-shipwreck sites. But in this case I will make an exception. Fossils are related to artifacts in that the represent relics of the past - nature's past instead of mankind's past. The vast majority of fossil hunting in South Carolina is conducted underwater: specifically in the Cooper River north of Charleston. Other rivers contain fossils, but they are not yet as popular or as well explored. The primary lure that brings divers to pan the river bed is the large concentration of shark's teeth - some up to seven inches in length! These dental masticators are millions of years old. Less common fossil finds include mastodon molars, saber-toothed tiger fangs, and ground sloth teeth.

Anyone visiting the Charleston area to explore the offshore wreck sites should take the time to dive the Cooper River. Not only do fossil shark's teeth abound, but the river bottom is littered with antique bottles, clay pipes, and china shards. Most of the diving in the Cooper River is conducted from small boats, sometimes on the drift. But there are near-shore sites as well, and these can be accessed easily by wading into the water from the banks. Once again, I direct the interested reader to the bibliography to see the only book on the subject.

According to the South Carolina Underwater Antiquities Act, "a Hobby license is required for persons wishing to conduct temporary, intermittent, recreational, small scale, non-commercial search and recovery of submerged property. It is a state-wide license. Recovery of submerged property must be by hand and must not involve mechanical devices or excavation. Hobby divers may recover a reasonable number of artifacts and fossils from submerged lands over which the state has sovereign control, but may recover only ten artifacts a day from a shipwreck site."

A hobby license is as cheap and as easy to obtain as a hunting or fishing license. To request an application, write to the South Carolina Institute of Archaeology and Anthropology, at P.O. Box 12448, Charleston, SC 29422; or call 803-762-6105; or call the Columbia office at 803-777-8170, 803-734-0567, or 803-799-1963. Allow two weeks for processing.

Below are a few of the fossils that Pete Manchee recovered from the Cooper River. At left is a mastodon molar. At right are a ground sloth jaw bone, three large sharks teeth, and a saber-toothed tiger fang.

Lionfish

The Popular Dive Guide Series covers marine life only tangentially, usually by means of fish photos that are used as fillers. But in this case I will make an exception - not only as a scientific observation but as a warning.

I specialize in shipwrecks, not in the fish that inhabit them. My species identification skills are severely lacking. I know my limitations and am willing to take advice from those who are more knowledgeable. In the mid 1990's, after returning from a dive to the Ore Freighter, I waxed ecstatic about the incredibly colorful sculpin or sea raven that I had seen on the bottom. After describing the long feathery fins and the vivid red and purple hues, someone exclaimed, "That's a lionfish!"

I was then informed that lionfish were venomous, and that a sting from one of the spines in the dorsal fin could be lethal. Sheepishly, I related how I had reached out to pet the multihued beauty, but had changed my mind before touching it because I had not wanted to disturb it.

Lionfish are indigenous to the tropical waters of the Pacific Ocean. They are not supposed to reside in the Atlantic Ocean - but they do. Mine was not the first sighting. And since then the lionfish has been proliferating and extending its habitat. There have been sightings everywhere between Florida and South Carolina, and, most recently, as far north as Morehead City, North Carolina.

Initially, marine biologists scoffed at reports of lionfish sightings, claiming that they were "anecdotal." In scientific lingo, "anecdotal" means "imaginary" or, with more forgiveness, "unfounded." "Anecdotal" is an arrogant term that scientists apply to sightings made by members of the general populace who do not possess a Ph. D. in their specific field. When the number of anecdotal sightings reaches some artificial critical threshold, scientists may begrudgingly accept the possibility that the reports have some basis in reality. Sometimes, when a scientist subsequently makes his own observation, he claims to have made a startling discovery - a discovery of a fact that many other observers have known for years. Such is the scientific ego.

Lionfish exist off the eastern seaboard of the United States. How they got here is a problem for scientists to solve. Perhaps they escaped from an aquarium, or were thrown out with the fish bowl water, or were released intentionally. We will probably never know. But as lionfish have no natural enemies in their new environment, the chances are that their numbers will continue to increase. I have seen them on the Ore Freighter on every dive since that initial observation. You can observe them for yourself. But do *not* try to pet them!

To see what a lionfish looks like, look at the top photo on the back cover.

Appreciations

As usual, I have several people to thank for their kind assistance in my research and survey work. Alphabetically, they are:

Christopher Amer, the current State Underwater Archaeologist, granted me access to the State's files on the *William Lawrence*, provided background information on the litigation that resulted in the State's assumption of ownership of the wreck, and offered memories and insights that were not in the written record.

Henry Ansley, Georgia's Artificial Reef Coordinator, furnished valuable insights about fishing and diving conditions on Georgia's artificial reefs, as well as some interesting background information on the Liberty ships.

Buddy Dennis, the affable captain of the *Safari IV*, provided laughs as well as location information.

Lynn Harris, a State archaeologist working in the Charleston office, provided background information on the *William Lawrence*. She also suggested additional sources of information.

Danny Long, on a last-minute note, transported me to several wrecks aboard his boat, the *Shark Attack*.

Pete Manchee - local diver, researcher, and long-time soul mate - shared with me his extensive files on South Carolina shipwrecks: files that took him years to accumulate. He also engaged in some additional research at my request. We spent many, many hours discussing the histories and mysteries of unidentified wrecks in our efforts to put names to some of these well-known dive sites. We also did archival and microfilm research together at local facilities.

Robert Martore, South Carolina's Artificial Reef Coordinator, furnished background information on the State's artificial reef program, and added much useful information about the artificial reef wrecks and their condition today. He let me go through his photo file and select some images for inclusion in this book.

Andy Ogburn, part owner of Wateree Dive Center, has supported my research and survey efforts throughout the years that I have dedicated to producing the current volume. His suggestions and insights have been invaluable.

Cameron Sebastian, owner of Coastal Scuba and the *Safari IV*, has been instrumental in putting me on wrecks that I needed to survey. In addition to the encouragement he offered for this book project, he furnished background data on some of the more popular artificial reef wrecks.

Mark Woods, owner of Freedom at Depth Diving, inspired me to add a section on fossil hunting.

Shipwrecks of South Carolina

The sinking of the *Weehawkin*. (From *Leslie's Illustrated Civil War*.)

CITY OF RICHMOND

Built: 1913   Sunk: October 5, 1964
Previous names: None   Depth: 50 feet
Gross tonnage: 1,923   Dimensions: 261' x 53' x 14'
Type of vessel: Passenger vessel   Power: Oil-fired steam
Builder: Maryland Steel Company, Sparrows Point, Maryland
Owner: Occidental Restaurant, Baltimore, Maryland
Port of registry: Baltimore, Maryland
Cause of sinking: Foundered
Loran 45343.8 / 59925.6   GPS 33-01.900 / 78-55.423

For nearly half a century, the *City of Richmond* led a venerated career as a luxurious passenger vessel, carrying people and freight from port to port along the protected waters of the Chesapeake Bay. The single-screw steamer was built in 1913 for the Chesapeake Steamship Company. The hull was constructed of steel, while the upper decks were fabricated entirely of wood. The three upper decks ran nearly the full length of the ship. Four water-tube boilers generated steam for the 4-cylinder, triple expansion, reciprocating steam engine.

The *City of Richmond* could accommodate 350 passengers in such splendor that she and her sister ship, the *City of Annapolis*, were often described as "floating hotels." A contemporary brochure provided the following description:

"Equipped with telephones in every room, they have all the latest improvements which can add to the comfort and safety of their passengers. The staterooms are well furnished, and all contain running water, electric lights, etc. Many of them have double brass beds and connect with bathrooms or shower baths. There are also a number of suites of two rooms with bath between. As a matter of fact, there are more bathrooms on the steamers of the Chesapeake Steamship Company than on any other line running on the bay. All bathrooms have both hot and cold fresh and salt water.

"The dining rooms are located on the gallery (upper) deck forward and have accommodations for 70 people.

"The line is noted for the excellence of its cuisine and has achieved a deservedly fine reputation on this account. Where the quality of the food is always of the very best, properly cooked by first-class chefs, and served by competent stewards, meals on this line are truly a pleasure which the passengers thoroughly appreciate.

"A large smoking room on the main deck and a music room on the gallery deck add to attractions of these beautiful vessels and nothing has been overlooked to make them stand in a class by themselves."

The anticipated service of the *City of Richmond* created quite a sensation, as noted in a local newspaper: "The Governors of two States, together with the

In her heyday. (Courtesy of the Steamship Historical Society of America.)

Mayors of Baltimore and Richmond and several hundred prominent citizens, will be the guests of the Chesapeake Steamship Company to-morrow at the festivities to mark the maiden voyage of the palatial bay steamer, the *City of Richmond*, which is to ply between Baltimore and West Point in connection with the Southern Railway from Richmond. No expense has been spared by the company in preparing for the entertainment of its guests."

Throughout the years, the routes that were traveled by the *City* sisters were changed to meet demands. Sometimes they plied a course between Washington and York, sometimes between Baltimore and Norfolk (with an intermediate stop at Old Point Comfort). The *City of Richmond* generally ran opposite her running mate. For example, on the Baltimore-West Point route, the *City of Richmond* departed from Baltimore at the same time that the *City of Annapolis* departed from West Point. They generally saluted each other midway, near Smith Point. On February 24, 1927, thick fog banks concealed portions of the Chesapeake Bay, with the result that the *City* sisters collided when they should have saluted. The *City of Annapolis* sank, while the *City of Richmond* returned to Baltimore heavily damaged, and carrying the passengers and crew members of both vessels. (For details, see *Shipwrecks of Virginia*, by this author.)

Other accidents occurred during her fifty years of service. In January 1920, the *City of Richmond* sideswiped the freighter Texan in a particularly dense fog. The *City of Richmond* was taken out of service while $25,000 worth of damage was repaired. In October 1923, she rammed and sank the schooner *James H. Hargrave* off Point No Point, in a thick fog. In February 1961, the *City of Richmond* was beset in the ice. She had to be freed by the Coast Guard cutter *Conifer*, which crisscrossed in front of the *City of Richmond* in order to break through the ice pack. Other "fender benders" dotted her career.

Perhaps the most ignominious accident of all occurred when the *City of Richmond* sank at her own dock, in June 1915. The crew was sleeping soundly as the tide dropped during the night. The vessel slipped partway under the wharf. When the tide rose, the rail got caught and the vessel listed. Water entered ports that had been left open by careless longshoremen after unloading the cargo. "All crewmen escaped safely." It took two weeks to pump the water out of the hull and to refloat the *City of Richmond*. Then she had to be towed to dry-dock for repair.

In 1930, the *City of Richmond* was converted from coal-fired boilers to oil-fired boilers. These new boilers provided an environment that was free from clogging coal dust, and enabled the company to reduce the number of boiler-room personnel. (Another source gives the year of conversion to oil-burning boilers as 1944.)

On June 20, 1941, all the holdings of the Chesapeake Steamship Company - including the *City of Richmond* - were purchased by the Baltimore Steam Packet Company, better known as the Old Bay Line.

In 1946, the *City of Richmond* became the first vessel to ply the inland waterways with a newfangled device that had been developed during the war: radar. This enabled the vessel to operate more safely at night and in fog. If she had been fitted with such electronic detection equipment in 1927, collision with her sister ship may have been prevented; and other collisions may have been avoided.

Cheap and reliable train travel brought a reduction in the bay passenger business. Then the proliferation of buses and automobiles brought a further reduction in business. Finally, in 1962, the Old Bay Line - the last line operating passenger vessels on the Chesapeake Bay - ceased operation. The company's three remaining vessels were purchased by B.B. Wills. In 1964, Wills sold the *City of Richmond* to the Occidental Restaurant, which owned a posh eatery and catering service in Washington, DC. The owners intended to send the *City of Richmond* to the Virgin Islands, where she was to be converted to a floating restaurant in Charlotte Amalie, in St. Thomas. The company envisioned plans that were grandiose, but practical and ahead of their time.

The *City of Richmond* was to be air-conditioned throughout, and all the staterooms were to be renovated. The top deck was to be converted to a night club "with the islands' biggest dance floor." The onboard restaurants would "serve the Occidental menu in a manner and atmosphere similar to the Occidental." The lifeboats would be refurbished "as motorized launches to take guests on trips to Honeymoon Bay and other secluded coves around St. Thomas."

The ship that was once referred to as a "floating hotel" was to become one in actuality: a combination hotel, restaurant, and night club, all rolled into one. The *City of Richmond* would be permanently docked "in a resort area which has been on the expensive side." However, without exorbitant land and construction costs, Occidental could charge moderate rates that would "cater to people who normally couldn't afford to think of the islands."

The owners planned to rename the *City of Richmond* the S.S. *Occidental*,

The owners planned to rename the *City of Richmond* the S.S. *Occidental*, with Charlotte Amalie as her new home port.

The *City of Richmond* was dry-docked at Bethlehem Steel. The hull was inspected and prepared for the long haul to the Virgin Islands, which was estimated to require eight to ten days. The propeller was removed to make for easier towing; the rudder was locked in the center position. Afterward, the holds were loaded with 700 tons of cargo: items that were needed for the final renovations. These items included "two sets of soda-fountain equipment, two trucks, lumber, doors, tiling, piping, valves, cafeteria equipment, &c." When everything was shipshape, the *City of Richmond* departed from Baltimore at the end of a hawser that was secured to the towing bitt of the tug *Lamberts Point*. Tug and tow arrived at Norfolk on August 13, 1964. Hurricanes Gladys and Hilda kept the *City of Richmond* in port for more than a month.

Not until September 23 did the tug *Sea Eagle* depart from Norfolk with the *City of Richmond* in tow. The two vessels proceeded southward at about six knots. The *Sea Eagle's* engine broke down off North Carolina, so she put out a call for help. The Coast Guard cutter *Chilula* raced to the rescue, and succeeded in towing both vessels to Morehead City. The *City of Richmond* waited a week for the arrival of another tug, the *Carville*. On October 3, the *City of Richmond* was once again secured to the end of a hawser.

Onboard the *City of Richmond* were a haphazard crew of six and one Carlos Queceda. Queceda had worked as the maitre d' of the Occidental Restaurant. He was going to oversee the ship's renovations, and then take on the job of operational manager when the S.S. *Occidental* opened for business. The riding master was Olin Smokey Stover, who "had never been to sea before except as a passenger." When the weather turned bad, no one aboard the *City of Richmond* was able to handle the situation with any degree of competence. For example, when one of the cargo doors was bashed in by big seas, and the ship began taking on water in great quantities, the crew chose to cry for help rather than to attempt to stem the flood and work the bilge pumps.

U.S. District Judge John MacKenzie wrote the following remarks pursuant to the subsequent lawsuit: "The inexperience of the riding crew was a major factor in the catastrophe. The lack of experience of the crew is plainly shown in their conduct in the darkness in the hours just prior to the sinking of the vessel. For instance, Queceda . . . , on the bridge of the *City of Richmond*, which was tossing about at the end of a 1,000-foot towline to the *Carville*, when unable to attract the attention of the *Carville* from the *City of Richmond*, suggested that he get out his rifle and attempt to shoot out the running lights of the *Carville*. The impossibility of such a task and its absolute inappropriateness is illustrative of the condition of panic existing aboard the *City of Richmond* in those early morning hours.

"The inexperience of the crew is further illustrated by the fact that the master of the riding crew Stover, about midnight on 4 October 1964, upon finding one of the trucks coming loose from its secured position on the cargo deck, chose to sit in the cab with his foot on the brake for ten minutes to keep the truck from moving, rather than seeing to its permanent securing and attending to the more pressing matter of the cargo port.

"The boarding up and securing of the hull openings and the stowage of cargo were improperly directed and supervised by the United States Salvage Association. As an example of this, motor vehicles and equipment being transported were not properly fastened to the cargo deck and came loose on the very first day of heavy weather after leaving Morehead City."

The penultimate struggle began at 2:30 in the morning of October 5. In seas that were reported to be running from ten to fourteen feet in height, the *Carville* turned north toward the Cape Fear River. At the same time, she notified the Coast Guard that the *City of Richmond* was taking on water and could not stop the leak. Soon afterward, the *Carville* altered course for Georgetown.

The Coast Guard dispatched the cutter *Cape Morgan* from Charleston. The tug and her tow limped toward shore for the next couple of hours. Shortly after 5 o'clock, the *City of Richmond* listed sharply in her final death throes. The tug got in position to take off the riding crew. The men leaped from the tow to the tug. Queceda, last to leave the sinking ship, had the presence of mind to take his briefcase, which contained important records and documents as well as his personal papers and credit cards.

Survivors reported that the *City of Richmond* "capsized," and "turned turtle," but neither description fitted the circumstance. They also reported that as the vessel sank, she "busted up like it had exploded," injuring two crew members with flying glass and debris. Trapped air "blew out the entire starboard side of the ship." At 5:23 a.m., the *Carville* advised the Coast Guard that the *City of Richmond* had sunk. The *Carville* then resumed her course for Georgetown, where she landed everyone safely. Queceda's credit cards came in handy: he used them to purchase new clothes for Queceda and the men, and to obtain lodging in a local hotel.

The *Cape Morgan* arrived at the scene of the catastrophe at 6:35 a.m. That the *City of Richmond* had not capsized was made evident by the fact that her smokestack protruded some twenty feet out of the water. The submerged hull constituted a menace to navigation. The *Cape Morgan* remained on site in seas that her captain called laconically "not altogether pleasing." After several hours of buffeting by monstrous waves, the stack was knocked down. Only a slowly spreading oil slick remained to mark the ship's final resting place. At 11:23, the *Cape Morgan* was recalled.

Storms washed the upper deck away within two days.

Judge MacKenzie rendered his opinion as to the cause of the loss: "In summary, the Court finds that the *City of Richmond* was unseaworthy on at least four counts; namely (a) the preparation for sea in the sealing of the elevator shafts was improperly planned, supervised and executed, (b) the cargo was improperly stowed and secured and the supervision of such stowage and securing was improper, (c) the provisions for pumping in the location of the pumps and lack of installed suction pipes to the lower holds was improper, and (d) with the ballasting and heavy cargo, the *City of Richmond* was overloaded from four to ten inches on a vessel of very limited freeboard.

"The crew was incompetent both in its failing to meet the requirements as to the number of rated AB Seamen aboard, and also in its failure to have been even cursorily instructed in the duties which would reasonably be expected to arise to a seaman as a matter of course. There were specifically no instructions to the men on board in how to use the pumps, or how or when to sound for water in the holds, and no instructions to inspect the interior of the ship and the stowed cargo for signs of shifting, nor any instructions in emergency procedures for damage control. The pumps themselves had never been tested on board the vessel. The weather encountered was not out of the ordinary for the area and the season of the year."

This opinion absolved the tug company from blame.

On October 7, Occidental formally abandoned the wreck to the underwriters (who had insured the hull for $75,000). The underwriters retained the salvage firm of Merritt-Chapman & Scott to conduct a survey of the wreck, with the idea of engaging the company to raise the hull on a "no cure, no pay" basis. The company conducted the examination, but declined to accept the job offer under the financial conditions that were proffered. Nor did the company display any interest in salvaging the cargo.

No attempt was made to demolish the wreck. According to a Coast Guard memorandum, "The Corps of Engineers, U.S. Army, reported they would take no action since the wreck lies outside of territorial waters. The Coast Guard decided to mark it as a menace to navigation. On 9 October, 1964, a Coast Guard helicopter from Coast Guard Air Station, Savannah relocated the wreck, and the tender class cutter *Papaw* established *City of Richmond* Lighted Bell Buoy WR2A in position 33-10.8N 78-55W with the wreck bearing 290° true, 100 yards from the buoy. This is an 8 X 26 buoy (8 foot diameter, 26 feet long) with a 200 MM lantern displaying a quick flashing red light. The Coast Guard knows of no plans to salvage the vessel."

The International Underwater Research Corporation displayed some interest in salvaging the hull and cargo, but that interest soon evaporated. The wreck was left to the devices of nature.

Researchers should note that in 1964 both the Merchant Vessels of the United States and the Record of the American Bureau of Ships listed the owner of the *City of Richmond* as the Tolchester Lines, not B.B. Wills. In 1964, the *City of Richmond* was listed as a steamship, whereas in 1965 she was listed as a barge. A barge is a vessel without means of propulsion. A steamship whose engine was removed is therefore a barge. The implication from this listing is that the propelling machinery of the *City of Richmond* was removed. However, such is not the case, as the engine is the most prominent feature on the wreck today.

The huge, quadruple expansion reciprocating steam engine rises to a least depth of 35 feet above a seabed which has a maximum depth (in washouts under the hull) of 52 feet. Thus the engine towers more than 15 feet above the surrounding sand. Abaft the engine lie four immense boilers in pairs. These are not typical Scotch boilers with integral furnaces, but rectangular boilers resting on individual furnaces, most of whose fire brick sides are still standing. Each boiler is topped by a cylindrical condenser that extends longitudinally. Parts of each boiler have rusted away to reveal the copper tubing.

The center portion of the wreck consists of approximately two-thirds of the length of the hull, and appears to stand upright. Yet at one time the entire wreck may have listed partway on its side. Both the bow and stern sections have broken away, each separated from the main wreckage by several feet of sand. At the present time, these extreme sections clearly list at least 30° to port. Also, most of the loose artifacts (tiles, silver platters, and sheets of blue slate) rest against the port side of the hull. Thus the most likely collapse chronology has the whole wreck originally listing to port. After the bow and stern broke away, the machinery spaces re-settled nearly upright. Then the sides of the hull toppled outboard. The upper portion of the rudder can be seen beneath the overhang in the stern.

I am told that most of the decks existed as late as the 1980's, and that Hurricane Hugo (which passed through the area in 1989) flattened the hull and generally demolished the wreck. Certainly, the *City of Richmond* exhibits but a sad remnant of her former grandeur. Yet as a shipwreck the site is visually stunning, and offers a rare example of Chesapeake Bay excursion steamer construction type.

The wreck is marked by the WR-2A buoy.

Courtesy of the Steamship Historical Society of America.

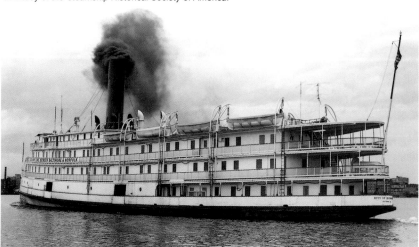

CITY OF SAVANNAH

Built: 1877
Previous names: None
Gross tonnage: 2,029
Type of vessel: Iron-hulled screw steamer
Builder: John Roach & Son, Chester, Pennsylvania
Owner: Ocean Steam Ship Company (Savannah Line), New York, NY
Port of registry: Savannah, Georgia
Cause of sinking: Blown ashore
Location: Off Hunting Island

Sunk: August 28, 1893
Depth: 10 feet
Dimensions: 254' x 38' x 24'
Power: Coal-fired steam

The *City of Savannah* was a stereotypic nineteenth century steamer, and a prime example of Yankee technological ingenuity. Her hull was fabricated from the strongest iron, with riveted construction throughout. Her spar deck was built entirely of iron, and her main deck partially of iron. "The deck frames were all fastened in the most secure manner known in naval architecture." She was powered by a compound engine that generated 350 horsepower. Steam was generated by four tubular, cylindrical boilers. "The capacity of her coal bunker was 600 tons."

"Her propeller was the Hirsch patent, having four blades capable of being removed, either singly or together, from the hub to which they were fastened by bolts. She had two donkey boilers and engines used in clearing the bilge, supplying the main boilers with water, and in case of fire. The vessel had three decks, besides the hurricane deck." Six watertight compartments provided a strong measure security against flooding in case of a hull breach.

Mechanical marvel that she was, the steamer nevertheless boasted two masts that were brig rigged. She was capable of spreading some 15,000 square feet of canvas, but it is unlikely that she ever relied solely on the wind as a means of propulsion. In 1877, when the *City of Savannah* was built, the rigging of sails was a holdover from early steamboating days, when steam engines were unreliable and were likely to break down at the most inconvenient times. The presence of sails was more of a backup that was designed to bolster the confidence of the passengers. Sometimes, however, sails were rigged in order to enhance the vessel's steering characteristics in contrary winds.

The *City of Savannah* could accommodate 150 first class passengers in elegant splendor, and an additional number in steerage in less opulent settings.

"Her dining saloon was 40 feet long and 29 feet wide. The interior was handsome in its appointments. The panneling [sic] was of mahogany, French walnut and amaranth, trimmed with gold, handsomely moulded and highly polished. All of the wood work was polished to the highest degree, and involved the outlay of many thousands of dollars. The ceiling of the saloons was frescoed to conform with the elegance of the apartments. The mirrors, glassware, table linen, silver service, carpets and general appointments were rich."

When she first went into service, the *City of Savannah* operated for the New York and Savannah Line. She then worked for a while on the Philadelphia Line. Then came a stint as "an emergency ship, running wherever the service of the company demanded." Toward the end of her career, she ran regularly between Boston, Massachusetts and Savannah, Georgia, for the Ocean Steam Ship Company.

The first major catastrophe in which the *City of Savannah* was involved was a collision with the bark *Gerald C. Toby*, in New York harbor. The date was January 17, 1880. The bark sank, representing a loss of $50,000, but the steamer suffered only minor hull damage and "derangement of the steam steering-gear."

On August 24, 1893, the *City of Savannah* departed Boston with only twenty passengers on board, and "a medium cargo consisting chiefly of shoes and furniture." Business was in a slump, but the steamship operated on a strict timetable according to regularly scheduled departure dates. There were forty-five officers and crew members to attend to the needs of the ship and her passengers.

Initially there were no indications that a storm was on the way. For three days the steamer proceeded quietly along her well-plied route. Not until dinner Sunday night did the first warning arrive. Captain George Savage was sharing a meal with the passengers when the vessel gave a sudden lurch and he was "thrown from his chair to the floor. He quietly excused himself with the remark that he was needed on deck." Captain Savage was not in the least bit intimidated, for the *City of Savannah* was a staunchly built steamship that had weathered many a storm during his assignment as her master.

But this was no ordinary storm. It developed into what might be called the "storm of the century." Gale force winds whipped the seas to froth. Captain Savage may have had a premonition of upcoming danger, or at least a pause for consideration, when he spotted a couple of empty lifeboats drifting aimlessly north of Cape Hatteras, North Carolina. After passing the Diamond Shoals, the wind commenced to blow from the northeast and the velocity increased to hurricane proportions. The *City of Savannah* continued on her course into the teeth of the storm.

Off Charleston, the intensity of the storm was so severe that the ship became difficult to maneuver. She crashed headlong into the bottom of deep troughs, then slammed into high walls of water that washed completely across her decks. Her speed was reduced to such a degree that she could barely maintain steerageway. Captain Savage gave the order to heave to. The *City of Savannah* bobbed like a cork in a swimming pool full of young boys doing cannonballs.

"Soon after the first heavy wave struck her, taking off the pilot house and sweeping clean over the vessel. Capt. Savage, who was in the pilot house at the time, was driven back through the partition wall into his own room in the rear. He was partially stunned by the shock and his room was filled with water, and for several minutes he did not know whether he was overboard or on deck. He

A woodcut of the *City of Savannah*. (From the author's collection.)

came out of this flow apparently uninjured, but in an hour afterward he was sore from head to foot.

"The gale continued all the afternoon with increased force. At 8 o'clock Sunday night the vessel shipped a sea that carried the smokestack overboard. This made the engines useless and rendered the vessel entirely helpless and at the mercy of the wind and waves. The water poured down the smokestack into the engine room and flooded everything. The cabins and the saloon had already been washed out by the waves and the passengers were making out as best they might, assisted all that was possible by the crew."

Now was the time to furl the emergency sails. While the *City of Savannah* was being blown helplessly downwind, Captain Savage ordered "all sail set, but the wind blew the sails away as fast as they could be hoisted." Tattered canvas whipped raucously from the masts, adding to the cacophony of the howling wind and crashing waves. Oddly, now that the ship was no longer bucking the seas, "the drifting was the easiest part of their experience of the storm." This was but a temporary respite. The worst was yet to come.

The anchors were dropped at 3:30 Monday morning, August 28. Soundings with the lead showed six fathoms of water. The *City of Savannah* lay dangerously close to the shoals that guarded St. Helena Island. The atmosphere was filled with a blinding spray as the wave tops were carried away by the tempest. The wind blew so hard against the hull that the anchors had little or no effect: they dragged through the soft sandy bottom as if their flukes were fish hooks. "The vessel began pounding about 5 o'clock and lodged about an hour afterward. . . . As soon as the vessel grounded Capt. Savage ordered her filled with water to hold her steady. The order was unnecessary however, as she filled without aid. She lay sidewise to the shore with her larboard side under water and the starboard side in the air. The passengers were gathered on the starboard side for safety. The vessel lay about three miles from shore. . . .

"The storm continued with severity Monday morning, and the sea soon began to sweep over the decks. The passengers realized their danger and behaved splendidly. Capt. Savage says a braver set of passenger he never saw. They could not have behaved better, he says, if they had been going to sea for 30 years. They remained quiet, made no complaints and obeyed the directions given them by the crew for their safety.

"The waves soon began to demolish the vessel. The saloon quickly went. The cabins were gutted entirely, and everything on the starboard side was carried away. That none of the passengers were swept away seems a miracle. To the good management of Capt. Savage and his crew their remarkable good fortune may be attributed."

The people huddled together on the starboard side of the vessel, notched in the corner that was created by the deck and the remains of the starboard bulkhead. At 10 o'clock Monday morning, Captain Savage dispatched a lifeboat for assistance. This boat was manned by two quartermasters and a boatswain.

"The passengers spent Monday night in the rigging. It was a terrible night, especially for the women and children, but all bore it bravely. The waves dashed over them and death was expected at every moment. All they had to eat Monday, was some herring, sardines, crackers and raw turnips that were found floating around in the vessel. They would have been without water entirely had not a barrel of mineral water floated up out of the stores. This was welcomed as a God send."

Throughout the night, "signals of distress were sent up and colored lights were burned," but to no avail.

"Tuesday morning, nothing having been heard from the boat that was sent out the day before and the vessel appearing likely to break up at any moment, Captain Savage determined to send the women and children ashore. There were only two boats left, three of the boats having been washed away on Sunday night. These were sufficient to accommodate only the women and children, and it was determined to send them and leave the male passengers on the vessel.

"Eight of the strongest sailors were picked out, four for each boat, and the boats were placed in command of First Officer Crowell and Second Officer Stovout. The women and children, nine in all, and the stewardess were also put in the boats. There being room for two more passengers, Dr. G.W. Lamar . . . and another gentleman, were selected to go with the party, being strong and able to render assistance to the sailors in managing the boats. The parting between husbands and wives and fathers and children under such circumstances, when the probability was that they would never see each other again, cannot be described. The boats were watched until they were out of sight. . . . The distance was so great, the mist so thick, and the seas so high that those remaining on the wreck were unable to learn whether the boats did or did not reach land."

At this point a deplorable and never explained incident occurred. A tugboat was sighted on the horizon offshore. The unidentified tugboat was described as having a smokestack that was encircled with a white band. The tugboat approached the wreck "with flags flying, with all the outward evidence of coming to the assistance of the castaways. So confident were they that this tug boat would rescue them that everybody on deck collected his little baggage together and made preparations to leave. All was joy and the experience of the preceding night and day were talked over and made light of. . . . What was left of the *City of Savannah* was resting in a bight with the breakers on both her starboard and port sides and at the stern. Leading to her bow there was a clear and safe channel cut to the sea with a least depth of 24 feet. The tugboat circled around the breakers, raising the hopes of the shipwrecked men to the highest pitch, and finally sailed away to the northward, leaving those behind to their fate. The tugboat never got nearer to the wreck than two miles." The anguish of the castaways can only be imagined.

Also proceeding to Savannah from Boston was the *City of Birmingham*, under the command of Captain Burg. She was one day behind the *City of Savannah*. After rounding Cape Hatteras, the City of Birmingham spotted a water-logged schooner that was in dire straits. The *Joseph Souther* "was going to pieces rapidly, and she gave the signal of distress. Capt. Burg at once sent out a lifeboat and took them all on board."

Captain Burg: "After that time we passed frequent wrecks. There were schooners and barks with their masts and everything on deck entirely swept away." Whenever a wrecked windjammer sent a signal of distress, "Capt. Burg would send out and offer them any assistance they wanted. Several of them wanted to be towed in, but that he refused to do. He was ready and glad to take the crews aboard, but almost all of them refused to desert their ships."

Captain Burg and his stalwart crew maintained a sharp eye for other vessels that were overcome by adversity. For some inexplicable reason that Captain Burg did not understand, he steered a course that took his vessel close along the coast, instead of heading for deeper water offshore. This course of action that was out-of-the-ordinary enabled lookouts to spot the *City of Savannah* "in the breakers about six miles south of St. Helena lighthouse." On such a razor's sharply honed edge are some human fortunes balanced.

"The *City of Birmingham* hove in sight about 6 o'clock Tuesday afternoon. Capt. Savage was on the watch for her, and attracted her attention by firing colored signal lights. Capt. Burg quickly hove the *Birmingham* to and sent out two boats. The *Birmingham* could not get nearer than about four miles. The boats approached the wreck about 8 o'clock, but could not come up to it on account of the storm and the darkness. They came up near enough to be spoken from the wreck, however. They were told that assistance was needed at the earliest possible moment and put back to the *Birmingham* with the information. The wrecked passengers spent another night in the rigging. They had nothing to eat all day, the water had given out and they were utterly exhausted. They could not have stood the strain much longer, but they knew that relief was at hand and that cheered their hearts.

"The *Birmingham* lay to all night and at the first break of day yesterday morning Capt. Burg sent out two boats well manned to take off the wrecked passengers and crew. This was accomplished in two trips, and by 12 o'clock those who had stared death in the face for thirty-six hours were safe aboard the *Birmingham*. The only regret then was that the women of the party had been sent off before the *Birmingham* appeared. The number of those taken aboard the *Birmingham* was 41, crew and passengers.

"Capt. Burg, as kind hearted as he is brave, and all the crew and passengers did everything in their power for the unfortunates. The first thing asked for by the rescued was water. They felt the want of this much more than that of food. After their thirst had been satisfied they were given food and at the first hearty meal they had eaten since Sunday at noon.

"They were destitute of everything. Their clothing, baggage and money had been left on the ship, and they had nothing but the bedraggled clothing they had on. The kind hearted passengers supplied them with everything, coats, hats, shoes, shirts and everything needed, drawing freely upon their own stores to do this. The *Birmingham* weighed anchor and steamed for Savannah at 1 o'clock, arriving in Tybee roads . . . at 2:30 o'clock. She lay to for awhile there, and then came up the river."

More than a thousand people thronged the wharf awaiting the arrival of their loved ones aboard the overdue steamship. Not until the *City of Birmingham* docked did anyone on land learn about the fate of the *City of Savannah*. The survivors of the lost steamer were taken to the hotel De Soto, "where they were registered by Agent Anderson of the Ocean Steamship Company."

What of the lifeboat that had been sent in search of assistance, and of the two lifeboats that carried the women and children?

Captain Savage wasted no time in chartering the tug *Paulsen* to search the barrier islands for the missing people. Despite the injuries he suffered from being slammed through the wall of the pilot house, and his exhaustion after spending two days and night in the rigging - without food and water - Captain Savage insisted on leading the rescue party. The *Paulsen* departed at five o'clock the following morning, while anxious husbands and fathers waited in the hotel De Soto for word of their loved ones.

The tug stopped at Beaufort, where Captain Savage "supposed that something would be known there with regard to the location of the stranded people, but they had no more information at Beaufort than we did. They kindly offered us any assistance they could give, however, and furnished us a pilot free of charge. We then left Beaufort for St. Helena, where we thought at least a portion of the party had landed and reached there about two o'clock in the afternoon. Myself and two of the men went ashore in a small boat and found that one of the life boats which had been sent out from the wreck had landed there. Three lifeboats in all had been sent out. One left the ship on Monday with three seamen in her to go and procure assistance, but they were stranded on one of the islands and we never heard anything from them. The other two left the ship early Tuesday morning. . . . It was one of these boats, the one in command of Second Officer Partelow, that had landed her on St. Helena Island." (In a previous report, Partelow's name was given as Stovout.)

"I found that this party, among which were about half the passengers who left the wreck, had been well cared for at Senator Don Cameron's place. In fact, it seemed they had been so well cared for that they did not like the idea of leaving when we came for them. They were glad to see us, however, and willingly went aboard the tug.

"This party could give us no information with regard to the others. They had not heard from them, and had no idea where they had gone. I felt satisfied that they were somewhere about on one of these islands, and I was determined to find them if it took a week. I would have gone to every one of those islands and searched it from one end to the other before I would have come back without them. With a small boat and two men we started out on the search. We rowed around all night.

"This morning about 4 o'clock we reached Hunting Island, about seven miles from St. Helena, where the other party had been found, and went at once up to the lighthouse. We found them all there in care of the lighthouse keeper and his wife, who had done everything in their power to make their forced stay comfortable."

Also in the lighthouse were the three men who had set out in the first lifeboat.

"They were about as surprised to see us as we were glad to find them, and know that they were safe. They had had no difficulty, it seems, in getting ashore, and Mrs. Lamar, upon whom the trip had been especially hard on account of her having her two children with her, looked as well as she did when she left Boston. As soon as we could get them all up and dressed we started for the tug, leaving the island about 5 o'clock this morning."

Mrs. John Norman, one of those who reached St. Helena Island, added detail: "We had little trouble in getting ashore after we left the ship. Two or three big breakers struck us on the way and some of us got pretty wet, but this was just as we were leaving the ship. Some of the waves that struck the boat I thought would turn us over, but the boat took in very little water.

"We reached the island about 8 or 9 o'clock in the morning, getting in without any difficulty. We walked for some distance, passing pieces of wrecks and houses that had been blown down, until some party came out to meet us and took us to Senator Don Cameron's place, where we were well fed and cared for. In fact we had turkey for dinner as soon as we arrived, the turkey that we didn't get for Sunday dinner, the day that the storm came up."

Once again more than a thousand people were waiting at the wharf for the *Paulsen's* arrival. It was a happy reunion for friends and family alike.

So grateful were the passengers of the *City of Savannah* for their providential rescue that they presented Captain Savage with a memorial which everyone but the infants gladly signed. The memorial read, "We the undersigned passengers on board the steamship *City of Savannah* on her trip from Boston to Savannah, August 24, 1893, take this means to testify to our high appreciation of the skill and bravery of Capt. George C. Savage and his officers and crew, as displayed during the terrible experience of the stranding and loss of his ship. We also wish to give expression to our feeling of thankfulness for the courtesy and kindness with which we were treated by all connected with the ship."

Times have certainly changed. Today, survivors would undoubtedly run for the nearest attorney to file extravagant lawsuits in their behalf, claiming "extreme mental suffering and duress" in addition to loss of time, wages, and belongings.

When all was said and done, every person who boarded the *City of Savannah* in Boston arrived safely in Savannah. But the loss of the steamship was merely a minor event in the much larger picture of devastation that resulted from the storm. Nearly *forty* other vessels were wrecked; these were largely wooden-hulled schooners and barks, but four were pilot boats and six were tugs. Dead bodies wearing life preservers were found floating in the turbulent sea. Massive flooding of coastal communities and on the barrier islands caused untold damage, with the confirmed number of fatalities reaching as high as *eight hundred* souls. The majority of these people were drowned. Many people disappeared without a trace: their bodies were either washed out to sea or were buried in sand and seaweed.

It was reported that the wind speed of the "cyclone" exceeded 120 miles per hour.

"Between Charleston and Savannah the storm wiped out most of the homes as well as the crops, and left the property in a terrible state." Entire forests were flattened. Cotton fields were flooded, putting vast numbers of people out of work. On some plantations the rice crop was declared a total loss. "The phosphate industry has been temporarily paralyzed by the loss of dredges and tugs and damage to drying plants." The inhabitants lost not only all of their possessions but their means of earning a living. "They are destitute of everything, even clothing, and what they have is rags, barely covering their bodies. They do not need money, what they need is food and clothing to keep them alive. . . . Their cattle and hogs and crops were swept away."

Huge tracts of cultivated land were destroyed. "The entire country along the rivers was flooded and the corn, potato and cotton crops are a complete loss." Most of the houses were obliterated. Thousands of island folk were isolated and stranded. Even inland people were cut off from relief efforts. The Tybee Railroad was damaged almost beyond repair. The roadbed was washed away in numerous places, and the "rails and ties were blown about." Washouts existed along the tracks of the South Bound railroad. A number of bridges were demolished. Some roads ceased to exist.

Plantation workers were hit especially hard. "The water which covered the lowlands to the depth of several feet came up into their cabins so high that they could not stay in their beds, but had to take doors and any planks that were obtainable, place them in the rafters above and crawl up there for what protection they could get. In a case of this kind where the cabins were blown down by the force of the wind during the most terrific part of the storm, some of the inhabitants were either crushed to death or were carried down into the water below and drowned."

It was feared that the death toll might rise into the thousands. "Every day some new account increases the death list and the number of those who are suffering from starvation on the places that were wrecked. The work of the storm along the Georgia and South Carolina coast will go down in history, and the entire number of those killed and wounded as a result of it will never be known."

Against this perspective of enormous tragedy, the relative cheerfulness of the steamship's survivors weighs harshly.

The *City of Savannah* was insured for $150,000; her cargo was insured for $50,000. Of this $200,000 total, only one tenth was insured domestically, the remainder of the risk being held in Europe.

After the storm subsided, the underwriters engaged the Merritt Wrecking Company to survey the wreck with an eye toward salvaging the hull and its cargo. Merritt dispatched the wrecking steamer *Cooley* from Norfolk. In the mean time, Captain Avery took the tug *Smith* to within a quarter of a mile of the wreck, off Hunting Island. "Her correct position is on Fripp's inlet shoal, off Hunting Island, about two miles off the beach, and about three miles from the Hunting Island light, southeast by south."

Lest the reader be confused by the multiplicity of islands and the wreck's actual location, St. Helena Island is situated to the west of Hunting Island, while Fripp Island is situated to the south of Hunting Island.

Captain Avery described the condition of the wreck: "Up forward the water is up to the pilot house door on the lee side. The saloon joiner work is gutted out on her main deck from the smokestack to the afterthwart ship passageway. Part of the spar deck and the social hall on the awning deck remain. Aft her main deck shows plainly at high water. . . . The *Savannah*, it appears, is listed only 20° to starboard instead of 45° as reported. She is comparatively flat bottomed and she stands almost straight up on the shoal." The wreck lay on a northerly heading.

Elsewhere it was reported that debris was found as far as ten miles from the site. "The wreckage of the steamer *City of Savannah*, cabin doors, saloon chairs, mahogany steps, washstands, mahogany balustrades and steps, as well as cushions, pillows and hundreds of life preservers, many stamped *City of Savannah*, strew the beach intermingled with fragments of the hard wood finish of the saloon, pieces of lifeboats and some of the heavy timbering of her superstructure." The sea was completing its job of demolition.

On September 12, after a week-long examination by divers, the wrecking crew made their report to the underwriters about the possibility of salvage. The news was short but not sweet: salvage in whole or in part was considered impracticable. "It was found that it had become buried in the sand and that the lower part of the hull had become partially filled with sand. The sides of the hull had been stove in and sand had covered everything in the lower part of the hull to such an extent that they found it would be impossible to raise her at any reasonable cost." Divers recovered no more than a few boxes and barrels. "The rest of the cargo down in the hold had also become covered with sand, and it was all under water."

A status report published on September 13 noted that the wreck "lies in about 7 feet of water, directly in front of Fripp's Inlet."

The owners abandoned the *City of Savannah* to the underwriters on September 15 because it proved "impossible to get her off."

An interesting sidelight occurred on or about September 5. A young man named King, who lived on Edisto Island, was walking on the beach near North Edisto Inlet and Botany Bay when he spotted a bottle lying on the sand. The bottle contained a piece of wrapping paper on which was written, "Lost on board steamship *City of Savannah* from Boston to Savannah on August 27, 1893, John Wade and John Armstrong, of Savannah." For one of the few times in recorded history, the proverbial message in a bottle was no joke.

In the 1972 book *Adventure in the Woods and Waters of the Low Country*, J.E. McTeer wrote: "The *City of Savannah's* boilers can be seen above the breakers on low tides. Many fishermen sit on them and bring in large catches of fish. During World War Two, some Beaufort men were doing just that when a Navy aviator, seeing for the first time what appeared to be the conning tower of a submarine, with the crew getting a breath of fresh air, opened fire with his 50 calibre machine guns on them. The men dove over board and clung to the *Savannah's* slippery sides, while 50 calibre slugs cut out chunks of metal all around them. Luckily their small boat was not sunk, or this story would have a much different ending, as it was, five miles off shore, and through the breakers. The pilot banked around the wreck, saw he had made a mistake, and went back to his base."

Today, some of the wreckage of the *City of Savannah* is still visible above the surface.

F.J. LUCKENBACH

Built: 1886
Previous names: *Marie, Euskaro*
Gross tonnage: 2,564
Type of vessel: Iron-hulled freighter
Builder: R. Thompson & Sons, Sunderland, England
Owner: Edgar F. Luckenbach (Luckenbach Steamship Company), New York, NY
Port of registry: New York, NY
Cause of sinking: Unknown
Location: Off Charleston

Sunk: May ?, 1914
Depth: Unknown
Dimensions: 282' x 38' x 18'
Power: Coal-fired steam

The circumstances surrounding the loss of the *F.J. Luckenbach* will forever be clouded in mystery. The freighter departed from Tampa, Florida on May 15, 1914 with a cargo of phosphate rock, on a route that she had running for the previous two years. She should have reached her destination - Baltimore, Maryland - six or seven days later. But she was never seen nor heard from again. Attending her loss was a flurry of conflicting reports, both official and unofficial.

According to the American Bureau of Ships, the *F.J. Luckenbach* was equipped with a wireless apparatus. Yet according to the Lloyd's Register, she was not. One New York City reporter, who may have obtained his information direct from the Luckenbach Steamship Company in that city, wrote: "She is not equipped with wireless and usually signals to the station at Sand Key, but did not do so on this voyage." Since Sand Key is located in Florida, the implication is that the freighter did not reach that point in her passage from the Gulf of Mexico around the Florida Keys.

The United States Life-Saving Service recorded that twenty-nine people were aboard at the time of her loss, whereas the Merchant Vessels of the United States recorded that there were fifty-eight people aboard. A New York City correspondent wrote that she "carried a crew of twenty-eight men. She was commanded by Capt. A.K. Webb of New York and George Arkebauer of Baltimore was chief engineer. She carried no passengers."

The *F.J. Luckenbach* was a week overdue when the crew of the steamer *Shawmut* saw "a great quantity of wreckage" floating in the ocean off Charleston. This wreckage consisted of "a large quantity of lumber and moulding and a canvas-covered hatch cover painted yellow." Baltimore "marine men said that her hatch covers were yellow, as reported by the *Shawmut*." This wreckage was "believed by shipping people to be from the steamer *F.J. Luckenbach*."

James Morris, an agent for the Luckenbach Steamship Company, said, "The vessel did not have deck loads of any kind and had no lumber aboard." Captain McGahan, master of the Luckenbach vessel *D.N. Luckenbach*, said, "If anything happens to a Luckenbach boat there is not likely to be much floating around.

Courtesy of the Steamship Historical Society of America.

They are pretty solid about the deck, with no deck cargoes, and with the exception of possibly a few lifeboats or rafts." Captain McGahan knew whereof he spoke, for he was the master of the *F.J. Luckenbach* only one year prior to her loss. It was his opinion that "if a Luckenbach boat sank it would leave a pretty clean wreckage."

In regard to the tarpaulin, Captain McGahan said, "the Luckenbach hatches were covered with brown tarpaulin. . . . They might have been painted yellow. . . . . They might have been described as yellow in any event."

A revenue cutter was dispatched to the area. She found no sign of the missing freighter. On May 30, "Capt. William S. Sims, commanding the torpedo flotilla, returning north from Vera Cruz, was ordered today by the Navy Department to search for the missing steamer *F.J. Luckenbach*. The nine destroyers and the tenders Birmingham and Dixie will form an extended line about seventy miles long as they proceed northward to search for the missing ship." Nothing was sighted.

The *F.J. Luckenbach* was insured for $97,200. The underwriters paid the claim, wrote off the ship as a statistic, then forgot about the freighter and the men who went missing with her.

It has been suggested to this author that a wreck known locally as the Anchor Wreck might be the remains of the *F.J. Luckenbach*, but I think otherwise. The *F.J. Luckenbach* was propelled by a compound engine. Steam was generated by two Scotch boilers, each measuring 11' 6" in length and 14' 6" in diameter. I have not measured the boilers on the Anchor Wreck, but I did observe that the engine was a triple expansion engine and not a compound engine. Nor did I see any evidence of phosphate rock. Pete Manchee recovered a piece of machinery connected to a flange on which was stamped "Goteborg." Since Goteborg is in Sweden, this suggests a vessel of Scandinavian origin.

See the section on Unidentified Wrecks for a more detailed description of the Anchor Wreck.

Some views of the anchors for which the Anchor Wreck was named.

FREDERICK W. DAY

Built: 1901
Previous names: None
Gross tonnage: 613
Type of vessel: Wooden-hulled, four-masted schooner
Builder: Kelley, Spear & Company, Bath, Maine
Owner: Frederick J. Hinckly, Bath, Maine
Port of registry: Bath, Maine
Cause of sinking: Foundered
Loran 45427.7 / 60471.7

Sunk: September 17, 1914
Depth: 55 feet
Dimensions: 172' x 35' x 18'
Power: Sail

GPS 32-36.025 / 70-40.141

On September 16, 1914, the *Frederick W. Day* was nearing the end of a routine passage from New York to Wilmington, North Carolina, when she ran afoul of a storm that struck the entire eastern seaboard. Captain William Oram and his crew of seven were unconcerned - the schooner had endured worse storms in the past. The vessel labored well against the high winds and heavy seas. Her holds were dry - and so was the cargo of cement in bags.

The schooner was rounding Cape Lookout when an awful thump sounded on the bottom of the hull. It was Captain Oram's opinion that he had struck a sunken wreck. The holds began to leak at once, and suddenly the *Frederick W. Day* was in trouble. The schooner was equipped with both steam and hand pumps. The crew immediately put the pumps into action.

Captain Oram signaled to a passing steamer - the *City of Montgomery* - which "aerographed" an urgent call for help. The SOS was intercepted by the Navy yard at Charleston, then forwarded to the Revenue Cutter Service. The revenue cutter *Yamacraw* was operating off Tybee, Georgia when she was notified by wireless of the schooner's difficulty. The *Yamacraw* radioed that she "was going with full speed to the assistance of the schooner."

The captain of the *City of Montgomery* offered to take the crew off the *Frederick W. Day*. He also advised Captain Oram to sail on, as he had received a wireless communication that prompt assistance was on the way. Captain Oram elected to stay with his ship. He released the *City of Montgomery* from further responsibility.

The waterlogged hull was less than fully maneuverable. Huge waves slammed against the sides, aggravating the damage that had been initially incurred. The schooner drifted southwest at the mercy of the wind - all night, and most of the following day. She passed her intended destination and kept on going. Soon she passed Cape Fear and entered the waters of South Carolina. Captain Oram strained his eyes to sight the revenue cutter, but no ship appeared on the horizon. The *Frederick W. Day* was alone on the wide, wide sea.

Water gained on the pumps with alarming celerity. After twenty-four hours

From the author's collection.

of frantic pumping, the water rose high enough in the hold to stop the steam pump. Soon after that, the water came up over the hatches. At nine o'clock in the morning of September 17, Captain Oram ordered abandon ship. The men launched the lifeboat, leaped aboard, and steered a course for Charleston - which by this time was not very far away. The lifeboat reached the *Charleston* lightship under power. Then the motor ran out of gasoline, and the men had to row the rest of the way into port.

Not one to give up easily, as soon as the lifeboat reached Charleston, Captain Oram engaged the tug *Cecelia* to tow the damaged schooner into port, "but during their absence the vessel sank."

A local newspaper reported, "Just why the *Yamacraw* failed to reach the schooner is not known."

The *Frederick W. Day* lay "in eight fathoms of water, the tops of her masts and bowsprits being above water." She was worth $30,000.

"Capt Oram said that everything of value on the schooner except the chronometer and compass, was lost. Many articles belonging to Mrs Oram, the wife of the master, were also lost, for Mrs Oram made her home on the vessel. This last trip of the *Day*, Capt Oram said, was the first that his wife had failed to make with him in a number of years."

The *Yamacraw* eventually located the *Frederick W. Day*, but not until the day after she sank. The wreck lay "in the path that is usually followed by coastwise shipping, especially vessels from Savannah." With the hull so dangerously exposed, the sunken schooner was considered to be a hazard to navigation. The lighthouse tender *Cypress* marked the site with a lighted gas buoy. Immediate plans were made to dynamite the hull.

On September 22, the *Yamacraw* completed the removal of the spars and masts so that "the water above the wreck is clear of obstructions to a depth of from four and one-half fathoms to five fathoms." Yet, on October 3, the steamer *City of Atlanta* reported that parts of the sunken hull were seen awash. On November 13, it was reported that the schooner "came to the surface at 2 PM yesterday, and is now a menace to navigation."

The wreck must have broken apart, as there is no way in which a hull that was filled with concrete could have refloated. More than likely, a portion of the deck separated from the hull and floated to the surface, perhaps along with the deck houses, rails, and rigging. No further reports ensued, but it might be presumed that the wreck was later demolished - or at least reduced in height - by means of explosives. The Coast Guard established a buoy on the site on June 22, 1942. There may have been some fear that, because shipping traffic was traveling so close to shore because of the numerous U-boat attacks, the wreck might have posed a menace to navigation for deep draft vessels.

Today, very little of the wooden hull remains. The site consists mainly of a massive pile of cement. The dry powdered cement was carried in sacks, and piled high in adjacent rows. The sack cloth has long since deteriorated, leaving behind thousands of solidified masses of cement in the shape of sacks. The main pile is approximately one hundred feet in length and twenty-five to thirty feet in width. Along nearly half the length of the main pile, the outer rows terminate in sheer walls that drop as much as seven feet. Surrounding the main pile is a ten-foot-wide perimeter of knocked-down cement masses. A few worm-eaten timbers are exposed at the bottom edge of the main pile, and among the knocked-down cement masses.

The bow is designated by a capstan that lies on its side, and by an anchor (or a pair of anchors) partially buried in the sand. At the stern, what appears to be a section of the rudder is exposed. The maximum amount of relief is thirteen feet.

FRED W. CHASE

Built: 1882
Previous names: None
Gross tonnage: 625
Type of vessel: Three-masted schooner
Builder: J.Manchester Haynes, Wiscasset, Maine
Owner: J. Manchester Haynes, Wiscasset, Maine
Port of registry: Augusta, Maine
Cause of sinking: Collision with SS *City of Atlanta*
Location: In the breakers three miles south of Morris Island Life-Saving Station

Sunk: February 4, 1887
Depth: 10 feet
Dimensions: 151' x 34' x 13'
Power: Sail

Captain John Nason was the master of the *Fred W. Chase* on her final voyage. Also on board were seven officers and crew members. The schooner was bound from New York to Charleston with a heavy cargo of granite for the construction of a jetty. She picked up a pilot outside of Charleston harbor. The pilot, Fred Fischer, did not advise attempting to cross the bar because of the uncommonly thick fog that obscured the markers. The *Fred W. Chase*, "like a good many other vessels," hove to in order to wait for better visibility. She rode her anchor "for several days."

The fog was eventually blown away - by a fierce northeast gale. On February 4, 1887, the tug *Monarch* steamed out of Charleston harbor and cast a towing hawser to the *Fred W. Chase*. Tug and tow then proceeded across the bar into the harbor.

Lying in Charleston harbor at that time was the SS *City of Atlanta*. The liner had been disabled on her previous trip to Florida, "and had been towed from Tybee to Savannah for repairs." She then steamed to Charleston. Under the command of Captain Lockwood, she departed for New York on the same afternoon on which the *Fred W. Chase* was being towed in. All three vessels converged on the "wreck buoy in South Channel" at around three o'clock.

Accounts of subsequent events differ. Captain Holborn, master of the *Monarch*, stated that the *City of Atlanta* "got on the inner shoal and became unmanageable, owing to the heavy sea and the gale that prevailed. The tug and the *Atlanta* had passed each other, exchanging the proper signals before the steamer got on the shoals and both vessels were on the proper course. The steamer, refusing to answer her helm, was blown around, and just as the schooner came abreast of her the two vessels collided. The prow of the *Atlanta* struck the *Chase* in the bluff of the port bow, cutting her through the 'quick' work down to the main plank sheer, knocking the anchor overboard and parting the hawser."

According to Captain Nason and Pilot Fischer, "We were making good headway when we met the *City of Atlanta*. She came on directly for us, and struck us on the port bow. The shock parted our tow line from the *Monarch*, cutting our vessel down to the water's edge. A strong northeast wind was blowing astern and we let go our anchor to prevent our getting ashore. As soon as possible the tug got round and threw us the line again, at the same time calling the cutter to her assistance. But we had already dragged the tug so far that it began to touch bottom and was obliged to cut loose to save itself. We do not know whether the *City of Atlanta* was unmanageable or not. All we know is that there was room enough between us and the obstruction buoy for the steamer to pass. The interval between us and the buoy was fully three lengths of the *City of Atlanta*. The wind was blowing *from* us towards the steamer. The *City of Atlanta* could have passed us on the opposite or west side of the obstruction buoy. Just a short time before she struck us she had been blowing salutes either for the tug *Monarch* or for an inward bound vessel that was just then passing (the *City of Columbia*.)"

Captain Lockwood had a completely different story: "The steamer was coming out of Charleston harbor, while the schooner was being towed in. The steamer passed the tow boat on the port side. Suddenly in passing the tow she erred on the right, head on into us, bringing us nearly head to head. We backed, but the schooner struck us right on the stern. I was on the bridge at the time, as I always pilot the boat in and out of the harbor. It was the schooner's fault. They should have gone more to the eastward. We were on the west side of the channel and our bottom was rubbing the bar at the time. So far over were we that I did not think that the schooner was much injured. The rail was broken and I saw the anchor, but I thought they had let it go. The steamer was not even scratched and did not feel the jar of the collision."

Without signaling for a situation report, the *City of Atlanta* proceeded on her way and left the *Fred W. Chase* to her own devices. The men aboard the schooner were in desperate straits. Captain Holborn swung the *Monarch* about and chased after his errant tow. The *Fred W. Chase* was driven by the wind into the Folly Island breakers. The hull bumped across the sandy bottom as the violence of the storm increased. The *Monarch* managed to pass another hawser to the schooner, but no sooner had this been done than the force of the wind against the schooner's sides commenced to drag them both onto the dangerous shoal. The *Monarch* was losing ground.

Instead of slipping the hawser and saving his tug, Captain Holborn signaled to the revenue cutter *McCulloch*, which was at that time crossing the bar. "The cutter went promptly to his assistance, a hawser was passed out to the *Monarch*, and both vessels attempted to drag the ill-fated schooner from her perilous position. They were unable to do so. They held on to the schooner until the *Monarch*, which only draws 10 feet of water, began to strike the bottom in 13 1/2 feet of water, imperilling [sic] her safety. Not until then did Capt. Holborn cut the hawser. The schooner was by this time high on the breakers off Folly Island; the sea was running mountains high, and it was impossible either to send a boat to the stranded vessel or to launch one from her."

Reluctantly, and with grave misgivings, the *Monarch* and the *McCullough* retreated to the safety of Charleston harbor. It was not as if they had abandoned the men on the schooner to whatever devices fate had in store for them. Rather, the perilous position of the schooner's crew was beyond the abilities of the men of the tug and the cutter to effect their rescue without unduly endangering the safety of their own vessels and, thereby, their lives. The surge over the shoal would have pounded their vessels to pieces.

The *Fred W. Chase* lay about a mile and a half from shore, and two to three miles southeast of the Morris Island Life-Saving Station. The schooner rolled and pitched with every wave. Her timbers creaked and groaned as if the hull were pulling apart at the seams. Slowly, inexorably, and despite the drag afforded by both anchors clawing the seabed, the schooner was forced ever higher upon the shoal. Her position became more untenable every minute.

The men did what they could to save themselves. They ran an ensign up the flagstaff as a signal of distress. First Mate Henry Stindt gave a gripping account of the terrible night that came to pass: "And so we waited, the water rising in the hold and the sea sweeping over us, and the pilot and the captain sweeping the sea with their glasses to see if, perchance, anything was coming our way. The signal must have been plainly visible to the life-saving station, and to that we turned as the last hope of despair. Nothing came, and the night closed in rapidly. The sky was thick overhead and of inky blackness. There was nothing to be seen except the Lighthouse beacon from shore. The night was bitterly cold and the gale drove the spray in our faces, blinding us and adding to the terror of the situation. The severe pounding that the schooner underwent broke two of the planks in the hull at last, and a flood of water entered. There was nothing then to do but go aloft.

"This was fully a half mile from where we were run into. We first all went up to the foretopmast, but afterwards, fearing the imposed weight might be too heavy a strain, we separated and divided the party, distributing ourselves on the three masts. We sat, or rather hung to the cross-trees, not knowing what an instant might bring forth. At about 10 o'clock the sea partially subsided at low water. We were then chilled to the bone and benumbed. With almost superhuman exertions we clambered, or rather fell down the masts and struggled to get a position on top of the forward house. There we used all possible endeavor to regain some of our strength by walking up and down on the roof. Even this was too dangerous, and at half-past 10 we went back to the rigging, and then began a vigil almost impossible to describe.

"Death stared us actually in the face; so painful all through the long hours that scarcely a word was spoken. Every feeling of anything except self-preservation had been frozen up. All this was terrible enough, but a new danger arose. At 2 o'clock in the morning our last boat was washed away, the other one having been swept loose on Friday evening. Then the cabin was smashed in and the poop deck, and the forward house. The vessel was, in fact, going to pieces.

"To increase, if possible, the confusion of the night, at 3 o'clock the masts on which we were clinging began to creak and sway. Then we gave up all, the very last hope. With the wrenching of the masts our falling into the sea was a foregone conclusion. But it was not to be, and our hopes began to revive as daylight appeared."

Meanwhile, from the life-saving station, Captain Merritt (the keeper) and Edward Bedgky (one of his crew) observed the sad travails of the drifting schooner. Merritt wasted no time in ordering his crew to prepare the lifeboat for launching. To do so, the boat had to be conveyed by wagon to the inlet, which was a mile and a half from the station. There the life-saving crew was met by John Wiecking (the lighthouse keeper) and Thomas O'Hagan (his assistant), both of whom had also observed from their lofty aerie the events as they unfolded. These two men helped the life-saving crew to launch the boat into Folly Inlet. By then it was five o'clock in the afternoon.

According to the Life-Saving Service report, "There was a tremendous sea running and the gale continued with unabated fury. The life-saving men strained every energy to reach the wreck." They pulled at the oars for two to three hours without let-up. Toward nightfall, they got to "within three hundred yards of her, where it was seen that she lay in the midst of the worst line of breakers, which were making a clean breach over her." At this point the life-savers were unable to make further headway against the fury of the storm. Exhausted, and "without the slightest chance of rescuing the imperiled people, the keeper at last abandoned the attempt, turned for the shore, and succeeded in landing several miles south of the place where he launched. The boat was then with difficulty tracked along the surf shore back to the inlet, which was crossed, and the crew returned to the station, where they changed their wet clothing. This being done a fire was built on the beach, which was vigilantly patrolled until daylight."

Captain Merritt neglected to mention in his report that, when he and his men towed their boat along the surf back to the inlet, they had to wade waist-deep in the water.

Nature raged furiously, thwarting every attempt to rescue the beleaguered men on the schooner. The would-be rescuers ashore, whose lives were not imperiled as long as they remained safely on land, suffered hardships and privations that were exceeded only marginally by the sailors who clung to the rigging of the *Fred W. Chase.*

With dawn came a slight moderation in the weather, and renewed attempts to reach the stranded schooner for the relief of the men who had endured such a horrible night in the wind, the spray, and the numbing cold. A massive, tripartite rescue operation commenced as soon as the sun shed its rays above the horizon.

A flotilla of boats departed from Charleston as soon as conditions permitted safe emergence from the harbor: the tugs *Hercules*, *Wade Hampton*, *Jacob Brandow*, *Thomas Morgan*, and the revenue cutter *McCulloch*. The *Thomas Morgan* soon returned with bad news: breakers were still sweeping over the deck of the *Fred W. Chase*, only three sailors were visible in the rigging, and it was yet impossible to approach the schooner in order to attempt the rescue the remaining men.

Then the *Jacob Brandow* returned to port. Her master, Captain Boyle, was not willing to relinquish the men to the fate that nature seemed to have bequeathed to them. He "called upon Messrs. Roach & Sons for a life-saving boat. Capt. Gus Crowell, of the steamship *Merrimac*, furnished the boat, and a crew was made up for it from *Pilot Boats 3* and *4*. . . . When the tug left the city, therefore, with the life-saving boat, there was a good chance that it would be of material assistance in the rescue of the imperiled sailors."

Nor was the life-saving crew lying idle. One man had been so debilitated by violent cramps as a result of the previous night's exertions that he was unfit for duty in the morning. "As there was a sea running, though the wind had somewhat abated, it was necessary to obtain a man to take the disabled surfman's place before going to the vessel and this occasioned some delay, the men having to row a mile up the inlet for that purpose. At once returning, however, they pulled off to the wreck and managed by skillful maneuver to get alongside."

Coincidentally, a lifeboat manned by sailors from the *McCullough* reached the wreck only moments before the arrival of the life-saving boat. Despite the earlier intelligence that only three men remained alive on the schooner, the rescuers were overjoyed to learn that every crew member had survived the awful tribulations of the night. The *McCullough's* boat took off three of the crew, while the life-saving boat took off the other six, including the captain and the pilot. The *McCullough* transferred her survivors to the tug *Wade Hampton*, which transported them to Charleston.

After a long, hard pull at the oars, the life-savers brought their boat alongside the *Hercules*, and delivered their survivors into the waiting arms of the men on the tug. All the survivors immediately received steaming hot coffee and a hale and hearty breakfast, which had been prepared for them in anticipation of their arrival on board.

The men were taken to the Seaman's Home. Since they had lost everything they owned except for the wet clothing on their backs, prominent merchants and businessmen donated a subscription of $228. In addition to praising the heroic efforts of their rescuers, "They spoke in the kindest terms of the treatment they had received at the Home and of the thoughtfulness of the gentlemen who had contributed so generously for their relief."

An allegation arose regarding the life-savers failed attempt to reach the wreck on the night of the catastrophe. One Joseph Brainovich voiced his opinion that the keeper and his men were not only cowardly but incompetent, and that they did not live up to the fine image of their Service. It developed, however, that these malicious accusations were made by a disgruntled ex-employee who left the Life-Saving Service after twenty-six days because "he could not get along with the officer in charge, Capt. Merritt, whom he did not regard as a proper person to have charge of such a station," and because "he would be unwilling to trust his life in a boat under the direction of Capt. Merritt."

The officers and men of the *Fred W. Chase* had nothing but praise for the efforts of the life-saving crew. As experienced seamen, they fully accepted the evident impossibility of reaching the wreck in a small boat during the height of the storm - and none had a better vantage point from which to voice an opinion than they.

The day following the harrowing rescue, after the storm had somewhat subsided, the life-savers returned to the wreck at extreme low water, with the intention of recovering for the schooner's crew whatever belongings they could find. Captain Merritt "found it under water up to the bulwarks." The masts were still standing, but the poop deck and a large portion of the main deck had been swept away, The life-savers brought away precious little: two bags of clothing that had been lashed to the mast, the flying jib, a flag, a deck bucket, and an oilskin coat.

There was no further mention of salvage. The *Fred W. Chase* represented a loss of $33,000. Her cargo of stone was stated to be worth about $400.

These photos of the exposed timbers of the site designated as the *Freida Wyley* were taken in 1989 by Chris Amer, South Carolina Institute of Archaeology and Anthropology. Hurricane Hugo temporarily washed away much of the sand that usually blankets the site. The wreck has since been sanded in. Occasionally, portions of the buried hull reappear.

FREEDA A. WILLEY

Built: 1880
Previous names: None
Gross tonnage: 507
Type of vessel: Barkentine
Builder: Dunn & Elliott, Thomaston, Maine
Owner: J. Willey, Thomaston, Maine
Port of registry: Thomaston, Maine
Cause of sinking: Foundered in a storm
Location: Between 41st and 42nd Avenues, North Myrtle Beach

Sunk: August/September, 1893
Depth: On the beach
Dimensions: 158' x 33' x 12'
Power: Sail

Local lore contends that the identity of a wooden hull that is sometimes exposed on the beach near 41st Avenue in North Myrtle Beach is the *Freida Wyley* (or *Freeda Wyley*, or *Freeda A. Wyley*), which foundered in the Great Storm of 1893. (See *City of Savannah* for particulars of the storm.) The South Carolina Institute of Archaeology and Anthropology has adopted that name for the site. Recent newspaper articles allege that the barkentine was struck by lightning, was abandoned off the mouth of the Cape Fear River, and then drifted to the location ascribed to her. If I accomplish anything at all in this chapter, at the very least I will provide the correct spelling of the vessel for which the site was named. According to the Record of the American Bureau of Ships, the barkentine was registered as the *Freeda A. Willey*.

Official documentation of the loss of the *Freeda A. Willey* is sparse. She was carrying a cargo of lumber from Pascagoula, Mississippi to New York when she got caught in the hurricane that came to be called the Great Storm of 1893. After the hull became waterlogged, the captain ordered the crew to cut the masts away in order to stabilize the vessel. She was abandoned on August 28, when the schooner *Anna E. Kranz* hove into view and took off the captain and his eight-man crew. No lives were lost. The *Anna E. Kranz* transferred the survivors to the steamer *Tallahassee*, which landed them at Savannah on September 1. The *Freeda A. Willey*, along with 437,000 board feet of yellow pine lumber, was left to the caprices of the wind and current.

The *Savannah Morning News* added vivid detail that was provided to that newspaper's correspondent by Captain Ichabod Willey, master of the *Freeda A. Willey*: "The *Willey* left Pascagoula, Miss., with a cargo of lumber for New York. The storm struck her Sunday morning [August 27] in latitude 30° 58', longitude 80° 09' [about ninety miles east of Brunswick, Georgia]. The storm was so severe that the seamen were unable to manage the vessel. Her deck load was shifted about so roughly by the storm that the crew was unable to remain on deck and tied themselves in the rigging. The vessel soon sprung a leak and filled with water, sinking nearly to the water's edge. The ship became water-logged and was in danger of going to the bottom. The storm moderating a little on Monday, Capt. Willey concluded to cut away the masts and clear the deck of its load, which was done. The *Willey* was fortunately equipped for a storm. There was a large box of sand on the deck, and a plentiful supply of matches and kerosene.

"A fire was built on the box and food cooked for the crew. There was plenty of beef and flour left and a full supply of water. The storm continued to moderate and the condition of the crew was comfortable, compared with their previous experience. Capt. Willey said the crew could have lived very comfortably for several weeks, provided no other storms were encountered.

"The schooner *Annie Kranz* came to their rescue on Tuesday. The fire on the sand box had been left burning, and soon after the crew were transferred to the *Kranz* the *Willey* caught fire. Capt. Willey says he did not set his vessel afire to remove her from the track of navigation, as he considered that bad policy under any circumstances. The vessel would only burn to the water's edge, he said, and leave a hulk more dangerous to navigation that the entire vessel.

"The *Annie Kranz*, Capt. Willey said, was bound for Savannah, and had been twenty days out from Cienfuegos [Cuba], being carried northward by the storms. On Thursday the crew of the *Willey* was transferred to the *Tallahassee* and brought to Savannah yesterday [September 1]."

Captain Willey told the reporter, "I wish you would say for me that we owe our deepest gratitude to the officers and crew of the *Annie Kranz*, and also of the *Tallahassee* for their kind and generous treatment of us."

According to official reports, the *Freeda A. Willey* was abandoned at north latitude 32° 45', west longitude 79° 55'. This must be a typographical error because that location is about half a mile inland from the north shore of James Island, south across the harbor from Charleston. The following day, on August 29, the partially submerged barkentine was spotted at north latitude 30° 57', west longitude 79° 26'. Incredibly, this also appears to be a typographical error, for that location is 100 miles east of Cumberland Island, near the Florida border. Not only is that a long distance for a derelict to travel in a day (some 120 miles), but the direction was contrary to that in which she had previously been drifting. The barkentine was next spotted on September 3, at north latitude 33° 17', west latitude 78° 26'. This position is about 35 miles southeast of Myrtle Beach. Official reports made no mention of the *Freeda A. Willey* having drifted ashore.

For nearly a month the *Charleston News and Courier* reported periodically on the strange peregrinations of the burned barkentine, as the hulk wandered to and fro among the shipping lanes. On August 31, Captain Foster, master of the steamer *William Crane*, "passed an abandoned vessel on fire. She was burnt to the water's edge. She was probably the bark *Freda A. Wiley*." (This is yet another misspelling of the vessel's name, plus an alteration in her rig.) The location given was "thirty miles north of Frying Pan."

On September 3, Captain Smith of the steamship *Nacoochee* passed "a burning wreck twenty-five miles off Frying Pan Shoals. It is supposed to have been the abandoned barkentine *Freda A. Wiley*." (Other than "off," no bearing from Frying Pan Shoals was given. At least the spelling error was consistent.)

On September 6, the captain of the steamer *Pawnee* "reports having passed wreck of a bark dismasted, lumber loaded, and stern partly burned off, twenty-five miles northeast of Georgetown bar."

On September 16: "The tug *W. P. Congdon* reports sighting the wreck of a vessel about 160 feet long, bottom up, twenty miles north-northeast of Georgetown bar. Its stern stands up 14 feet out of the water and the bows about 7 feet. It is probably a foreign bark from the build. An attempt was made to right her, but it could not be done. She is drifting north, and will probably go ashore on or near Murrell's Inlet." The captain thought that the wreck was loaded with Spanish cedar.

Notice that the latter two accounts make no speculation about the floating wreck's identity. If these various sightings all referred to the *Freeda A. Willey*, the barentine must have been drifting in large amorphous circles. This is not necessarily impossible, for there is no prevailing current in the area shown on the nautical charts as Long Bay, which stretches from Georgetown to Cape Fear (from which Frying Pan Shoals extend south-southeast). Fingers of the Gulf Stream occasionally poke into the bay, but eddies, counter-eddies, and curling ribbons of water create a virtual, slow-moving maelstrom. Once trapped in the reaches of Long Bay, the peripatetic hulk may very well have plied such a dizzying course. How she got into the bay from north of Frying Pan Shoals, where the Gulf Stream predominates and flows consistently northeast, is another matter. Perhaps two or more vessels were responsible for the wide range of these espials.

The *Savannah Morning News* named thirty-four vessels that were stranded or damaged by the storm. (The *Freeda A. Willey* was not one of them.) Most were either salvaged or repaired and returned to service. Contemporary local newspapers did not report that the *Freeda A. Willey* - or any other vessel - had drifted ashore. This begs the question: how did knowledge come down through time that the hulk buried under the sand in North Myrtle Beach was the barentine in question?

Oral history or racial memory recalls that a newspaper article published *after* the turn of the twentieth century established the identity of the wreck on the beach, at which time it was largely exposed. A calendar that was published in the 1950's repeated the appellative assignation. Now, despite evidence that appears to be purely circumstantial, the identification is commonly accepted. Lacking proof to the contrary, the 41st Avenue wreck has *become* the *Freeda A. Willey* (or one of its orthographic guises).

In 1989, Hurricane Huge moved so much sand off the beach that the wreck was almost entirely exposed, right down to the keelson. The SCIAA conducted an "in depth" survey of the hull, and added it to the register of State archaeological sites.

Is the hull that is buried near 41st Avenue the remains of the *Freeda A. Willey*? Your guess is as good as mine.

GENERAL GORDON

Built: 1886
Previous names: None
Gross tonnage: 1,696
Type of vessel: Iron-hulled four-masted ship
Builder: R. & J. Evans & Company, Liverpool, England
Owner: T. H. Skogland & Son A/S, Haugesund, Norway
Port of registry: Haugesund, Norway
Cause of sinking: Ran aground
Loran 45580.1 / 61096.0

Sunk: February 24, 1919
Depth: 35 feet
Dimensions: 258' x 38' x 22'
Power: Sail

GPS 32-10.107 / 80-33.212

Particulars of the loss of the *General Gordon* are sparse. According to the solitary mention in official documents, she was making a passage from Buenos Aires, Argentina to Charleston when (on February 24, 1919) she went ashore "off Hilton Head, Port Royal Sound, SC. Feb 27 The crew of the ship *General Gordon* was landed here by tug *W B Keene* last night. The captain of the *Gordon* is standing by on the beach." This slender entry makes it appear as if the crew remained aboard the stranded vessel for two days before abandoning ship.

Local newspapers added some additional if conflicting detail. According to one story, "The Norwegian bark *Gen. Gordon* was driven on the North Breakers in Port Royal sound some time on Sunday. She was sighted by a local steamer Sunday about noon and the position given is about six miles east of the lightship. The captain and crew abandoned her."

According to another story, "While proceeding slowly through a heavy fog the ship lost her way and without being aware of the close proximity of the shore went aground. It is understood that the vessel is now in a waterlogged condition and that the cargo has been damaged by water. The *General Gordon* was carrying a cargo of grain, consigned from South American ports to Charleston, at the time it went aground. Tugs have been sent to the rescue from the port of Savannah."

In his book, *Adventures in the Woods and Waters of the Low Country*, J.E. McTeer stated that he discovered the wreck accidentally in 1968. McTeer and his partner, Leroy Keyserling, owned a fishing boat called the *Edwin*, which they operated in conjunction with a purse seine dory. The boats were running the purse seine around a large school of bluefish and mackerel when they came to an abrupt halt. The net had snagged the wreckage of what supposedly was the *General Gordon*. More shipwrecks have been located in this manner than by any other method. I have seen numerous wrecks that still have trawler doors or the remnants of nets and floats clinging to their rotted ribs or rusted beams - jagged structural members that project outward like the thorns on a sticker bush to catch anything that approaches too close.

Today the wreck is the centerpiece of an artificial reef site. It lies less than one hundred feet from the buoy that marks the reef. In addition to the *General Gordon*, the reef consists of a thirty-foot barge and N-shaped concrete structures approximately four feet by four feet by four feet. Visibility on the site may be poor, so divers are warned that it is possible to swim underneath and into portions of the *General Gordon's* iron hull. The average depth around the wreck is 30 feet. Washouts occur, some going as deep as 37 feet - either under the outward slope of the hull or inside partially intact compartments. In dark or in conditions of poor visibility, one can enter these overhead environments without knowing it. Penetration of more than ten feet is not possible, yet it can be disconcerting to suddenly find oneself under a broad overhang or inside the confinement of a narrow corridor in conditions of near-zero visibility.

The keelson and most of the bottom plates are buried. The upper part of the frame slopes outward, much like webbed fingers from a pair of spread hands that are touching at their heels. Some vertical supports rise to a least depth of 18 feet. The remains of at least two iron tubular masts lie among the wreckage: they look like elongated barrels without lids, or like hollow metal logs. The *General Gordon* was equipped with a donkey boiler to generate steam for auxiliary equipment such as winches and the windlass, but I saw no sign of it.

The upper and side surface areas of the wreck are beautifully carpeted with bright white sponges and colorful hard corals. The undersides and interior sections have only a thin veneer of encrustation - this because marine fouling organisms are filter feeders, and thrive only in areas that have a constant flow of water to ensure a continual supply of nutrients. Fish abound on the site.

From the author's collection.

GEORGE MacDONALD

Built: 1943

Previous names: *Escalante*

Gross tonnage: 10,165

Type of vessel: Tanker

Builder: Bethlehem Steel Company, Sparrows Point, Maryland

Owner: Sinclair Refining Company, Wilmington, Delaware

Port of registry: Wilmington, Delaware

Cause of sinking: Foundered

Location: 32-25 North

Sunk: June 30, 1960

Depth: 450 feet

Dimensions: 501' x 68' x 30'

Power: Two oil-fired steam turbines

78-50 West

The *George MacDonald* began her career as the *Escalante*, in 1943, at a time when the world was torn by global conflict. By contemporary standards she was a supertanker - although today she would be a midget compared to tankers that are twenty times her tonnage. She was also ultramodern in that she was propelled by two steam turbines. For seventeen years the tanker enjoyed quiet anonymity, leading a career that was no more exciting than that of a tank truck plying the nation's interstate highway system.

June 27, 1960 found the *George MacDonald* on a routine voyage from Houston to New York City. Her tanks were filled with 130,000 barrels of crude from the Texas oil fields, bound for the refineries in northern New Jersey. This cargo of oil, however, was not destined the reach the cracking plants.

The tanker was 160 miles east of Savannah when the water box of the main condenser exploded. No one was injured by the blast, but seawater spurted uncontrollably into the engine room through a ruptured hull fitting. The engine room flooded at such an alarming rate that, as a precaution, Captain Eldridge Burnthorn transmitted an SOS. The rising tide soon disabled the engine. The *George MacDonald* went adrift. The time was 6:32 p.m.

The response to the captain's call for help was immediate. Both the Coast Guard and the Navy dispatched rescue craft to the scene. Nearby merchant vessels altered course and poured on steam in order to reach the beleaguered tanker before she sank. Twenty-eight of the forty-four crew members abandoned ship in two lifeboats. These men did not depart from the area, but stayed nearby. Those who volunteered to remain onboard did what they could to keep the pumps operating in the hope of saving the ship.

First to reach the drifting tanker was the *Esso Scranton*. She picked up the men in the lifeboats without much ado. Within short order the slowly foundering *George MacDonald* was surrounded a flotilla of vessels of all descriptions: U.S. Navy destroyer *Robinson* (DD-562), Coast Guard cutters *Papaw* and *CG 95313*, and tank steamer *J.E. Dyer* (another vessel of the Sinclair fleet). Aircraft flew by the scene like vultures waiting for a victim to die. A tug that had been dispatched

from Savannah had to turn back to port because of mechanical difficulties. The Sinclair Refining Company hired the salvage outfit of Merritt-Chapman & Scott to go to the rescue of the *George MacDonald*. Merritt-Chapman & Scott immediately dispatched the salvage vessel *Curb* from its New York base. It was expected to take a day and a half for the *Curb* to reach South Carolina.

The *Robinson* removed another ten or twelve men (accounts vary) from the *George MacDonald*, then later transferred them to the *Papaw*. The *Esso Scranton* was released from duty; she continued on her way and took the men she had rescued to Jacksonville, Florida. Still on board the stricken tanker were Captain Burnthorn and two to four officers and seamen (again, accounts vary). They were fighting desperately to save the ship.

The *George MacDonald* was settling at the rate of one foot per hour. By dawn of the twenty-seventh, her stern was submerged to the point at which the engine room was completely flooded, and her after deck was awash. Like a seesaw, the sinking of the stern had raised the bow some twenty feet higher. At that angle the tanker attained a precarious equilibrium - she stopped sinking. She and her escorts drifted northeast with the current.

Scattered rain squalls hampered salvage operations. Late in the day the weathered moderated, the sky cleared, wind speeds fell, and the waves subsided. At eight p.m., Captain Richard Dutson, master of the *J.E. Dyer*, managed to get two ten-inch towing hawsers aboard the *George MacDonald*. According to Captain Lenczyk, master of the *Papaw*, "The excellent seamanship on the part of the master of the *Dyer* was largely responsible for the successful rescue. He put his hull within two feet of the MacDonald with the risk of damage to his own ship. He did a wonderful job."

The *J.E. Dyer* proceeded toward shore at a speed of three knots with the deadweight of the tanker in tow. At first, Captain Dutson hoped to make it to Charleston, where the Maryland Shipbuilding and Drydock Company had a local subsidiary that could effect repairs. Later, when it was ascertained that the draft of the *George MacDonald* was now more than forty-five feet - deeper than the Charleston channel could accommodate - he steered toward a point between Cape Romain and Charleston, with the idea of beaching the *George MacDonald*.

The towing operation proceeded sluggishly for nine hours. Then, while still some sixty miles from shore, the towing hawsers "snapped like strings" in a fierce rain squall. The time was 1:55 a.m., June 29. The *Papaw* took off the remaining crew members and transferred them to the *J.E. Dyer*.

The stern lost its buoyancy. Slowly, almost gracefully, the *George MacDonald* slid backward under the choppy surface of the sea. The bow rose high into the sky. Trapped air burped and bubbled from the submerged compartments. The hull dived downward until the fantail crashed into the seabed some 450 feet below. Because the length of the vessel exceeded the depth of water, the wreck came to rest on its stern, and remained that way - much like a rocket poised for take-off on a launch pad - with the stem pointed to the sky. This was the vision that appeared after dawn.

The hull remained nearly vertical with thirty feet of the bow protruding above the surface of the sea. A spreading slick of oil streamed downcurrent of the wreck. In some places the oil was several inches thick. "As the *Papaw* cruised the area, it appeared to be traveling in a sea of oil."

The *Curb* was still proceeding southward. There was a faint possibility that divers could connect salvage hoses to the deck pipes and pump out the tank compartments. At the very least this would save the oil, and perhaps, by lightening the vessel, it would enable the *Curb* to tow the hulk by dragging it along the bottom to shallow water, from where it could conceivably be raised. "The Sinclair company dispatched the *Miss Donna* from Charleston at 4 p.m. Wednesday [June 29] with orders to stand by with a line on the ship's prow until a New York salvage boat could reach the scene. . . .

"Two hours later the duty watch on the trawler felt the boat lurch. The loose hawser and connecting lines tightened like steel rods." According to Garland Toler, master of the *Miss Donna*, "It jerked our boat like a toy." Then the line snapped and the *George MacDonald* disappeared from sight. This occurred at 2:15 in the morning of June 30.

The *Curb* was subsequently recalled. The tanker was abandoned to the insurance underwriters. The hull was valued at $1.5 million, the cargo at $200,000. Both hull and cargo were fully insured.

The *George MacDonald* reportedly went down at latitude 32° 25' north, longitude 78° 50' west. The depth of water was given in one source as 72 fathoms (432 feet), in another source as 456 feet, and in yet a third source as 470 feet.

From *Early American Steamers*, by Erik Heyl.

GOVERNOR

Built: 1846

Previous names: None

Gross tonnage: 644

Type of vessel: Wooden-hulled side wheel steamer

Builder: Samuel Sneeden, New York, NY

Owner: Caleb Snow and others, Boston, Massachusetts

Port of registry: Boston, Massachusetts

Cause of sinking: Foundered

Location: Off Santee Point, south of Georgetown?

Sunk: November 3, 1861

Depth: 78 feet

Dimensions: 235' x 28' x 10'

Power: Coal-fired steam

For fifteen years the *Governor* led a varied and undistinguished career in the transportation of passengers and freight between ports along the New England coast. During that time she operated on various routes for three different companies. Like many early wooden-hulled steamships - propellers and paddle wheelers alike - the concentrated weight of the boilers and propulsion machinery exerted a strain on the timbers used in the construction of the hull. Braces were secured longitudinally to the vessel's upper deck for additional strength. These braces - called "hogging arches" - prevented the ends of the vessel from bending downward and breaking the keel.

In 1861, when war broke out between the States, a group of entrepreneurs headed by Caleb Snow - of Boston, Massachusetts - purchased the *Governor* and promptly chartered her to the U.S. War Department for use as a troop transport. She may have remained in relative obscurity had it not been for a terrible storm that struck the eastern seaboard on November 1, 1861 - a storm that resulted in the loss of the vessel and one of the most dramatic rescue operations in maritime history.

In October 1861, Flag-Officer Samuel Dupont amassed a huge fleet of vessels at Hampton Roads, Virginia for a Great Expedition to attack coastal Confederate strongholds. On the twenty-eighth, Dupont dispatched a convoy of twenty-five coal vessels under the escort of the aging sloop-of-war *Vandalia* (laid down in 1825). The following day the main fleet departed. This fleet consisted of fifty vessels: Dupont's flagship *Wabash*, Navy escorts, and army transports, including the *Governor* and the *Peerless* (q.v.). More than 15,000 soldiers were aboard these vessels; these ground forces were under the command of Brigadier General T.W. Sherman (not the more famous William Tecumseh).. They were anticipating an amphibious assault - but they did not know where, for the destination was held as a closely guarded secret. Indeed, in order to confuse Confederate spies, the coal vessels were ordered to rendezvous off Savannah.

In command of the *Governor* and her crew was Captain C.L. Litchfield. On board were Major John Reynolds and his marine battalion consisting of 385 men, all fully armed and ready for battle.

For three days the fleet proceeded southward without a hitch. Then the wind began to freshen, on the morning of November 1. Within two to three hours the breeze developed into a full-fledged tempest. "The fleet was utterly dispersed." The next day, only a single sail was in view from the deck of the *Wabash*. "As the vessels rejoined, reports came in of disasters. I expected to hear of many, but when the severity of the gale and the character of the vessels are considered, we have only cause for great thankfulness."

The *Governor*, separated from the main body of the fleet, found herself completely alone. She commenced to creak and groan with the strain: "working" as the hull was wrung like a soggy dish cloth, first one way and then the other. Major Reynolds provided a blow by blow account, stating in his report that the wind "blew so violently we were obliged to keep her head directly to the wind, and thereby leave the squadron, which apparently stood its course.

"Throughout the afternoon the gale continued to increase, though the *Governor* stood it well until about 4 o'clock. About this time we were struck by two or three very heavy seas, which broke the port hog brace in two places, the brace tending inward. This was immediately followed by the breaking of the hog brace on the starboard side. By great exertions on the part of the officers and men of the battalion these braces were so well stayed and supported that no immediate danger was apprehended from them.

"Up to this time the engine worked well. Soon after the brace chains [guys] which supported the smokestack parted, and it went overboard. Some 3 feet of it above the hurricane deck remained, which enabled us to keep up the fires. Soon after the loss of the smokestack the steam pipe burst. After this occurrence we were unable to make more than 14 pounds of steam, which was reduced as soon as the engine commenced working to from 3 to 5 pounds. The consequence was we had to stop the engine frequently in order to increase the head of steam. At this period the steamer was making water freely, but was easily kept clear by the pumps of the engine whenever it could be worked. About 5 o'clock we discovered a steamer with a ship in tow, which we supposed to be the *Ocean Queen*. To attract attention we sent up rockets, which signals she answered. When our rockets, six in all, were gone, we kept up a fire of musketry for a long time, but, the sea running high and the wind being violent, she could render us no assistance. She continued on her course, in sight the greater part of the night.

"About 3 o'clock Saturday morning the packing round the cylinder head blew out, rendering the engine totally useless for some time. The engine was finally put in running order, although it went very slowly. The rudder chain was carried away during the night, the water gaining constantly on us and the boat laboring violently. At every lurch we apprehended the hog braces would be carried away, the effect of which would have been to tear out the entire starboard side of the boat, collapse the boiler, and carry away the wheelhouse. Early in the morning the rudderhead broke, the engine was of very little use, the water still gaining on us rapidly, and we entirely at the mercy of the wind. It was only by the untiring exertions of our men that we were kept afloat. Nearly one hundred of them were kept constantly pumping and bailing, and the rest were holding fast the ropes which supported the hog braces."

Captain Litchfield proved himself incapable of assuming command of the situation. As a consequence, he was relieved of the duties that he was failing to perform as captain of the *Governor*, and John Weidman took over as Acting Master. Weidman wrote, "Of the crew, the least I can say is that they were very, very worthless. The chief engineer and the chief mate conducted themselves as cowards and traitors." Thus it fell to the men in Reynolds' battalion to work the ship.

"Toward morning the weather, which during the night had been dark and rainy, seemed to brighten and the wind to lull. At daybreak two vessels were seen on our starboard bow, one of which proved to be the U.S.S. *Isaac Smith*, commanded by Lieutenant J.W.A. Nicholson, of the Navy. She descried our signal of distress, which was ensign half-mast, union down, and stood for us. About 10 o'clock we were hailed by the *Smith* and given to understand that if possible we should all be taken on board. A boat was lowered from her and we were enabled to take a hawser. This, through the carelessness of Captain [C.L.] Litchfield, of the *Governor*, was soon cast off or unavoidably let go. The water was still gaining on us. The engine could be worked but little, and it appeared that our only hope of safety was gone.

"The *Smith* now stood off, but soon returned, and by 1 o'clock we had another hawser from her and were again in tow. A sail (the propeller bark *Young Rover*) which had been discovered on our starboard bow during the morning was soon within hailing distance.

"The captain proffered all the assistance he could give, though at the time he could do nothing, owing to the severity of the weather. The hawser from the *Smith* again parted, and we were once more adrift. The *Young Rover* now stood for us again, and the captain said he would stand by us till the last, for which encouragement he received a heartfelt cheer from the men. He then stood for the frigate, made signals of distress and returned."

The frigate was the USS *Sabine*, Captain Cadwallader Ringgold in command. The *Sabine* was on blockade duty when the terrible storm struck the coast. Rather than expose his vessel to the beating of the waves "in an exposed roadstead like that off Georgetown," Captain Ringgold weighed anchor and steered for deeper water offshore. This action fortuitously placed the *Sabine* within sight of the *Young Rover* when the bark went looking for help for the *Governor*. Captain Ringgold's suspicions were aroused. There was every likelihood that the "rakish barque" could be a blockade runner, whose movements, "in view of the blockade, made it proper to watch and chase her." In fact, the *Young Rover* was a Union gunboat.

The *Sabine* proceeded to investigate. She had not gone far before she spotted two steamships in the distance, over the shoulder (so to speak) of the approaching bark. The *Young Rover* came about with the wind aft, "displaying flags union down as signals of distress," then turned and headed back toward the steamers. Captain Ringgold followed and, as the bark was now forced to tack in order to claw her way upwind (with some assistance from her auxiliary engine), the *Sabine* soon left the beneficent herald behind.

Captain Ringgold: "I found my worst fears painfully realized. A side-wheel steamer, rolling heavily, rudder gone, smoke-stack overboard, her decks crowded with human beings, lay before me a helpless wreck, and a small screw steamer, evidently much damaged and scarcely able to take care of herself, was nobly standing by her in her misfortune. The wind being high and the sea very heavy it was extremely doubtful whether any boat could live either to reach the wreck or to regain the ship.

"Notwithstanding the hazard, I promptly dispatched Lieutenant Balch, executive officer, with Acting Master Beattie [in another boat], to the scene of the disaster, for the purpose of assuring the officer in charge of our determination to stand by and succor them to the last extremity. Lieutenant Balch passed within hail - it being impossible to board - exhorting the vessel's company to rely upon our exertions and the power of the ship to save and provide for them. The encouragement thus given was responded to with a shout that rent the heavens. This fearless officer with great difficulty regained the ship."

In actuality, both officers as well as the men at the oars regained the ship, but it proved impossible to hoist up the boats because of the heaving seas. The time was now about 3 o'clock in the afternoon. Captain Ringgold positioned the *Sabine* upwind of the *Governor* and dropped anchor. He then passed orders for the *Governor* to do the same, which Captain Litchfield did.

Reynolds: "About 8 or 9 o'clock the *Sabine* had paid out enough chain to bring her stern close to our bow. Spars were rigged out over the stern of the frigate and every arrangement made for whipping our men on board, and some thirty men were rescued by this means. Three or four hawsers and an iron stream cable were parted by the plunging of the vessels. The *Governor* at this time had 3 feet water, which was rapidly increasing. It was evidently intended by the commanding officer of the Sabine to get the *Governor* alongside and let our men

From *Frank Leslie's Illustrated Newspaper.*

jump from the boat to the frigate. In our condition this appeared extremely hazardous. It seemed impossible for us to strike the frigate without instantly going to pieces. We were, however, brought alongside and some forty men succeeded in getting on board the frigate. One was crushed to death between the frigate and the steamer in attempting to gain a foothold on the frigate.

"Shortly after being brought alongside the frigate the starboard quarter of the Sabine struck the port bow of the *Governor*, and carried away about 20 feet of the hurricane deck from the stem to the wheelhouse. The sea was running so high, and we being tossed so violently, it was deemed prudent to slack up the hawser and let the *Governor* fall astern of the frigate with the faint hope of weathering the gale till morning. All our provisions and other stores, indeed every movable article, were thrown overboard, and the water casks started to lighten the vessel."

The reader must understand that these operations were conducted in total darkness. The fury of the gale increased during the night. As the *Governor* "lurched first to port and then to starboard, burying her sharp bow deep into the trough of the sea, each plunge seemed to be her last." The two boats that had been left in the water "were literally stove to atoms by collision with the wreck and my ship." Several times the hawsers were parted by the *Governor's* sharp stem. Each time, Beattie and a group of volunteers "gained the deck of the *Governor*, (passing over the stern of the frigate,) and the hawsers were soon again made fast." Still the hawsers kept breaking. Yet, "Providentially, a single hawser stubbornly held on, preventing the wreck from drifting off."

Reynolds: "At daybreak preparations were made for sending boats to our relief, although the sea was running high, and it being exceedingly dangerous for a boat to approach the guards of the steamer. In consequence the boats laid off and the men were obliged to jump into the sea, and were then hauled into the boats. All hands were thus providentially rescued from the wreck with the exception, I am pained to say, of 1 corporal and 6 privates, who were drowned or killed by the crush or contact of the vessels. Those drowned were lost through their disobedience of orders in leaving the ranks, or abandoning their posts."

Both from the *Isaac Smith* and the *Sabine* worked together to effect the rescue of the men. Captain Litchfield and Captain Reynolds were the last to leave the *Governor*, which they did at 8 a.m.

Both the *Young Rover* and the *Isaac Smith* then left the scene. The *Young*

Rover departed without further communication. The *Isaac Smith* had been so disabled by the storm that she had been forced to jettison her heavy battery. She steamed for Port Royal with intelligence for Flag-Officer Dupont about the safety of Major Reynolds' battalion.

Most shipwreck sagas usually end at this point - but not this one. Despite the hardships that the men had endured over the previous forty-eight hours, and the incredible stress of impending death, they now determined to save from the wreck that portion of the battalion's property that had not already been thrown overboard. Neither captains' reports stated precisely how this task was accomplished, but it must be presumed that the fierceness of the gale moderated enough to permit small boats to lie alongside the sinking steamer.

Reynolds: "After the troops were safely reembarked every exertion was directed to securing the arms, accouterments, ammunition, and other property which might have been saved after lightening the wreck. I am gratified in being able to say nearly all the arms were saved and about half the accouterments. The knapsacks, haversacks, and canteens were nearly all lost. About 10,000 round[s] of cartridges were fortunately saved, and 9,000 lost."

Salvage operations were secured at 11:30. The *Sabine* remained by the *Governor's* side with the intention of scuttling her, either by setting her afire or by shelling her. Neither expedient was necessary. "At 3:30 p.m. she fell on her side, (carrying the walking beam and platform with her,) went to pieces and sunk, covering the surface of the sea with the shattered fragments of her upper-works."

And *still* the story is not over. Confusion reigned on deck as the deployed hawsers were heaved aboard and the ship was restored to order. The *Sabine* now had "about nine hundred souls on board." Victuals were insufficient for such a crowd, and the supply of wood and water was "extremely limited." (Wood was needed to cook the food.) Also to consider was what to do with Reynolds' battalion. The nearest ports were held by the Confederates. The Carolinas were enemy territory. The *Sabine* could not abandon her post unjustifiably because she was under orders to prevent the incursion of blockade runners. Furthermore, the loss of Reynolds' battalion to Flag-Officer Dupont might create a shortcoming to the Great Expedition - the objective of which Reynolds was yet ignorant.

Reynolds decided that he must break the seal of his confidential orders. That was when he - and Captain Ringgold - learned of the proposed assault against Port Royal. With this intelligence in hand, Captain Ringgold felt that he had "no alternative but to assume the responsibility of quitting the station and proceeding forthwith to Port Royal, for the object of adding a powerful body of troops to Flag-Officer Dupont's command."

Captain Ringgold furnished eight volunteers from his own command to replace the seven marines from Reynolds' command who had perished, and one whose arm had been broken. Captain Ringgold also dug into his own stores in order to equip Reynolds' men with the arms and accouterments they required in order to engage the enemy in the upcoming invasion.

Where there is a will, there is not necessarily a way - especially where the weather is concerned. The *Sabine* ran into another gale that greatly retarded the progress of the vessel. Water rations were reduced to one-half gallon per person per day, "a privation to which all submitted with cheerfulness." The *Sabine* fought the storm for the next five days. The morning of November 8 found her within thirty-five miles of Port Royal, from which point the men could distinctly hear the "reports of the guns of the bombardment." Captain Ringgold immediately cleared his ship for action.

If this book were a novel, the *Sabine* would next dash through the shot of Confederate guns, disembark her contingent of marines to establish a beachhead, and cover the men with supporting fire while Reynolds and his battalion stormed the Southern fort and overwhelmed the defenders. The truth, however, is anticlimactic.

The firing ceased at 1 p.m. - a clear presage of Union victory. Even the rearguard action had ended by the time the *Sabine* gained the approaches to Port Royal later that evening. Reynolds' battalion missed the whole shooting match. By wresting Port Royal from Confederate control, the Union commanded a splendid base of operations from which to wage future assaults against Southern insurgency.

The officers and crew of the *Governor* were returned to Hampton Roads aboard the *Vandalia*, along with the injured marine and another one who had contracted typhoid fever.

Captain Ringgold and his officers and men received a testimonial from the Life-Saving Benevolent Association of New York City. The gold medal had the following inscription: "Presented to Captain Cadwalader [sic] Ringgold, in commemoration of his successful efforts, and those of the officers and crew under his command on board the U.S. frigate *Sabine*, in saving over 400 lives from the transport steamer *Governor*, on the 2d and 3d of November, 1861."

The Common Council of New York (City) expressed its appreciation by composing a preamble and resolution that was read to the men aboard the *Sabine*, "in order to incite, emulate, and encourage others to the performance of like deeds under similar circumstances." The legislature of the State of Maryland followed suit

Captain Ringgold was later promoted to Commodore. On March 7, 1864, the United States Congress passed a resolution in the same regard. It read (in part), "Resolved by the Senate and House of Representatives of the United States of America in Congress assembled, That the thanks of Congress are hereby tendered to Commodore Ringgold, the officers, petty officers, and men of the United States ship *Sabine* for the daring and skill displayed in rescuing the crew of the steam transport *Governor* . . . "

The reader should note that two other vessels that are covered in the present volume were sunk in the same storm that caused the demise of the *Governor*: the *Osceola* and the *Peerless*, both of which went down on November 2. Most modern references also give November 2 as the date of the *Governor's* loss - but this is in error. I do not know for certain how the discrepancy arose, but I suspect that it may be because it was the last date mentioned by number in most official correspondence: that is, the date on which the *Governor* was totally wrecked and went adrift, and on which she was approached by the *Sabine*. It is clear from the account that is quoted above that the *Governor* did not actually sink until the following afternoon. Yet November 3 was seldom written as such in contemporary narratives, either in official records or in the reports that were submitted to Congress. Only the gold medal presented by the Life-Saving Benevolent Association, and associated correspondence, mentioned November 3.

Today, the *Governor* is one of the most sought-after shipwrecks in the waters off South Carolina. Captain Ringgold took a sounding when the *Sabine* anchored ahead of the *Governor*. The depth of water was 13 fathoms, or 78 feet. Captain Ringgold noted that when he first spotted the *Young Rover* to the north of him, he observed the "Georgetown light-house bearing N.W., 35 miles distant." I do not know if it was possible to sight the lighthouse from a distance of 35 miles. If not, Captain Ringgold may have been estimating his position by means of dead reckoning - pure guesswork at best, considering the tempest in which the ship was then embroiled.

Also in doubt is how soon Captain Ringgold noticed the steamers beyond the Young Rover during her approach to ask for assistance, and how far he could see the masts of the steamers in the distance. Five miles? Ten miles? Fifteen Miles?

If Captain Ringgold's estimate was accurate - or even approximately so - the wreck of the *Governor* could lie somewhere in the area that is ten miles north of the spot that is 35 miles southeast of the lighthouse. Triangulation of these positions puts the wreck about 25 miles offshore of Santee Point, south of Georgetown. Searching the 13 fathom curve in that vicinity might be productive.

When the Civil War Wreck was first discovered, many people jumped to the conclusion that it was the *Governor*. The depth was certainly right if not the location, even when making allowances for the inherent inaccuracies in Captain Ringgold's report. I suspect, however, that most people who made the claim for the *Governor* did so because of its widespread notoriety. I think the evidence points to the likelihood that the Civil War Wreck is the *Suwanee* (q.v.). Other than historians and ardent researchers, few people had ever heard of the *Suwanee* at the time of its discovery.

A cannon that was recovered from the Civil War Wreck was stamped with a date that postdated the loss of the *Governor*. Additionally, there was no mention in the records of the *Governor* being armed - she was, after all, a chartered passenger vessel being employed temporarily as a troop transport.

Researchers should note that the Governor was fitted with a vertical beam engine whose cylinder measured 48 inches in diameter, with a stroke of 11 feet. The diameter of her paddle wheels was 30 feet.

Pete Manchee has suggested the possibility that a wreck known locally as the Pipe Wreck may be the remains of the *Governor*. He and three of his buddies recovered a bell from the Pipe Wreck. The date stamped on the bell was "1857." A vessel that was built in 1846 would not normally have been equipped with a bell that was dated eleven years later, unless the original bell was damaged or lost. See the section on Unidentified Wrecks for a description of the Pipe Wreck.

Official U.S. Coast Guard photo.

HEBE

Built: 1916
Previous names: None
Gross tonnage: 1,140
Type of vessel: Freighter

Sunk: April 11, 1942
Depth: 110 feet
Dimensions: 250' x 36' x 23'
Power: Coal-fired steam

Builder: Boele's Schpsw & Mcb, Bolnes, Netherlands
Owner: Royal Netherlands Steamship Company, New York, NY
Port of registry: Amsterdam, Netherlands
Cause of sinking: Collision with HMS *St. Cathan*
Loran 45237.4 / 59612.7   GPS 33-08.451 / 78-20.421

The *Hebe* departed New York City on the morning of April 7, 1942. She was bound for the Caribbean island of Curacao with a general cargo. To the thirty-one members of the crew, this would have been a routine passage had it not been for the fact that the eastern seaboard had recently become a war zone. In the previous three months, German U-boats had torpedoed and sunk more than sixty merchant vessels in the Eastern Sea Frontier alone. The ESF extended from Maine to Georgia. U-boats were also marauding merchant shipping off the coast of Florida and in the Caribbean with equally devastating results. All merchant vessels were at risk, even those registered to ports in neutral nations, for the Germans did not respect the laws of neutrality - or any of the laws of civilization, for that matter. U-boats sank indiscriminately any vessel that came within sight of their periscope crosshairs. Thus the Dutch officers and West Indian crew had much to fear, for the *Hebe* had to run this gauntlet of foreign aggression in order to reach her destination.

The *Hebe*'s cargo consisted largely of canned goods and flour. She was also transporting 266 bags of mail. There were no military supplies aboard. Nor was the vessel armed. She proceeded south at nine knots, hugging the coast in the hope of staying out of harm's way - and in accordance with routing instructions that were issued by the British Routing Office in New York. She was also blacked out: running without navigation lights in order to make her hull a more difficult target to spot.

The *Hebe* put into the Delaware Bay overnight as a temporary safe harbor, then put into the Chesapeake Bay the following night. From there she was instructed to proceed as close to shore as safe navigation would permit. She brushed past the Diamond Shoals and Cape Lookout, then followed the contour of Onslow Bay. On the night of April 10, the *Hebe* rounded Cape Fear and altered course to 233° - approximately west southwest - in order to parallel the shore of Long Bay. Captain J. van der Ploeg, master, relinquished command to his chief officer and retired to his bunk.

Proceeding northeast was Her Majesty's Ship *St. Cathan* (q.v.). The *St. Cathan* was one of twenty-four armed trawlers that Great Britain had loaned to the United States to aid in convoy escort duty. The ex-fishing trawler was armed with two depth-charge racks on the fantail, and a 3-inch, 23 caliber gun mounted on the foredeck. Lieutenant John MacKay, Royal Naval Reserve, was in command of an all-British crew. The *St. Cathan* was also running blacked out.

The night was dark with no moon, and the seas were rough. First Mate B. Visser was on the bridge of the *Hebe*. "I went into the helmsman to check the course. I was in there maybe five or ten seconds - just long enough to look - then the lookout sounded out, 'Ship on port.' It took me only ten or fifteen seconds to get to the lookout. When I came up to him I was looking out on a white and green headlight on the bow of the trawler. Then it was maybe twenty to thirty feet away. . . . I couldn't do anything. It was only a question of seconds. I had come right out of the wheelhouse as soon as I could and there was nothing to do. I was not blinded when I came out and I could see the approaching vessel. It looked like a submarine or a corvette to me. . . . She was straight ahead. The middle of the trawler was right off our bow. Just after I came on the bridge we collided." The time was two hours after midnight.

The running lights of the *St. Cathan* were switched on a moment prior to impact, but by that time a collision was already unavoidable.

The stem of the *Hebe* crashed into the starboard side of the *St. Cathan* abaft the smokestack, and sliced through the hull like a knife through butter. Visser sounded the siren and ordered the *Hebe*'s engines stopped. Captain van der Ploeg rushed onto the bridge. Visser reported the situation to him. The captain instructed the radio operator to transmit an SOS. The captain maneuvered the freighter toward the *St. Cathan*, which now lay dead in the water some two hundred yards away. Some of the *Hebe*'s lights were switched on, and by the faint illumination the freighter's crew could see British seamen swimming for their lives.

Within five minutes of the collision there was six to seven feet of water in the *Hebe*'s forepeak and forward hold. The second engineer reported that the pumps were losing headway. The freighter was settling by the head.

Captain van der Ploeg: "We started lowering a boat to pick up survivors, but word came from the engineers that we were getting water in the boiler room. We had to stop our boats and couldn't pick up all the survivors. We were maneuvered close to try to pick them up, but when [we] found our ship was sinking we stopped lowering boats and tried to look after our own ship. We could not pick up survivors, as we needed the boats ourselves. We picked up five with lines."

The five sodden seamen were taken to the galley to get them warm. One of the survivors was the *St. Cathan's* master, Lieutenant MacKay. He had been asleep at the time of the collision. "I was awakened by what I at first thought was a torpedo explosion. I hastened to the bridge and dimly saw a ship off our starboard quarter, which made me realize we had been in a collision. The Officer of the Watch, Sub-Lieutenant Hodgshon said, 'I put the wheel hard to port.' Also from the confusion of the moment I remember the S.D. rating Coultard saying, 'We had just picked up hydrophone effect ahead.' I asked what had happened, and one of the lookouts said the boat had been carried away.

"Not then realizing how quickly we were sinking I told the Officer of the Watch to inspect the damage, then I looked aft on the starboard side and saw the stern settling quickly. I shouted for Mr. Weston, on the forward deck. He was releasing the Carley float and answered at once. I told him to get the boat ready, but within one minute the ship plunged down stern first. I was sucked down when the bridge went under, but then seemed to be thrown up and clear. When I came to I saw what must have been the stem of the ship above water for a second, illuminated by one of the flares which had ignited in the water. Then it disappeared. From my own calculations, and the impressions of other survivors, I estimate that the ship sank in from four to five minutes."

Lieutenant MacKay's escape was little less than miraculous. In addition to his own observations, he interviewed the other survivors in the hospital. This enabled him to report some additional facts to the U.S. Naval Board of Investigation. Engineman Smith was on duty in the engine room at the time of the collision. "The ship was struck on the starboard side in the way of the engine room, but Smith managed to escape. He says that Stoker Watson, also on watch, managed to reach the deck, but Watson was not seen again. . . . Leading Seaman Humphries and Seaman Parry saw the Carley float, which had been launched, being sucked back under the rigging and gun platform with some men on board."

The impact knocked Donald Smith onto the thrust block. He heard water rushing into the engine room but he could not determine its origin because the lights went out. A sudden rush of water knocked him off his feet. In total darkness he found the life guard and made his way along it until he came to a ladder. Just as he gained the deck he was washed overboard as the ship went down. "I managed to pull clear an oar from the Carley float and I hung on to that and swam around, and after I had been in the water about 20 minutes I picked up a lifebelt. I made two attempts to get to the merchant ship, but the tide was too strong. I swam around in the water for half an hour, and then made a final attempt and came up on the starboard side of the merchant ship. They threw me a line and I was taken aboard." Smith survived only because he was an exceptionally strong swimmer.

On the *Hebe*, Captain van der Ploeg ordered abandon ship. While the boats were being lowered and the emergency survival rafts were being freed from their chocks, Second Officer A. de Bruyn put the British Navy codes and other confidential documents into a weighted bag, and threw it overboard. The entire crew of the *Hebe*, plus the rescued men from the *St. Cathan*, crowded into the two lifeboats. They backed away quickly in order to avoid being swamped in case the freighter capsized suddenly on top of them. Only twenty minutes had passed since the moment of impact.

The *Hebe* continued to settle for the next five to ten minutes. Then she rolled onto her port side and disappeared. The emergency lights were extinguished, leaving the survivors in the near utter blackness of night. When asked about the life rafts, Captain van der Ploeg answered, "After it sunk, they were floating. We were drifting and maybe after 15 minutes got the motorboat ready and started picking up our men. There was just the lights that turn on when the rafts hit the water. Didn't see anybody else. Then we headed for the coast."

Lieutenant MacKay described his rescue: "After I was thrown in the water and swam clear, I saw a man holding on to some wreckage and I joined him at the other end. Then I had to shout for help, and then I swam some distance, I don't remember how far, and helped one of our stokers, Calder, to get to this piece of wreckage. Before I got back I became exhausted and kicked myself clear. Then I got hold of a piece of wood which I passed to him and he was able to join us. I don't know how long I was in the water before I was cramped and very cold. We observed the *Hebe* approaching us, then she seemed to stop. I thought she was picking up survivors, but she stopped. Eventually, both to get there more quickly and to keep from getting cramped, I swam to her. I got to the ship's side and somebody threw me the end of a line. I was joined by two other men, Parry and Humphreys. The men on the deck of the *Hebe* just looked over at us, and we cried for a ladder but they did nothing at all. Eventually Humphreys climbed up, but I could not manage it. After a while they lowered the life boat and I managed to swim over to it and they hauled me on board. Things are rather vague after that. The boat pulled away from the ship and I remember them saying their ship was going down. Some of them spoke English. I lifted myself from the bottom of the boat and I think I saw her go down, but I am not sure. The Chief Officer of the *Hebe* was in the boat and I told him that there were 39 men on my ship and they were all in the water, and he said he would look out for them. I went back into the boat and I remember we were taken in tow by the other boat, which was a motorboat."

Sub-Lieutenant Alexander Weston had this to say: "I got a call from the Captain from the top bridge to unlash the No. 2 lifeboat which was on the starboard side forward. I tried to undo a shackle, but it was a bit tight and I called for a spike. Then I started to unlash the ropes and the next thing I knew the water was up to my neck. After that I was in the water. I was sucked down a little and lost my breath and when I came to the surface, all I could see of the ship was the mast and forecastle. The sea was choppy and I swam around in a circle past two groups of men. I was really looking for what men I could find to bring them together and then I came across an empty lifebelt with a flare. In a very short while I passed close to a raft with the Captain and two or three others. At the same time I remember sighting this ship. I swam to the ship and was hauled aboard. I asked if the lifeboats were being lowered and their reply was that they themselves were sinking. In a few minutes they took to the lifeboats."

Seaman Jack Parry elaborated: "The crew tried to get the floats away and we managed to get one away. As my ship was sinking very quickly, the water brought the float inboard again, and it was sucked underneath the forecastle head and the ship went down. I was on the float at the time and when I saw what was happening to the float, I got clear of it. I was in the water with all the rest of the men, swam about for a while until I found some wreckage and saw the merchantman which I swam to. When I got to the merchantman, the Captain and the gunner were hung on the ship's side with a rope. We asked aid of the merchantman to throw us a ladder, but they never lowered anything to us until they found that they were sinking themselves and then they lowered the lifeboats. The Captain and myself made for the lifeboats and were pulled aboard."

The *Hebe's* motor lifeboat was equipped with a wireless set, but when the operator tried to establish contact he could not obtain a reply. The second lifeboat was tethered to the motor lifeboat by means of a line. Slowly, the boats proceeded eastward.

Lieutenant MacKay was still concerned about his crew. "When we got underway, I mentioned the other men to the Chief Officer again and he said the boat was proceeding to a flare which was bobbing in the water and thought it might be someone, but nobody was picked up there. So far as I know the boat just proceeded, I am not sure of the direction, but I think it was into the wind because I remember a spray coming over the boat. Later in the morning we were picked up, by I think the *Azurlite*."

Seaman Patrick Raitt was washed off the *St. Cathan* when she sank. He made this confusing statement: "I saw one or two dead in the water and got a life belt for one in the water who was unconscious and I managed to pull him up through it and I carried on on my own." Raitt managed to stay afloat for six hours, and to keep Stoker John Lipscomb afloat, until they were picked up by a whaleboat belonging to a passing freighter, whose name he could not recall. "They were foreign people, that is all I know. They transferred me to an American patrol escort yacht."

These ships did not find Raitt and Lipscomb by chance. The *Hebe's* distress call was intercepted by the radio station in Charleston, which relayed the message to all ships in the vicinity. A small convoy consisting of the SS *Kosmos* and her two escorts, the USS *Azurlite* (PY 22) and the USS *Beryl* (PY 23), proceeded directly to the designated area. Lookouts reported a suspicious object. The *Azurlite* ordered the *Kosmos* to move away from the object lest it prove to be a periscope, then maneuvered to interject herself between the *Kosmos* and the object. The "object" was two ratings in lifebelts, whom the *Azurlite* promptly rescued.

In the process of moving away, the *Kosmos* discovered "two men on a wooden potato locker." The *Kosmos* lowered her starboard whaleboat, which plucked the British seamen from the water and transported them to the *Beryl*. The whaleboat also picked up the dead body of a sailor.

Meanwhile, an Army patrol bomber flew over the *Hebe's* lifeboats. The plane circled, dipped its wings, then flew off and directed the *Azurlite* back to the location. The *Kosmos* and the *Beryl* remained on station and conducted a systematic search through a broad field of flotsam.

Lieutenant Commander Charles Thorwall, master of the *Beryl*: "Wreckage sighted consisted of potato locker, several small boxes, seven life rings, two drums, and considerable amount of small boards. Three nude corpses in life jackets were seen 500 yards northwest of the wreckage. An attempt was made to lower lifeboat, but due to rough confused sea, and violent motion of the ship, it was impossible to do so. A further attempt was made to get them aboard with boat hooks, but the life jackets would not hold. Corpses were abandoned and search continued for survivors."

After the search was abandoned, the *Beryl* transported the two survivors and the corpse to Charleston.

The *Azurlite* rescued the thirty-six men in the lifeboats. She hoisted the *Hebe's* motor lifeboat onto her deck by means of her davits, and sank the other lifeboat.

Only nine of the *St. Cathan's* complement lived through the ordeal. Thirty men died in the awful calamity. The survivors were taken to a hospital in Charleston where they were treated for shock and exposure. One crew member of the *Hebe* was treated for two damaged fingers.

A Board of Investigation was held in Charleston two days after the collision. None of the *Hebe's* officers or men attended the investigation. The Board soon learned that the *Hebe's* "officers were very unwilling to cooperate in the questioning." Lieutenant Philip Dennler, master of the *Azurlite*, elaborated: "I received a message to get as many statements as possible . . . which I proceeded to do. I would approach an officer of the *Hebe* and he would just shrug his shoulders and wave his hands in a matter of fact way as if to say 'what's it to you people'. I went to the Master of the *Hebe* and he told me that he was not going to sign anything. Then he did give a statement but very reluctantly." This statement, along with a transcript of Lieutenant Dennler's interrogation of witnesses, was submitted to the Board as an exhibit.

It developed that the "*Hebe* was not following the route prescribed by the routing instructions covering her voyage but was about twenty-five (25) miles to seaward of the prescribed shipping lane at the time of collision."

After three days of testimony the Naval Court formed its opinion. "Proper lookout watches were being kept in H.M.S. *Saint Cathan*," and, "Lookout watches in the S.S. *Hebe* were insufficient and not alert." These opinions do not appear to reflect the fact that lookouts from neither vessel spotted the oncoming vessel until moments before collision was imminent.

Additionally, "The collision and resultant losses were not due to the fault, negligence or inefficiency of any person serving in H.M.S. *Saint Cathan*."

Furthermore, "Lack of prompt rescue action by the S.S. *Hebe* contributed to the loss of life. . . . The officers of the S.S. *Hebe* were unduly reluctant to impart information immediately upon their rescue. . . . The master of the S.S. *Hebe* was at fault in that he did not comply with his instructions concerning the route to be followed as prescribed in his routing instructions."

There is no doubt that the crew of the *Hebe* could have provided better assistance to the men in the water by the freighter's side, and that they could have conducted a more thorough search for survivors before departing. Yet, it must be remembered that, had it not been for the prompt transmission of the SOS, along with the precise location of the disaster, four of the *St. Cathan's* ratings would undoubtedly have perished.

The U.S. Naval Court's opinion appears to be tainted with subservience to the British Navy - an appeasement, or perhaps an apology, intended to soothe the soul of the British government for the deplorable demise of British subjects who died in the performance of their duties in the fight against Nazi domination of the world. If true, it demonstrated an amazing prescience in light of the fact that three more British armed trawlers were lost off the eastern seaboard during the following five months. The HMS *Bedfordshire* was torpedoed by a German U-boat on May 12. (For details, see *Shipwrecks of North Carolina: from Hatteras Inlet South*, by this author.) The HMS *Kingston Ceylonite* struck a German mine on June 15 (see *Shipwrecks of Virginia*). The HMS *Pentland Firth* was sunk by collision on September 19 (see *Shipwrecks of New Jersey: North*).

Despite Captain van der Ploeg's reluctance to speak about the collision and its aftermath, he was remarkably forgiving with respect to the true underlying cause of the disaster. "I have no criticism. This was just a matter of circumstances, a matter of war. It would not have happened if it had not been for the war. Absolutely a simple war matter, no ships would be blacked out except for the war. Even dim lights can be seen several miles on a dark night. Dim lights are no good. Must black out everything. It was absolutely war circumstances. Even with conditions it is better to have black out, especially going along the coast. If you put your lights on you can see it too far. We don't smoke, use flashlights, or any lights on the bridge, on deck. You can see a cigarette for a mile or a mile and a half distance. If you get thick weather, or foggy, you have to use dim lights, otherwise, no."

When all is said and done, black-out conditions were a necessary evil. We will never know how many ships were saved from a watery grave by making themselves invisible to German lookouts.

Today, the wreck lies stretched out on the bottom in near picture perfect imitation of the ship that she once was. The hull is contiguous from stem to stern. The starboard hull rises some 15 feet off the seabed, while the port side is broken down into a debris field that reaches out twenty to thirty feet. Cargo booms are sometimes exposed in this debris field.

Although the decking is gone, both the forward hatch coaming and the after hatch coaming are clearly delineated. Sand rises to within a few feet of these coamings - a strong indication of how far the wreck has settled into the seabed. The two boilers lie side by side amidships, and the engine stands tall directly behind them. The propeller shaft is partially exposed, from the engine block through the after hatch, at which point it disappears under the stern. The stern section is high and penetrable on two levels. All this makes the *Hebe* a fun and exciting dive to explore.

Beer bottles may be found anywhere within the hull and in the debris field. They were part of the cargo. All are embossed with Spanish writing. The lucky diver might also find the occasional brass ingot that was part of the cargo. Each ingot was stamped "FMC".

HECTOR

Built: 1909   Sunk: July 14, 1916
Previous names: None   Depth: 35 feet
Gross tonnage: 11,250   Dimensions: 403' x 53' x 24'
Type of vessel: Collier   Power: Coal-fired steam
Builder: Maryland Steel Company, Sparrows Point, Maryland
Owner: U.S. Navy   Official designation: AC-7
Cause of sinking: Foundered
Loran 45380.3 / 60027.1   GPS 32-59.984 / 79-06.108

The *Hector* was one of three ultramodern sister ships that were designed to meet U.S. Navy specifications with regard to cargo carrying capacity. The other two colliers were the *Mars* and the *Vulcan*. Each was capable of hauling 7,200 deadweight tons.

"They are single-decked self-trimming vessels, with poop bridge and forecastle, with a pilot house above the bridge, two masts and ten derrick posts; each having two booms, arranged to lift hatch covers and to handle cargo. There are ten large hatches with steel covers, especially fitted to be water tight. A double bottom runs from the after boiler room bulkhead to the forward peak bulkhead, and upper wing ballast tanks are formed in the triangular space between the deck and the side, outboard of the cargo hatches. The machinery space, containing four Scotch boilers, two triple-expansion engines and auxiliaries, is placed aft. The bunker coal is carried in longitudinal bunkers abreast the boilers and on the main deck around the boiler casing. a donkey boiler is located on a flat forward in the boiler room. Fresh-water tanks are in the engine room, while a refrigerating plant is located on the main deck aft. The officers' quarters are in the bridge house, the engineer's in the after-deck house on the poop deck, and the crew on the main deck aft. The forecastle contains the windlass engine and storerooms. The hull and machinery are constructed in accordance with the requirements of the American Bureau of Shipping for their highest class."

There were seven bulkheads which divided the hull into eight watertight compartments. The forwardmost compartment was the forepeak, then came the five cargo holds, then the boiler room compartment and the engine room compartment, far aft. The bridge straddled the third bulkhead from the bow, which separated hold #2 from hold #3. The after deck house was perched above the boiler rooms and the engine rooms.

The heavy-duty winches and clamshell buckets of the coaling gear could offload between one hundred and two hundred tons of coal per hour per hatch. "If now, the clamshell bucket is introduced on all of our colliers it is clear that coal may be delivered in bulk at various parts of a battleship. Therefore, the necessity for winches and booms, and also for rigging on battleships, will disap-

pear, because it is clear that the problem will then be one of taking the coal from piles on deck and shoveling it either to the chutes that are nearest the piles or shoveling it into bags or baskets and dragging them across the deck to other parts of the battleship. In the old method, also, the sailors were sent into the hold to shovel coal into bags, and it is worthy of note that the old colliers seldom delivered more than 25 tons of coal per hour per hatch, and even that required from 20 to 25 men. The *Mars* can easily discharge 1,000 tons of coal per hour - the work of a thousand men - and only twenty men will be required to perform this."

The *Hector's* propellers were nearly fifteen feet in diameter. The blades were made of bronze.

Despite these innovations, the *Hector* did not see as much service as one would expect. She was officially commissioned on October 22, 1909. For the next three years she "carried fuel and stores for the ships of the Atlantic fleet in routine operations. Then she was laid up for more than a year. She was placed in full commission on February 16, 1914. For the next year and a half she traveled around the world to such wide-flung ports as Manila, Honolulu, and Guam. "Subsequently, she did intermittent duty in Haitian and San Domingan waters transporting passengers and carrying stores and fuel."

The *Hector* was designated as a naval auxiliary vessel. Instead of being commanded by regular naval officers and manned by a naval crew, she had a merchant captain and merchant officers and crew.

On July 10, 1916, the *Hector* departed Norfolk, Virginia. She was deeply laden with 11,000 tons of soft coal that was bound for the U.S. Navy station at Guantanamo Bay, Cuba. On board were twelve officers and sixty seamen. The collier had orders to take on a detachment of marines from Port Royal: the naval port attached to the marine base at Parris Island, just north of Hilton Head on South Carolina's southern seaboard. These marines were needed for "urgent duty" in San Domingo, the port city of the Dominican Republic. On July 12, the *Hector* dropped anchor off the *Charleston* lightship to await the arrival of the marines. Sixty marines were transferred aboard that afternoon.

The *Hector* was released to continue on her way. She did not go far before she found her stem driving into the teeth of a gale that was working its way north from the Caribbean. The gale developed into a furious hurricane. High winds whipped to seas to a froth, and thick rain severely reduced visibility. The *Hector* was in trouble before she knew it. Her hull was battered brutally, and she began making water through the cargo hatches, which became loose because of the heavy seas that broke completely over the ship. This caused the vessel to take on a starboard list. Tremendous waves struck the side of the hull so hard that the seams worked loose. Water now squirted into the holds through the ruptured seams. The wet coal shifted to port, which increased the list even further. Eventually, the *Hector* listed over so far that her starboard rail was "about awash."

Disabled and unmanageable, the *Hector* hove to and dropped her anchors. So strong were the wind and current that the collier was dragged northward at speed that estimated to have been three to four knots. She was clearly at the mercy of the storm.

On July 14 came the final calamity: the *Hector* was driven onto a sandbar - no one knew where.

The stern was solidly aground but the bow floated freely. Captain G.F. Newell, the merchant master of the *Hector*, ordered the wireless operator to communicate the ship's perilous condition to naval authorities. He thought the *Hector* was located ten miles south-southeast of Charleston light. However, he had no way of determining the distance that the vessel had dragged. The captain could not establish his position with any accuracy because of the rain and the dark overcast sky. A sextant and a table of calculations were useless without a sighting of the sun. In essence he was lost - a circumstance that thwarted rescue vessels and salvage tugs from locating the beleaguered collier with any promptitude.

The Navy dispatched vessels from various quarters to search the seas between Charleston and Georgetown for any sign of the *Hector*. The Navy also broadcast a general alert to vessels that were anywhere near the area to alter course to coincide with the collier's most likely track, and to post a sharp lookout. Seven vessels converged on this broad stretch of ocean: *Alamo*, *Vigilant*, *Cypress*, *Paducah*, *Somerset*, *Relief*, and *Seminole*.

Naval authorities intercepted various transmissions from the *Hector*. At 3:55 p.m.: "Sent wrong position will verify think we are 20 miles from Cape Romain." At 4:04 p.m.: "Send help at once I am aground have more men than boats will hold all now lowering boats." (The marine contingent boosted the number of personnel aboard to one hundred thirty-two.) At 4:25 p.m.: "Can't get to Captain now. He is forward on the bridge, and we are breaking in two. . . . Please hurry before it is too late." Then: "We are aground and broken in half; heavy sea running, men now in boats." Further transmissions were unintelligible due to a grounded antenna.

The naval station in Key West, Florida plucked this transmission out of the air, but could not identify the vessel that had sent it: "USS *Hector* in sinking condition forty-five one seven zero true from *Charleston* light vessel." Interpretation: 45 miles from the *Charleston* lightship on a bearing of 170°, or practically due south. The last reported position received from the *Hector* was twenty miles *north* of Cape Romain. Charleston and Cape Romain were about thirty miles apart. The straight line distance between the two most distant positions reported was nearly one hundred miles. The *Hector* could lie anywhere in between - or possibly farther afield.

The hurricane complicated the coordination of rescue efforts by breaking telephone lines, knocking down telegraph poles, and disrupting landside communications sporadically. At 7:05 p.m., when a worried Admiral Benson was finally able to place a long distance call from Washington, DC to Charleston, he was told, "Wind has gone down, hurricane seems to be over, are at present having a thunder storm." Admiral Benson asked, "Have you any reason to believe that the *Hector* knows her position?" The reply was, "No she does not. She is only guessing at it."

It now seemed likely that the men were adrift in small boats - and in seas so rough that pilot boats were forced to turn back to port, leaving several ships at anchor outside Charleston harbor to weather out the storm as best they could. Via wireless, rescue vessels maintained a running commentary on the locations they were searching. As the night wore on, the only news they had to report was where the *Hector* was *not*. They kept crisscrossing the most likely grid in the hope that they would stumble over the stranded collier.

Finally, at 1:00 a.m. this welcome news was received from the lighthouse tender *Cyprus*: "*Cyprus* has on board captain and 20 of crew of *Hector*, rest taken into Wilmington. *Hector* abandoned 12:35 a.m. 7 miles N.E. of Cape Romain gas buoy both anchors down vessel broken in two."

Naval authorities thirsted for additional information. They wondered which vessel or vessels had picked up the rest of the men, and why the survivors were being taken to Wilmington. Elucidation followed in a subsequent transmission from the *Cyprus*: "Tug *Wilmington* has remainder of crew and marines aboard heading for Charleston." Later it developed that *Wilmington* was a typographical error. The name of the tug that rescued the men was the *Wellington*.

All hands were saved. With a collective sigh of relief, the Navy broadcast this final message to all ships: "No further search necessary. Services rendered very highly appreciated."

From *Scientific American*.

This view of the after section is undated, but the white hats imply that these men are U.S. Navy personnel, not civilian salvors. Note the vessel lying against the *Hector's* starboard stern. (From the author's collection.)

The diagram on the opposite page is from *Scientific American*.

Wreck of USS.

No sooner were the grateful men landed in Charleston than the Navy initiated salvage operations. The U.S. gunboat *Paducah* (AG-7) examined the wreck on July 15. The *Hector* was solidly aground. The starboard hull was separated just abaft the bridge, and the deck was torn clear across to the port side. The hull was sagging amidships. Worse than that, the bow section was slewed thirty degrees to port with respect to the stern section. It appeared as if the waves had pounded against the floating forward section until it snapped in two like a broken pencil. Huge waves surged into the open break.

Naval inspectors landed on the forward section. They found that every compartment was flooded except for hold #2, which contained the ship's storerooms. Due to the heavy seas they "could not attempt to visit after part without undue risk." They recovered some navigational instruments. The inspectors recommended that an expert salvage outfit examine the hull "in smooth weather" to determine the possibility of raising the *Hector* in two sections.

Merritt and Chapman Derrick and Wrecking Company was hired to make a more thorough examination of the hull. On July 17, the salvage vessel *Relief* transported the company's salvage experts to the wreck. They boarded the stern section and found that all the compartments were completely flooded except for the engine room, which was only partially flooded: the water was twelve feet below the outside level. They recommended the salvage of the sixteen coaling winches and booms, the five anchors, the chain, the windlass, and "other strippings." In their opinion, however, the hull was a total constructive loss.

By July 18 the wreck was fast falling to pieces. The storerooms were no longer accessible. Rivets located under water were loose. The hull was flooded throughout. And the ocean was still too rough to attempt to offload removable items by means of launches.

Nonetheless, the Navy thought it might be possible to salvage the two halves separately, tow them to the Navy yard at Charleston, and rejoin them. They hired Merritt and Chapman for the job. "The wrecking tug *Rescue* and an ocean wrecking barge, with all necessary apparatus, including 15 pumps, air compressors, etc., were dispatched to the wreck. Operations for saving the ship were begun. Anchors were laid, cables bent on, and the pumps, compressors and boilers were set up on the quarter deck. . . . The engine and boiler compartments in the extreme after portion of the wreck, and the adjoining hold, number five, were pumped out, bringing the stern up. . . . Then, by means of the anchors and cables, the stern was pulled around until it lay in a northeast direction and faced the prevailing seas. This was done to enable the wreck to take the seas stern on and save the hull from the severe buffeting it would receive if it took them on broadside.

"It was the purpose of the wrecking company to make tight the bulkhead between holds four and three; jettison the coal in holds four and five; pump them out and float the after section, compressed air being used to assist in bringing the wreck to the afloat condition. The same methods were to be used on the forward section. All that was necessary was a suitable spell of calm weather . . . "

The salvage plan was certainly viable. The salvors went to work with a will. Nine consecutive days of good weather gave them a good start. Then a storm blew in. "The successive spells of calm were very short, and the work of repairing the smashup of gear and plank during the recurring rough weather occupied the whole of the following period of calm." And so it went. Each storm destroyed the work that had been accomplished in the preceding calm. Merritt and Chapman stayed on the job until October, when a northeast gale struck the coast.

The salvors were stuck in port for a week. When they returned to the wreck they found that the bow section had settled so much that it was almost completely submerged at low tide. The stern section had settled considerably, and had swung back to westward with the stern pointing north. The cofferdams around number five hold were washed away, and the materials were badly damaged.

The salvors worked intermit-

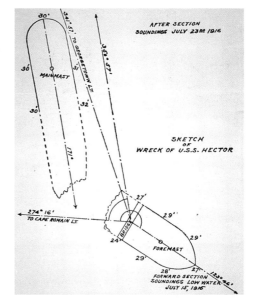

In this view the stern is still riding high. (From the author's collection.)

tently for another month. Finally, on November 11, they secured operations for the winter - and, as it developed, forever.

Today, the wreck has been designated as an artificial reef site; it lies inshore of shoal buoy WR-4. Storms have taken their toll over the years. No sections of the hull are contiguous. Discrete quantities of wreckage lie sprawled about the bottom like the hollow building blocks of a Cyclopean child. It is difficult to visualize anything on the site that resembles a ship, or even segments of a ship. Two hawse pipes were the only parts that I recognized. Room-sized structures lie on a white sandy bottom, each structure separated from its neighbor by five to ten feet or more.

These large structures provide ample safe havens for fish that like to hide: grouper, spadefish, flounder, and so on. Many of these structures are large enough for divers to swim through. One such structure was fifty feet in length, twenty-five feet wide, and eight feet high; its interior was a crosshatch of vertical beams and diagonal supporting members. Inside, barracudas cruised slowly through schools of darting fish. Outside, I saw amberjacks, cobias, and stingrays.

The wreck is sprawled liberally across a huge swath of seabed. The highest point of relief is 12 feet.

In this view the stern has settled to the bottom. (Courtesy of the Naval Photographic Center.)

MADGIE

Built: 1858
Previous names: None
Gross tonnage: 220
Type of vessel: Wooden-hulled screw steamer
Builder: Philadelphia, Pennsylvania
Owner: U.S. Navy
Cause of sinking: Foundered
Location: 12 miles southeast of the *Frying Pan Shoals* lightship

Sunk: October 11, 1863
Depth: 110 feet
Dimensions: 122' x 22' x 8'
Power: Coal-fired steam

Classification: 4th rate screw steamer

After the commencement of the War Between the States, the U.S. Navy found itself with a serious shortage of ships. For the most part, this was due to the fact that the Confederate States confiscated any naval vessels that were in their possession at the time of secession. To make matters worse, the federal strategy to blockade Southern ports required a large number of steamships in order to enforce the blockade and to capture Confederate blockade runners. To make up for this shortage, the U.S. Navy purchased merchant vessels and converted them for military purposes.

The *Madgie* was a small coastal steamer that operated on the Philadelphia Line to Hartford, Connecticut. She possessed one deck on which was perched a small cabin. Her wooden hull was constructed of oak that was sheathed with copper. She was propelled by a single-piston, direct-action steam engine.

On October 14, 1861, R.F. Loper sold the three-year-old *Madgie* to the Navy for $13,000. The Navy installed a two-gun battery on November 9. This battery was exchanged on March 29, 1862 for one 30-pounder Parrott rifle and one 20-pounder Parrott rifle. Her battery was increased on May 4, 1863 to include two 24-pounder broadside howitzers and one light 12-pounder smooth bore. These were the guns with which the *Madgie* was armed at the time of her loss. She carried a crew of forty-five officers and seamen.

The *Madgie* was assigned to the South Atlantic Blockading Squadron. She was not particularly fast, but her shallow draft permitted her to navigate creeks and inlets that deeper draft vessels could not navigate without fear of running aground. On more than one occasion the *Madgie* was taken on reconnaissance patrols along the inland waterways of Georgia and South Carolina. Her guns were put to good use against Confederate forts and batteries.

Ironically, during her two years of naval service, the government spent more than twice the amount on repairs to the *Madgie* than it had originally paid to purchase the vessel.

In 1863, the *Madgie* experienced mechanical breakdowns that required the engine to be overhauled. This put her out of action for several weeks. Subsequent to that she began to leak. On August 1, Acting Master Woodbury Polleys submitted a report to Rear Admiral John Dahlgren - who was in command of the South Atlantic Blockading Squadron - with regard to the condition of the hull: "When I joined her some two months ago she was leaking at the rate of 2 inches per hour in smooth water; in a seaway, much more. The leak has steadily increased till at present she leaks from 4 to 6 inches. On the 26th instant [sic] I received permission to examine her bottom from Lieutenant Kittredge, senior officer present. On the morning of the 28th I put her on the beach, with tackles at the masthead to keep her upright, so that I could examine the offshore side and then list her over to examine the inshore side. On the starboard or offshore side I found about twenty or thirty sheets of copper off that had probably been off since she was ashore on Cape Lookout some sixteen months ago. She has so flat a floor that we could not well get at it, but by cleaning the grass off with brooms we found that where the copper was off her bottom was a perfect honeycomb, it is so badly eaten by the worms. I send you a sample of her bottom planking and keel enclosed in a box. She has no shoe on and no copper on the bottom of her keel that we could see. On the port side the copper was not off so bad, but where it was off is badly worm-eaten; in one place clear through the timbers, leaving a hole 4 inches square, over which I put a patch of board and canvas. It is astonishing to me how she has kept afloat so long. In all my experience of twenty-five years at sea I have not seen a vessel's bottom in so bad a condition. When we heeled her offshore the water came out of her bottom like out of a sieve. The iron extension that the rudder is shipped on is only held by one bolt, the others having rusted off. Otherwise she is in good condition as regards said, rigging, anchors, chares, etc., with a good and efficient battery I don't think she is safe to go to Port Royal without a tug in company. We have only the deck pumps to keep her free, as the donkey pump has given out and the engineer reports he is not able to repair it, and her engine is so bad that she will not steam ahead in a head sea and will only go 3 knots in still water. Enclosed you will find the reports of the carpenter, engineer, etc. We are lying at present without fires, being out of coal."

Admiral Dahlgren accepted the opinions of his subordinates in the field. On September 14, he wrote to Secretary of the Navy Gideon Welles from his flagship outside of Charleston: "The *Madgie* is here in a condition to be towed home, but not fit to go home by steam, and it is my opinion that she is not worth tow."

Gideon Welles, from his safe sanctuary in Washington, DC, believed otherwise. He ordered the *Madgie* to "come north," adding the proviso that she should "not carry over 15 pounds of steam."

Admiral Dahlgren complied with Welles's request. However, he was cautious enough to assign an escort for the *Madgie*, "because it is represented that her bottom is in such condition as to render it advisable that some vessel should be with her."

At 5 p.m. on October 10, 1863, the *Madgie* departed from the Charleston bar under tow of the USS *Fahkee*. Their destination was Hampton Roads, Virginia. The weather was fine, the sea was smooth, and a breeze blew gently from the north-northeast. The *Madgie* was leaking at the rate of six inches per hours.

According to the brief report filed by Woodbury Polleys, the acting master

of the *Madgie*, "At 4 a.m. on the 11th wind increased, with a heavy sea, ship pitching heavily and the leak increasing at 9 a.m. Heavy head sea during the day, but by keeping the engine and deck pumps constantly going could keep the ship free. At 5 p.m. I saw a piece of her sheathing come up alongside, and the water at once commenced gaining on the pumps. Thinking the sheathing came from a hole in her bows . . . I immediately lightened the ship forward by bringing the chain cables aft on the spar deck. The water still increasing and gaining on the pumps. At 6 p.m., after consulting with the officers, I concluded to abandon the ship, as we could not keep her free. Communicated with the *Fahkee* and sent the paymaster with his books, papers, and funds on board.

"At 6:30 water was over the berth deck; pumps still going. At 6:40 engine pumps reported choked; ordered away all boats to save the effects of officers and crew. At 6:45 ordered the men to leave the pumps, it being useless to try to keep the vessel free with deck pumps alone, the water being then over the fire-room floor. At 7 p.m. I left the ship with the last boat and mustered the *Madgie's* crew on board the *Fahkee*.

"At 8:45, the *Madgie* having entirely filled, rolled heavily to starboard and sank in 18 fathoms of water, the *Frying Pan Shoals* lightship bearing by compass N.W., 12 miles distant. The *Fahkee* laid by her till the last, only cutting the towing hawser when the *Madgie* disappeared beneath the water. I can not speak in too high praise of the officers and men. Although very dark, every one obeyed orders to the last, and the men never left the pumps until ordered to do so by me. But very few of the officers and men saved anything except the clothing they had on. Of the effects of the ship, I saved only the chronometer and three boats."

Two weeks later, a contemporary Confederate correspondent wrote: "Doubtless her heavy battery carried her instantly to the bottom, where, in company with the *Cumberland*, *Congress*, *Monitor*, and thousands of other vessels, she will lie till judgment day." If he intended to imply that the gunboat would never be salvaged, either in whole or in part, his prediction is holding true. The wreck of the *Madgie* has so far not been located.

From *Harper's Weekly.*

MINNEHAHA

Built: ?
Previous names: ?
Gross tonnage: ?
Type of vessel: Two-masted schooner
Cause of sinking: Foundered
Location: Off Charleston

Sunk: October 4, 1866
Depth: Unknown
Dimensions:
Power: Sail

On September 29, 1866, the schooner *Minnehaha* departed Savannah in good weather. She was bound for Richmond, Virginia. In those days, there was no way to transmit information from the Caribbean that a tropical storm was working its way toward the North American continent. The *Minnehaha* experienced "nothing remarkable" during her first day of northing, because the seas were relatively calm. The following day, however, the sky assumed a black and ominous appearance, and the wind picked up until it was blowing with the full force of a gale. As the wind was coming out of the east northeast, it tended to halt the schooner in her tracks, and perhaps it drove her back in the direction from which she had come. At that time, the captain estimated that the *Minnehaha* lay wallowing approximately eighty miles east of Charleston.

The captain "lay the vessel to under three-reefed foresail." The gale "soon increased to a hurricane with a tremendous sea." Gigantic waves washed over the deck with ever-increasing strength. Seawater seeped into the holds through the hatch covers, and the hull began to leak as a result of the powerful stresses that were imparted by the mountainous seas. For three days the crew labored unceasingly at the hand-operated pumps. Even though they worked in rotation the men were soon exhausted.

The mainmast splintered with an ear-shattering crack and fell by the way-side, bringing down with it a cat's-cradle of rigging. The foremast and the bowsprit were sprung. Suddenly the *Minnehaha* lay in desperate straits. She was "shipping large quantities of water, and laboring very heavy. At midnight the gale moderated to some extent; got reefed jib and double-reefed foresail on, and head-ed to the westward, the vessel still leaking badly."

On October 4, the steamer *George Cromwell* hove into view. She was on a passage from New Orleans, Louisiana to New York. In addition to her own pas-sengers and crew, she had onboard all eighteen passengers and twenty-five crew members of the steamer *Daniel Webster*, which had foundered in the same storm off Cape Canaveral, Florida, on the previous day. Captain Vaill, master of the *George Cromwell*, now undertook to save the captain and the four-man crew of the *Minnehaha*. This he accomplished without loss of life, thus acting the savior of forty-eight thankful souls.

Stated the captain of the Minnehaha, "To Capt. Vaill and officers I hereby tender my sincere thanks for their kind attention to myself and crew."

The location of the *Minnehaha* has not been established.

NORTH CAROLINA

Built: 1838
Previous names: None
Gross tonnage: 370
Type of vessel: Wooden-hulled side wheeler
Builder: New York
Owner: Wilmington & Raleigh Rail Road Company, Wilmington, North Carolina
Port of registry: Wilmington, North Carolina
Cause of sinking: Collision with SS *Governor Dudley*
Loran 45372.2 / 59650.6

Sunk: July 26, 1840
Depth: 65 feet
Dimensions: 160' x 24' x 9'
Power: Coal-fired steam

GPS 33-24.185 / 78-40.557

The *North Carolina* was a steam packet that traveled between the ports of Wilmington, North Carolina and Charleston, South Carolina. When she departed Wilmington on July 25, 1840, the sea was perfectly calm and "the night was one of the finest we have ever witnessed." It was estimated that thirty to forty individuals were on board for that final, fateful passage. Among the passengers were seven distinguished members of Congress, who were returning to their constituencies in Georgia, Alabama, and Louisiana. Captain Davis was the master of the *North Carolina*. The only woman on board was the wife of the Honorable Mr. Hubbard (Alabama), who was accompanied by their son.

Plying the identical but reciprocal course was the SS *Governor Dudley*. Shortly after midnight, the captains of both vessels retired to their bunks. Each ship was then in command of her respective chief mate. Around one o'clock in the morning, the signal lanterns of the two approaching vessels became visible to each other. There was no immediate cause for alarm: the vessels were yet three to five miles apart, and it appeared that they were aligned properly for a port to port passing. Soon, however, it became apparent that the vessels were steering directly toward each other, each at a speed of about twelve miles per hour.

There was strong disagreement about the maneuvers that preceded the collision. Some observers stated that the *Governor Dudley* altered course in order to pass to the starboard of the *North Carolina*, and in doing so, crossed the path of the oncoming vessel. Others stated just the opposite: that the *Governor Dudley* maintained a straight course, and that the *North Carolina* turned into her path. Chief Mate McQuade, who was in command of the *North Carolina*, stated that when collision became imminent he rang the ship's bell and ordered the helmsman to turn to starboard in order to avert collision.

Be that as it may, the bow of the *Governor Dudley* pierced the *North Carolina's* after port quarter abreast of the saloon. The *North Carolina* was instantly bilged. The hull flooded so quickly that "before half of the passengers could get out of their berths, the cabins were filled with water, and most of those on board were compelled to leap from the hurricane deck."

The *Provincial* is a near lookalike of the *North Carolina*. (From *Early American Steamers*, by Erik Heyl.)

Both vessels wasted no time in launching lifeboats. The Honorable Mr. Chinn (Louisiana) suffered a concussion, and the Honorable Mr. Dawson (Georgia) was injured "by leaping off one boat to the other." Passenger D.J. Dowling jumped overboard in his shirt, "but was instantly picked up by one of the boats in charge of Capt. Davis, who displayed considerable presence of mind during this awful disaster." The lifeboats rescued everyone in the water, and conveyed them to the *Governor Dudley*.

The *North Carolina* sank within ten to fifteen minutes of the collision. The bow of the *Governor Dudley* was "a good deal shattered, but she made no water except while under way." Elsewhere it was noted that the hole was four feet square, "and at first leaked badly, but the aperture was in a measure closed with blankets, tarpaulins, and other articles of a like nature."

The passengers of the *North Carolina* beseeched Captain Smith, master of the *Governor Dudley*, to remain in the vicinity of the wreck in order to recover whatever items could be found floating on the surface. Most of the passengers were without any belongings except for the nightclothes they were wearing at the time of the collision. Some of these trunks that went down with the ship were of special worth, not because of the clothing inside but because of the money "and other valuable articles" that they contained: estimated to be worth between $15,000 and $20,000.

The *Governor Dudley* remained on site until daylight. It was reported that "seven leather, and two canvass bags, containing the mails, were saved." This amount was less than half the mail bags that were known to be on board. "Those whose trunks were picked up found their contents so completely saturated that they were of no service." The *Governor Dudley* arrived in Wilmington around half past three that afternoon.

Immediate plans were made to return to the site of the collision in order to retrieve additional items from the wreck. Captain Davis returned on a pilot boat, and the steamship *Vanderbilt* was dispatched from Wilmington. The *Vanderbilt* found timbers and part of the hurricane deck, but nothing of any value.

On August 14, the *Charleston Courier* reported, "Several pieces of the ill fated *North Carolina*, have been found on the front beach of North Island." On September 2, the same newspaper reported, "A trunk belonging to the Hon. Mr. Nisbet, of Georgia, and which was lost on the *North Carolina*, has been picked up on Baldhend Beach." One might wonder how many other trunks floated free of the wreckage only to disappear: either when they lost their buoyancy and sank again, or when they washed up on the beach and were covered by sand.

The most nagging question, however, has always been this: how much of that $15,000 to $20,000 was paper money, and how much of it was gold? The bills would long since have deteriorated, but gold lasts forever!

The site has long been known to local recreational divers as the Copper Pot, so called because of the wreck's copper boiler. Pete Manchee identified the Copper Pot as the *North Carolina* in the 1980's - not by anything that was recovered from the site, but by the age of the machinery and by the location of the wreck, which lay almost directly along the *North Carolina's* route between Wilmington and Charleston.

Not much of the wreck remains (or is exposed) after more than a century and a half: the shaft of the paddle wheel, an anchor, and the eponymous copper pot, or boiler. The wreckage is widely dispersed, leading one to believe that it might have been torn apart accidentally by the nets of draggers. The distance between the paddle wheel shaft and the boiler is 260 feet. Nothing but white sand intervenes.

I had an interesting encounter on the site. The boiler was one of antique construction: a metal cylinder some twelve to fifteen feet in length, from which the perpendicular tube of the flue extended at the level of the seabed to a distance of six feet. (The boiler lies on its side.) I could clearly see large copper rivets where the sand had been washed away from the curved base of the boiler. After circling the boiler, I saw noticed that the flue was large enough to enter: about four feet in diameter. I crawled inside the flue with the intention of penetrating to the boiler, in order to see if the internal copper tubes were still in place, or if they had dropped to the bottom with the collapse of the mounting frame and thereby left the boiler a hollow shell. I pushed my camera inside ahead of me. I got only my head and chest inside when I saw that a light gray or silvery shark was resting inside the main cylinder of the boiler - by which I can assume that the copper tubes must have fallen away. I could see only four feet of the shark's tail and lower abdomen, to the point at which it barely began to fatten. From experience with sharks and with what I could observe, I estimated that the shark exceeded eight feet in length, and was possibly as long as ten feet or more. I did not recognize the long tapering tail, but the slender girth and the lack of dark splotches made it seem apparent that it was not a sand tiger shark - one that is not (under normal circumstances) a species that attacks man.

After a moment of irrational contemplation, during which I thought stupidly of tweaking the shark's delicate tail, I decided that it was not a healthy course of action to pursue, especially in light of the fact that my body effectively blocked its only means of escape. I did not relish being trapped inside a boiler with a startled shark of monstrous proportions. Arriving at (for me) the rare conclusion that discretion was the better part of valor, I cautiously refrained my tripping my camera's strobe, and quietly backed out of the tube to let the sleeping shark lie.

In 1996, treasure salvor Herbo Humphries proposed to conduct a commercial recovery operation on the *North Carolina*. Humphreys owned an underwater salvage company called Marex International. On August 12, he applied to the Federal Court in Savannah, Georgia for exclusive salvage rights to "the unidentified, wrecked and abandoned vessel, her hull, cargo, tackle and appurtenances," whose location was the same as that of the Copper Pot. As no competitors contested Humphreys' claim, he was duly appointed by the Court as the wreck's Substitute Custodian. This action enabled Marex to work the site without interference.

Humphrey's plan was to either airlift the sand off the embedded hull or to blast it away with prop wash deflectors, then scoop up the gold and silver that lay loose underneath. In its promotional material, Marex claimed that the treasure was originally worth some $77,000. Company executives estimated its present value at more than $20 million. That's a fairly high rate of inflation, but factored into the equation that was used to determine the current market value were such multipliers as numismatic rarity, prior ownership by Congressional delegates, and the fact that the gold was recovered from an historic shipwreck.

The *Beacon's* mammoth prop wash deflectors.

Marex worked on this ambitious project off and on for the next two years - as weather and other circumstances permitted. Operational costs were between $5,000 and $10,000 per day when the salvage vessel *Beacon* was engaged on the job. After several months on site, divers moved enough sand away to reveal the wooden hull. They dug down to the keel in what they believed to be the cabin area. In all they recovered eighteen gold coins, two gold watches, many ornate trunk latches, and a quantity of copper ore. Each coin was touted to be worth some $57,000. How much each coin actually realized on the open market is corporate information.

OSCEOLA

Built: 1848
Previous names: None
Gross tonnage: 177
Type of vessel: Screw steamer
Builder: Hogg & Delamater, Brooklyn, New York
Owner: P.N. Spofford, New York, NY
Port of registry: New York, NY
Cause of sinking: Ran aground
Location: Off North Island, near Georgetown

Sunk: November 2, 1861
Depth: Unknown
Dimensions: 117' x 22' x 7'
Power: Coal-fired steam

The *Osceola* was a small screw steamer that transported freight between the port of New York and Caribbean ports in Cuba and Honduras. After the onset of the Civil War, she was chartered by the U.S. Quartermaster Department. She was operating in that capacity when the Great Expedition to take Port Royal from Confederate hands was organized by Flag-Officer Samuel Dupont and Brigadier General T.W. Sherman (not William Tecumseh). Captain Morrill, master, received no instructions as to where his vessel was destined to proceed. He was ordered simply to follow the fleet. (See *Governor* for more details about the Great Expedition.)

Captain Morrill rendered an account of the loss of the *Osceola*. "The *Osceola* sailed from New York on Thursday, October 24th, for Hampton Roads, with a cargo consisting of fifty head of beef cattle, five hundred barrels of potatos [sic] and sundries, arrived at Fortress Monroe, October 27th, where eleven head of cattle were landed, leaving thirty-nine on the vessel. At New York we were ordered to take on board water and provisions for only fifteen days, which made it evident we were not to proceed South of the coast of Georgia, as such a supply would not have answered for a trip to the gulf. Remained in Hampton Roads until Tuesday, October 29th, when the entire fleet sailed, consisting of from fifty to sixty sail of vessels of all classes, from the powerful steamships *Vanderbilt*, *Baltic*, *Wabash*, *Minnesota* and *Roanoke*, to the ordinary sized tug boat.

"On Wednesday it blew heavily from the Southwest, lasting twelve hours, when the wind changed Northwest, and continued stormy, but the smaller vessels were somewhat protected from its force by keeping close under the shore. Early on Friday, the 1st instant, the wind shifted to Southwest, and increased to a most severe gale, in which the squadron got separated. While keeping close in shore early on Saturday, say between 2 and 3, A.M., the *Osceola* got ashore on the Day Breaker, off North Island near Georgetown, and in two hours she bilged, the cattle soon taking to the water, and many of them reaching shore. The vessel having become a wreck, the officers and crew, twenty in number, took to their boats, in which they reached North Island, and were taken prisoners."

Captain Morrill was taken to the Guard House in Charleston by Captains Pinckney and Mazyck. It was from there that he answered the questions of interrogators, and issued the statement just quoted. If Captain Morrill knew anything about the planned amphibious assault against Port Royal, he did not apprise the Confederates of it. He simply said that some of the large transports had troops on board, "but he was not informed as to their number and had no correct idea." (More than 15,000 troops participated in the raid against Port Royal.)

On November 4, the boats of a Union blockader boarded the stranded steamer, but what the sailors did on the wreck went unrecorded. North Island was in Confederate hands, and remained in Confederate hands despite the Union success in taking over Port Royal. On November 11, the Confederates claimed that the *Osceola* was being salvaged. "Several hundred barrels Potatos [sic] have been recovered, together with other valuables. It is expected that her boiler and machinery will be got off and secured."

Captain Morrill and his crew were held in Richmond, Virginia as prisoners of war until the following May, when they were either released or exchanged for Confederate prisoners. They then found their way across the Mason-Dixon Line to Washington, DC, where they requested passes to go home.

Whatever remains of the *Osceola* has not been located nor identified.

Researchers should note that the *Osceola* "was fitted with vertical direct-acting engines, with two cylinders, each 24 inches in diameter, and a stroke of piston of two feet; she was also supplied with one tubular boiler, and her propeller was seven feet in diameter, and made of iron. Her rig was that of a schooner." Her hull was constructed primarily of oak and chestnut.

Both images of the *Overbrook's* final moments are official U.S. Coast Guard photos.

OVERBROOK

Built: 1918
Previous names: None
Gross tonnage: 5,724
Type of vessel: Tanker
Builder: Chester Ship Building Company, Chester, Pennsylvania
Owner: Gladstone Transportation Company, New York, NY
Port of registry: New York, NY
Cause of sinking: Fire
Location: 32° 15' North

Sunk: 1928 April 28
Depth: Approximately 350 feet
Dimensions: 400' x 54' x 31'
Power: Oil-fired steam

77° 50' West

At the time she was built, the *Overbrook* was one of the largest and most modern oil tankers in the country. The steel frame and plates that comprised her hull were riveted together at the Chester Ship Building Company in Chester, Pennsylvania. She was propelled by a steam turbine that was constructed nearby at the shop of the Westinghouse Engine and Manufacturing Company. Steam was provided by three Scotch boilers that were the workmanship of the New York Ship Building Company - which, despite the allusion of its nomenclature, was located in Trenton, New Jersey: across the Delaware River from Philadelphia, Pennsylvania. Heat was generated by clean-burning fuel oil instead of smoke-producing coal. Her wheel house was equipped with the latest wireless set. Yet, despite these innovations, she had less than seven feet of freeboard - typical for tankers whose hulls, designed to hold liquid cargoes, were essentially connected watertight compartments encased within a hull.

The *Overbrook* plied her work-a-day trade for a decade before she was overcome by the disaster that is feared the most by those who go down to the sea in ships: fire!

She was on a routine voyage from Texas City, Texas to New York when an explosion occurred in the pump room. The time was 4:15 in the morning of April

26, 1928. Flames spread quickly and rampantly. And nearly as quickly the radio operator transmitted an SOS. At the time, the tanker was located at 28° 55' north latitude, 79° 31' west longitude - approximately east of Jupiter Inlet, Florida. The first to answer the call for help was the steamship *Fred W. Weller*. She arrived and hove to as thirty-four crew members abandoned ship in lifeboats and boarded the *Fred W. Weller*. Every life was saved.

The *Fred W. Weller* stood by the *Overbrook* as the fire raged out of control. Shore stations dispatched the Coast Guard cutter *Tampa* and the destroyer *Wilkes* to the scene. The *Wilkes* was an ex-Navy vessel that had been transferred to the Coast Guard in order to help "suppress the illegal, but lucrative, traffic in alcoholic beverages spawned by Prohibition." She was engaged in what was known descriptively as the "Rum Patrol." The *Wilkes* reached the scene about noon. She took the *Overbrook's* survivors off the *Fred W. Weller*, and relieved that vessel of her duty of standing by so she could continue on her way. The survivors were later transferred to the *Tampa*.

The *Overbrook* continued to burn but was in no immediate danger of sinking. Consequently, she was taken in tow with a view toward saving the ship, if not the cargo. Thanks to the low freeboard, the fire was extinguished by mounting seas that washed over the tanker's deck. What followed was a trenchant, two-day ordeal as the stalwart Coast Guard vessels proceeded with agonizingly sluggish progress toward Charleston. They were still more than 150 miles short of their goal, and more than 200 miles east of Hilton Head, when the *Overbrook* poised before taking her final plunge.

The tanker gradually settled by the stern until her poop deck was completely submerged. The weight of the machinery in the after compartment, combined with tons of inrushing water, proved to be heavier than the buoyancy of the hull could offset. The *Overbrook* took a sudden tail dive. Her bow rose high in the air, and her stern slipped raucously beneath the waves - much like a sword sliding into its sheath. As the fantail crashed against the sandy bottom, the tanker nearly measured her length. Air trapped in the forward compartments kept the bow

afloat. The *Overbrook* stood vertical like a missile in a silo. The hull careened drunkenly like a falling spire, then, in a gulp, disappeared beneath the surface of the sea.

The tanker's final resting place was given as 32° 15' north latitude, 77° 50' west longitude. Judging by the length of hull that protruded above the surface before the upended tanker canted over and vanished, the depth of water must exceed 350 feet. The wreck has not been located.

PEERLESS

Built: 1853
Previous names: None
Gross tonnage: 600
Type of vessel: Iron-hulled side wheel steamer
Builder: Alexander Denny, Dumbarton, Scotland
Owner: J.T. Wright, New York, NY
Port of registry: ?
Cause of sinking: Collision with *Star of the South*
Location: Unknown

Sunk: November 2, 1861
Depth: Unknown
Dimensions: 175' x 26' x 10'
Power: Coal-fired steam

There were some marvelous engineers in the middle of the nineteenth century. In fact, the time period might be called the "age of mechanical marvels," much as today is the computer age. Inventors were making vast improvements on existing mechanical systems, such as steam engines for ships and trains, and were creating machines that were based upon alternative modes of operation, such as John Ericsson's caloric engine. Machine tooling was coming into its own with the fabrication of parts whose tolerances required ever more precision. It was in this atmosphere of fearless subservience to mechanics that the *Peerless* came into being, in 1852.

Construction of the *Peerless* originated in Scotland, at the yard of Alexander Denny. The iron hull was knocked together and partially pre-assembled, to ensure that all the parts fitted together perfectly. The engines were built at the nearby yard of Tulloch and Denny. Afterward, the ship was disassembled and shipped to Canada in five thousand separate pieces. The various components were then re-assembled by the Niagara Dock & Harbor Company, in Queenston, Ontario. The *Peerless* was launched on January 6, 1853. She was valued at $50,000 and was rated A1.

For the next eight years the *Peerless* operated on Lake Ontario, principally between Niagara and Toronto. According to *History of the Great Lakes*, published in 1899, "About the beginning of May, 1861, she was purchased by J.T. Wright, of New York, from the Bank of Upper Canada, for $36,000. On May 10 she left Toronto, under command of Capt. Robert Kerr. On reaching Montreal she had to be dismasted in order to enable her to pass under the Victoria bridge, and on May 27 she reached Quebec, where it was ascertained that under British laws she could not sail for a foreign port without an Imperial charter, which the officer at Quebec could not give, as she was owned by an American. Mr. Wright thereupon made application to the American consul at Quebec for a sailing letter; but this was declined on the ground that the vessel might be destined for service in the navy of the Confederate States."

Indeed, the U.S. Department of State issued the following memo to the Navy

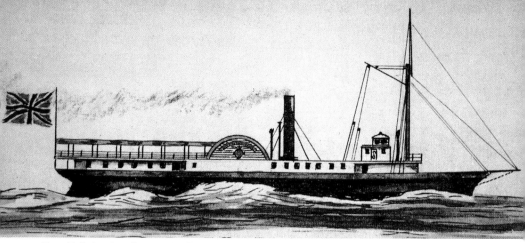

From *Early American Steamers*, by Erik Heyl.

on May 1: "If you have reliable information that the *Peerless* has been sold or contracted for and has been delivered, or is to be delivered, to the insurgents to be used against the United States, seize and bring her into port and detain her there under whatever flag or papers she may bear and refer the parties to this Government." This memo was written by no less a person than William Seward, the Secretary of State. Seward was a staunch abolitionist and expansionist. He eventually secured consent to purchase Alaska from Russia in 1867. This transaction was known as Seward's Folly at the time, but it is perceived today as a perceptive investment that is still paying enormous dividends.

In the event, the allegations against Wright proved to be false. "Mr. Wright was finally enabled to get his vessel out of port by giving heavy bonds that the *Peerless* should not be used for war-like purposes, and he was allowed to clear her on condition that Captain McCarthy, a native of Nova Scotia, but a naturalized citizen of the United States, should command her."

To prove his point, Wright chartered the *Peerless* to the U.S. Quartermaster Department for use as a freighter. He was paid $8,250 to transport a cargo of cattle and stores in support of the Great Expedition to capture Port Royal from the Confederates. (See *Governor* for more information in this regard.) The *Peerless* departed from Hampton Roads on October 29, 1861, in consort with fifty vessels under the overall command of Flag-Officer Samuel Dupont. The army leader in charge of the amphibious assault was Brigadier General T.W. Sherman (not the more famous William Tecumseh).

The fleet proceeded southward in weather that Flag-Officer Dupont described as "unsettled . . . though it promised well when we sailed, but off Hatteras it blew hard. . . . On Friday, the 1st of November, rough weather soon increased into a gale, and we had to encounter one of great violence from the southeast, a portion of which approached to a hurricane. The fleet was utterly dispersed."

Nearly all the vessels managed to rejoin after the storm abated, but the *Governor* and *Peerless* went missing. The *Peerless* was struck so hard by mountainous waves that she commenced to leak. So wildly did the *Peerless* pitch that the eighty-seven cows mooed pitifully, and the twenty-six people onboard feared for their lives. The captain ran up a signal of distress.

In the area at the time was the *Star of the South*, one of whose passengers was an artist who worked for *Frank Leslie's Illustrated Newspaper*. Not only did this artist draw a graphic sketch for publication, but he added some descriptive detail that was missing from the official report of the rescue. "The *Star of the South* ran down to his aid, but came too close, and ran into the *Peerless* on the quarter, inflicting severe damage. The captain of the *Peerless* then lightened his ship by throwing the cattle overboard, and thinks she would have ridden out the gale in safety had she not been injured by the *Star of the South*. However, he found that his ship was sinking, and he was obliged to leave her."

Around that time the USS *Mohican* hove into view. Commander S.W. Godon took in the situation at a glance: "I at once prepared a boat for lowering, although the sea made it very doubtful if the boat would live. Lieutenant Henry W. Miller volunteered at once, and the crew of the boat were in place in a moment. The boat barely escaped swamping, and in the meantime the steamer had swamped her boat in lowering it. We relieved, through the skillful management of the boat, the entire crew of the distressed vessel by their jumping overboard to our boat and being hauled from our boat to the ship. My officer, Lieutenant Miller, and boat's crew were taken on board of this ship in the same way from the boat, which we were obliged to tow astern to await the moderation of the gale. I regret to say the boat has been so damaged as to render her quite useless. As the distressed crew came on board with nothing but what they stood in, I ordered the purser to issue such clothes as were needful to relieve them in their destitute condition."

While Commander Godon's account is clear and succinct, it lacks the drama

From *Frank Leslie's Illustrated Newspaper.*

that undoubtedly prevailed in so harsh a sea. The newspaper artist added some additional graphic detail, which the reader may decide is pure journalistic hyperbole rather than unvarnished truth: "The captain was the last to leave his ship, and, when he did so, he created no little merriment, in spite of the storm, by quietly launching his lifeboat, putting his trunk into it, and getting on board the *Mohican* without wetting a hair. The *Peerless* went down within the hour."

Wright purportedly received $100,000 in compensation for the loss of the *Peerless* - and that was in addition to the money he was paid for the cattle that were never delivered! He obviously made out on his investment, earning in a single uncompleted voyage three times the amount that he paid for the vessel.

No accounts provided positional data. The location of the wreck could be as far south as Port Royal and as far north as North Carolina. However, a case could be made for the *Peerless* going down off South Carolina by drawing a parallel to the *Osceola* (q.v.) with respect to timing. The *Osceola* was steaming in the same convoy as the *Peerless*, and ran aground off North Island, near Georgetown, on the same day on which the *Peerless* was lost. The same parallel can be drawn with the Governor, whose southward progress was halted on November 2 (although she did not founder until the following day). The Governor is supposed to have gone down offshore and south of Georgetown.

To add to the confusion, there is conflicting information with regard to the tonnage and dimensions of the *Peerless*. According to *Canadian Coastal and Inland Steam Vessels, 1809-1930*, the *Peerless* admeasured 600 tons and stretched 175 feet in length. These are the figures that I used in the statistical sidebar. Erik Heyl, in *Early American Steamers*, agreed with the length but placed the tonnage at 478. The *New York Times* (for what it is worth by means of comparison) gave the tonnage as 690 and the "length on deck" as 227.5 feet.

Tonnage is irrelevant with respect to identifying a wreck because it is invisible. Besides, tonnage is a calculation based upon a number of formulas that are at variance with each other. Length, however, is an important measurement when it comes to properly identifying a wreck - particularly when that length is seen to differ by as much as 52.5 feet.

Researchers should note that the *Peerless* was fitted with two direct-acting trunk engines whose cylinders measured 57 inches in diameter, each with a stroke of 5 feet 10 inches. The paddle wheels measured 26 feet across. According to the NYT, "She was also supplied with tubular boilers, located in her hold. Her rig consisted of a foresail and a jib. She had three water-tight athwartship bulkheads.

PERCY THOMSON

Built: 1873

Previous names: None

Gross tonnage: 1,228

Type of vessel: Full-rigged ship

Sunk: June 15, 1874

Depth: 130 feet

Dimensions: 198' x 38' x 22'

Power: Sail

Builder: William P. Flewelling, Clifton, New Brunswick

Owner: Robert Thomson, Jr., St. John, New Brunswick (plus 9 other shareholders)

Port of registry: St. John, New Brunswick

Cause of sinking: Foundered

Loran 45177.7 / 59713.6

When the Composite Wreck was first discovered it was called the Unknown Schooner. I dived it shortly thereafter (in 1993), and instantly recognized its composite hull construction. A composite hull is one in which the vertical supports are constructed of ferrous metal beams, to which horizontal wooden planks are secured along the outboard side of the uprights. Think of a fence or railing consisting of posts to which boards or slats are nailed. I began referring to the site as the Composite Wreck - an appellation that was more descriptive - and the name eventually superseded the misnomer Unknown Schooner. There is no evidence that the Composite Wreck was ever a schooner: no masts or rigging are exposed. It may have been a barge, a schooner-barge, or a square-rigged sailing vessel with any number of rigging schemes and whose sails were not rigged fore-and-aft.

The wreck is 150 to 200 feet in length. The keelson is exposed and runs along the centerline of the wreck. On each side there exists a low parallel line of wooden beams, each representing the turn of the bilge. Outboard of the turns of the bilges, the curved vertical support beams stand eight feet in height. Thick brass dowels extend twelve inches or more from each beam; these dowels are spaced equidistantly along the height of each beam. The only planking that has survived the ravages of teredoes and other wood-devouring organisms are the planks that lie adjacent to and under the white sandy bottom.

The visual effect of the composite hull is one of the ribcage of a sperm whale carcass from which the flesh has been flenced and only the bones remain.

A vertical post rises eight feet above the sand beyond the forward termination of the wreck; this may be the stem. A large clump of concreted anchor chain lies on the port bow. A capstan lies on its side abaft the midship line on the starboard side. A gudgeon at the stern attests to the one-time existence of a rudder. Chunks of rock lie scattered about the inner confinement of the hull. No other features are exposed, nor does a debris field extend outboard of either side of the upright support beams.

Four sailing vessels are known to have been sunk in the immediate vicinity of the Composite Wreck:

Selah B. Strong	144-ton schooner	1869 August 9	32-12 N / 78-25 W
H.C. Brooks	162-ton brig	1870 September 19	32-?? N / 78-?? W
Percy Thomson	1,228-ton ship	1874 June 15	32-49 N / 78-25 W
H.B. McCaulay	335-ton schooner	1876 February 4	32-55 N / 78-24 W

Information on each of these losses is meager. I quote official notices in full.

"Schooner *Selah B. Strong*, (144 tons of New York), Murray, from Charleston for Delaware City, with a cargo of phosphate, foundered at sea Aug 9th in Gulf stream; crew saved in the boat, and were picked up by bark *J M Churchill*, at Baltimore 19th from Havana." Elsewhere it was stated that the crew abandoned the vessel in the Gulf Stream, and then were picked up later at the location given above. This implies that the vessel did not sink at the quoted location. She was built on Long Island, New York in 1855.

"Brig *H C Brooks*, Briggs, from Charleston for Providence, was abandoned at sea, (no date &c given). The crew arrived at Charleston in sch *Zeta Psi*, for Philadelphia, which put back to Charleston Sept 28th. The *H C B*, registered 162 tons, was built at Columbia, Me, in 1856, and hailed from Fall River."

"*Percy Thompson* (Br), Deck, from Bull River, SC, for London, with phosphates, sprung a leak in a gale June 14, in lat 32,49, lon 78,25, and sunk 15th. Crew saved and landed at Vineyard Haven 22d." She was built in 1873 at Clifton, New Brunswick. She was owned by R. Thomson, Jr. (Note that in this and subsequent notices, Thomson was spelled with a "p" - Thompson.)

"*H B McCauley*, from Baltimore, with 400 tons phosphate, valued at $20,000, for Savannah, was abandoned waterlogged, January 31, in lat 32 55, lon 78 24. Her crew having been at the pumps two days, were exhausted, and were

taken on board the sch *Express Tilton*, from Baltimore, and landed at Savannah Feb 3." She was built in 1867 at Milton, Delaware. She was owned by Hill & Company.

The cargo of the *H.C. Brooks* was not given, but the astute reader will have noticed that the other three vessels were carrying phosphate rock. The rock found on the Composite Wreck has not been assayed, but it is rough-cut rock (not rounded ballast rock) and could very well be phosphate ore.

Three of these vessels are too small to fit the size of the site. Only the *Percy Thomson* is large enough to suit. The *Charleston News and Courrier* published two elaborations of her loss. June 23: "The Capt. & crew of the ship *Percy Thompson*, from Bull River for London, report that the ship was abandoned in sinking condition, on the 14th inst. in lat. 32.49, long. 78.25." June 26: "Ship *Percy Thompson*, (of St. John's, N.B.) Dick, from Bull River, S.C. for London, with a cargo of 200 tons of phosphates, sprung a leak on the 14th inst., in a gale, and sank on the morning of the 15th, in lat. 32.42, long. 78.25. The crew were taken off by schr. *Henry Norwell*, from Mobile for Boston, which arrived at Vineyard Haven, 21st. 20 crew were rescued.- Ship went down 20 minutes later."

A brass cover that was twelve inches square was recovered from the wreck. On this cover was stamped "T. McAvery & Son" and "St. John, N.B." Since the *Percy Thomson* was the only one of the four stated vessels that was built in New Brunswick, it is deceptively easy to conclude that this is likely to be the Composite Wreck.

There is a problem with this quick and easy conclusion, however. According to the Record of the American Bureau of Ships, the construction remarks given for the *Percy Thomson* were abbreviated "M;Icf;S". According to the abbreviation code, "M" stands for "sheathed with yellow metal," "I" stands for "iron" as the hull material, "Cf" stands for "copper or composition fastenings," and "S" stands for "steeple." The steeple refers to the superstructure, but the other three terms refer to the hull. A literal translation of these abbreviated terms means that the hull was constructed of iron, that the outside of the hull was sheathed with yellow metal (an alloy of copper such as brass or bronze), and that the fastenings were made of copper or an alloy of copper.

If I have interpreted the code correctly, the abbreviation for a composite hull (a phrase that was apparently not in use at the time, as it was not given in the code key), should be "Ifr," which stood for a hull that was "iron framed.". Incidentally, there is no such abbreviation as "cf" (small "c"). The proper abbreviation calls for a capital "C" in "Cf." Thus the printed remarks contain an internal inconsistency.

Iron-hulled vessels were neither sheathed nor fastened with copper or composition fastenings. Instead, wooden hulls were sheathed in order to protect them from barnacles and wood-boring organisms. Iron hulls were fastened with iron rivets. The purpose of this long-winded discussion is to support the proposition that a typographical error might have been made in the Record.

In my opinion, the *Percy Thomson* seems to be the mostly likely contender for the Composite Wreck. Pete Manchee agrees.

From *Early American Steamers*, by Erik Heyl.

RALEIGH

Built: 1865
Previous names: None
Gross tonnage: 868
Type of vessel: Wooden-hulled side wheeler
Builder: Lawrence & Foulke, Brooklyn, New York
Owner: Livingston, Fox & Company, New York, NY
Port of registry: New York, NY
Cause of sinking: Fire
Location: 20 miles off Charleston

Sunk: December 24, 1867
Depth: Unknown
Dimensions: 172' x 35' x 17'
Power: Coal-fired steam

There was no cause for celebration aboard the *Raleigh* on Christmas Eve, 1867. On board at the time were fifty-five persons, passengers and crew combined, and an unspecified general cargo. The sidewheel steamer was on a routine passage from New York to New Orleans, Louisiana when, around noon, fire erupted below deck. She was then some twenty miles off the coast of South Carolina.

Police captain Nathaniel Mills, a passenger, thought "the fire must have been smoldering for a long time, for when it broke out it spread with inconceivable rapidity, involving the whole deck in a very short time."

Captain Charles Marshman, master, wasted not a moment in issuing the order to abandon ship. The crew members rushed to their emergency stations and launched all four lifeboats in a trice. Captain Marshman stood calmly on the paddle guards distributing life preservers, wooden chairs, and anything that would float, to the passengers. He was especially mindful of the women and children.

"Captain Mills got into one of the boats as it was being lowered, but she was swamped at once, and all were struggling in the sea. He was washed by a heavy sea up against the steamer, and succeeded in catching a ladder-rope, to which he clung, and thus his life was saved, for he cannot swim. He scrambled on deck again. . . . Captain Mills then fastened a life-preserver to his own waist, and proceeded to lower himself into the sea as steadily as possible for fear of getting under water, which he thought would be the death of him. As he was thus lowering himself a boat came just under him and he let himself drop into it. . . . After five hours pulling in a boat, which had to be baled constantly with the hats of the men, they reached a lightship off Charleston. Here they met with every mark of attention that their forlorn condition called for."

Two other lifeboats were launched successfully. Purser McManus took charge of boat No. 2. Before shoving off, McManus's wife pleaded with the captain to join them. Captain Marshman was adamant: "No, my child, I cannot leave my ship while there is a soul on board. I have given orders to Mc. to save you, and I think he will do it."

Mills gave a similar account of his own efforts to convince the captain to abandon ship with him. According to Mills, the captain steadfastly refused to leave his ship "until everyone else had gone. He had done so once when there was no hope of saving the vessel, and left her temporarily in charge of an inferior officer, and he had been called a murderer and a coward from one end of the country to the other, and he could not again pass through such an ordeal."

Such is the onus of the tradition of the sea. Captain Mills was not seen again, and it was supposed that he went down with his ship.

Boats No. 2 and No. 3 remained in the vicinity of the burning sidewheeler for five or six hours. The wind was very fresh from the northeast, with a heavy sea running. McManus claimed that it required every exertion to keep the boats' heads to the wind and sea. Despite the efforts of the crew members at the oars, the lifeboats gradually lost headway. McManus transferred three occupants from his lifeboat to boat No. 3, and gave them an extra oar and four tholepins, after which he was able to return to the vicinity of the still-floating steamer.

McManus: "When I rounded the wreck, I saw five men upon a raft. They hailed me and I told them I could not take them in, but told them that boat No. 3 was astern of me, and could take about thirteen more into her. I asked them if they saw her, and they replied yes, 'We see her.' Soon after [I] lost sight of boat No. 3, and the raft. . . . [I] saw the burning wreck up to 10:30 at night, at which time it disappeared from view. At that time the wind was light and the sea smooth. Guided by the North star, we made the Lightship off Charleston harbor, about 4 A.M. Christmas morning."

The lightship was now crowded with the occupants of two lifeboats: No. 1 and No. 2. McManus signaled a passing tug - the *Christiana*, under the command of Captain Sly - which transported the survivors to Charleston.

Boat No. 3, in charge of Chief Officer C.W. Bartlett, reached Kiowah inlet. These people were then picked up by the brig *Fauquier*, which transported them to Charleston. One of the occupants of this lifeboat was Charles Marshman, Jr.: the captain's son.

A final tally was taken after the crew and passengers were reunited in Charleston. There were thirty-one survivors. That left a death toll of twenty-four people: fourteen passengers and ten crew members. Although the reports did not state so explicitly, it appears that the majority of these fatalities must have occurred when No. 4 lifeboat capsized during the launching, at which time there was too much way on the steamer.

According to Erik Heyl, "The Raleigh was valued at $175,000.- while her cargo was worth about $350,000.-; both were a total loss, tho covered by some insurance. It was believed that an over-heated boiler ignited a wooden bulk-head." The report filed by the Steamboat Inspection Service differed from Heyl with regard to value: "The vessel and cargo were estimated at $130,000, all of which was a total loss."

The present whereabouts of the *Raleigh* are unknown. On December 27, "The Capt. of the steamer *Ashland* reports seeing off Charleston a vessel so low in the water that he could not make out her name, supposed to be the wreck of the *Raleigh*." This implies that when the flames were extinguished and McManus lost sight of the steamer, the vessel continued to float - and consequently, to drift. She may have drifted a long way before finally settling to the bottom. Researchers should note that the *Raleigh's* speed of twelve knots was provided by a vertical beam engine that generated 350 nominal horsepower. The engine cylinder measured 44 inches in diameter and had a stroke of 11 feet. Walking beam engines are quite distinctive and should be readily recognized. Charred bulkheads, especially in the vicinity of the boiler room, should arouse suspicions of the wreck's identity.

ROBERT B. HOWLETT

Built: 1860
Previous names: None
Gross tonnage: 120 (or 246)
Type of vessel: Two-masted schooner
Builder: in Baltimore, Maryland (or in Mathews County, Virginia, or in Boston, Massachusetts)
Owner: Not given on certificate of enrollment
Port of registry: Philadelphia, Pennsylvania
Cause of sinking: Foundered
Location: Northern Charleston Bar

Sunk: December 9, 1864
Depth: Unknown
Dimensions: 106' x 27' x 9'
Power: Sail

The *Robert B. Howlett* was a small coastal schooner that was chartered by the Union Navy to furnish coal for the blockading squadron off Charleston during the Civil War. Captain James Brewer was in command of a crew of six men. Together they sailed the vessel to a position offshore of the city but inside the Charleston bar. For two months the *Robert B. Howlett* delivered coal whenever it was needed. Then the captain was ordered to anchor his vessel in the channelway for employment as a lightship. One crewman departed, leaving the captain, a mate, and four able-bodied seamen to man the vessel.

This was the schooner's position when a storm blew up in the morning of December 9, 1864. By 9 a.m., they were experiencing "the full fury of the hurricane. The stock of the anchor which held the schooner, broke through the force of the gale, and the vessel began to drag. An attempt was then made to let go the other anchor, but the chain fouled at the hawse hole after 2 1/2 fathoms (15 feet) had run out, and it was impossible to extricate it. In this plight the vessel began to drive toward the northern bar, when Captain Brewer made an effort to get her under sail, but she would not 'wear,' owing to the dead weight of the anchor, and nothing further could be done to save her from going ashore.

"Presently she struck, and the first blow knocked her stern completely out. Heeling over on her bilge, the second blow snapped all her lee timbers like pipe stems, and in half an hour afterwards she was broken to pieces. The entire company got on the foremast while it remained standing, and when it fell all managed to secure small pieces of the wreck, but the sea ran so high, and an ebb tide setting off shore, made it impossible for a human being to long escape drowning under such circumstances.

"For an hour or more [Seaman John] Cruse and his companions buffeted the waves, gradually becoming separated by the angry sea, and the last that he saw of them convinced him that not one could hold out a great while longer.

"Dean, the mate, was on a piece of the poop deck, and Cruse drifted near him, succeeded in getting upon it, thus obtaining a better support than the deck

From *Harper's Weekly.*

plank which he had seized when the vessel went to pieces. Upon this small piece of the deck he and his companion were carried out to sea, passing through the breakers off Stono Inlet, where they were several times washed off.

"Dean had been severely bruised on the head by a plank when he was thrown into the water, and only survived the injury and his desperate circumstances until 10 1/2 o'clock on Friday night. For hours before his death he was senseless and helpless, and Cruse's strength was nearly exhausted in his attempt to hold him on the raft. After the decease of his companion, Cruse divested him of his clothing, to add to his own comfort, and lashed the corpse to the wreck, having already contemplated the horrible necessity of feeding upon it, if another day passed without relief came to him."

Cruse spent the night and all the following day without resorting to cannibalism. He clung to his meager fragment of decking alongside the grisly remains of the mate. Then, at dusk, after thirty-three hours adrift without food or drink, a steamship hove into view. The *Eliza Hancox* was Colonel Mulford's dispatch vessel, Captain Post commanding, on route from Port Royal to Charleston with a special correspondent on board. The steamer was overdue, having been detained at Hilton Head by the storm that demolished the *Robert B. Howlett*. After passing "immense pieces of wreck" off Edisto, the pilot of the *Eliza Hancox* was being especially watchful lest he stave in his hull on flotsam or floating wreckage. "No sun was visible, and a dense fog shut in our horizon to very narrow limits."

Despite the poor visibility and the falling darkness, the pilot spotted a section of decking - larger than any he had seen so far - and "made the suggestion that we should run down to it and ascertain if it supported a human being. Capt. Post acceded, and we had scarcely changed our course when a thrill of joy passed through all on board, at the sight of a poor creature running frantically around his narrow raft like an imprisoned animal in a cage, and waving his hands imploringly.

"Ever and again the man would be hidden from our view as a mighty wave with curling crest, curled over his frail support. The *Hancox's* boat was lowered and gallantly manned by volunteers from the crew, who did not weigh the risk to themselves in braving the angry sea, while they sturdily pulled toward the shipwrecked sailor. With some difficulty they laid their boat alongside the raft, with not only getting the living man on board, but in obedience to their humane impulse, bringing off the ghostly corpse that lay bound to the wreck beside him.

Cruse was given dry clothes and hot coffee that "got the chills out of his bones." He was the sole survivor.

Ironically, the *Eliza Hancox* had about thirty coffins on board "for the burial of deceased soldiers released by the rebels." The body of A.H. Dean was placed in one of these convenient coffins, "and will be interred on Morris Island. Col. Mulford intends to send the survivor of this frightful disaster home by the steamer *United States*, which leaves on Monday with released prisoners for Annapolis."

The *Robert B. Howlett* must have been uninsured, for she was not listed in either the Record of the American Bureau of Ship or Lloyd's Register. Her certificate of enrollment does not give complete statistical information about her construction - in particular, her builder and owner. Various sources give conflicting information about her tonnage and about the location of the shipping yard that built her.

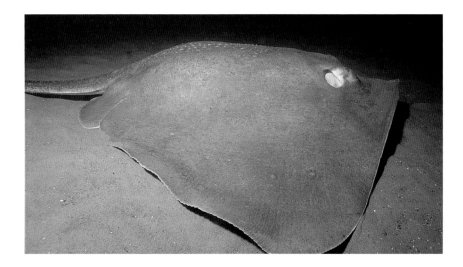

As the *Marie di Giorgio*. (From the collection of Pete Manchee.)

RUNA

Built: 1911
Previous names: *Marie di Giorgio*
Gross tonnage: 1,611
Type of vessel: Steel-hulled freighter
Builder: Nylands Vaerksted, Kristiania, Norway.
Owner: Hagb Waage, Christiania, Norway
Port of registry: Christiania, Norway
Cause of sinking: Foundered?
Location: On or Off Frying Pan Shoals

Sunk: December 15, 1923
Depth: 120 feet?
Dimensions: 250' x 34' x 22'
Power: Coal-fired steam

The *Runa's* first run with catastrophe occurred in January 1920. The freighter was on route from New York to St. John's, Antigua and Barbuda (in the Caribbean) when she ran into a blizzard that drove her to the middle of the Atlantic Ocean, and forced Captain Gundersen to steer his ship for the Azores for coal. "The fuel was exhausted before land was reached and all available wood-work was burned in the furnaces. The Captain said it was impossible to cook in the galley, and for four days the crew lived on hardtack and water. The waves swept the decks, carrying away the lifeboats, smashing doors, and flooding the cabins. The battered steamship finally made Fayal and got coal to carry her to St. John's."

During the height of the storm, crewman Ludwig Larsen was washed overboard and lost.

In 1923, the master of the *Runa* was Captain Iversen. According to reports, the *Runa* filled her bunkers with coal on December 9 - in Norfolk, Virginia - then proceeded south to Savannah, Georgia. She departed from Savannah on December 12, bound for Liverpool, England. She "was wrecked on Frying Pan Shoals at 4 PM December 15." The time span of these events appears contrary to logical calculation. The distance between Norfolk and Savannah is more than twice the distance between Savannah and the Frying Pan Shoals. If three days were required to steam from Norfolk to Savannah and take on a cargo, it should not have taken three days to proceed from Savannah to the Frying Pan Shoals.

Be that as it may, the first outside knowledge of the catastrophe was obtained by the steamer *W.W. Mills* when she came upon one of the *Runa's* lifeboats. In the lifeboat were six seamen, two of whom were dead. The *W.W. Mills* effected the rescue of the survivors, and plucked another hapless seaman out of the water. She then proceeded on her passage to Sabine, Texas. She communicated the incident to the steamship *Munsona*. On December 16, it was reported that the *Munsona* proceeded up the Cape Fear River to Wilmington, North Carolina "about noon yesterday, and brought a story of a tragedy off Frying Pan Shoals." The chronology of events is clearly out of place. If the *Runa* was wrecked at 4 p.m., knowledge of her loss could not have been ascertained by noon of the very same day.

Little additional information was forthcoming. The Coast Guard cutter *Modoc* was dispatched to search for more survivors. The *Modoc* located another lifeboat from the *Runa*, but all six of its occupants were dead. No explanation was given as to how these seamen died. Floating bodies were observed by the *W.W. Mills* and by the steamship *Berkshire*, "but it was not disclosed whether either steamer stopped to pick them up. Officials here are doubtful whether this could have been done in the rough seas."

On December 18, it was reported, "The *Modoc* found nothing except considerable dressed lumber, a part of the *Runa's* cargo. The *Runa* is supposed to have capsized in rough seas near the gas buoy a the far end of Frying Pan Shoals, about 33 miles southwest of Cape Fear River Bar."

The *Modoc* found no other survivors, and recovered no bodies. The official tally of lives lost was twenty-two. On December 24, it was reported, "A clinker built ship's boat, badly battered and without any identification marks, was picked up by the cutter *Modoc* on her cruise along the Carolina coasts during the past week. It was found many miles to the southward of the spot where the *Runa* went down."

As if this story is not already full of enough contradictions, consider this report from December 14 - one day *prior* to the conjectured time of the *Runa's* loss: "Mystery still surrounds a large metallic lifeboat found adrift and deserted last Friday [one week earlier] by Coast Guard cutter *Modoc* off Cape Romain, South Carolina. Food, clothing, tools, ships stores were found in the boat." Of course, this may have been simply a coincidence.

The astute reader will have noticed that in one of the reports quoted above, the location of the catastrophe was given as *on* the Frying Pan Shoals, while in another report the location was given as *off* the Frying Pan Shoals. This is not a simple case of semantics. There is a big difference between "on" and "off." *On* the shoals implies that the *Runa* ran aground, whereas *off* the shoals implies that she foundered somewhere nearby, or perhaps in the vicinity. This distinction between "on" and "off," coupled with the fact that most of the seamen were already dead when the lifeboats were found, and with the possibility that the given locations referred to the position at which the first lifeboat was sighted (after drifting for an undetermined period of time) and not to the actual wreck site, make it apparent that the correspondents were merely guessing. There is too much conflicting data to make an intelligent extrapolation.

Exactly when, where, and under what circumstances the *Runa* went down will forever remain unknown. She may have sunk many miles away from where the lifeboats and bodies were found floating.

However, if we lend credence to the report that specified the distance and bearing from the Cape Fear Bar, we find ourselves suspiciously close to a wreck known locally as the Ore Freighter, or the 18 Fathom Wreck, which lies at a depth of 120 feet. There exists the possibility that this wreck could be the *Runa*.

The wreck is contiguous and approximates the length of the *Runa*. The width cannot be determined because the hull plates have long since fallen outboard, creating a debris field that is more than 75 feet across at amidships. The forward part of the bow lies almost perfectly on its port side. (I have been told that, prior to Hurricane Hugo - which struck the coast in 1989 - the bow stood practically upright.) Both anchors are stowed in their hawsepipes. The starboard anchor can be seen from above, but to look at the port anchor you have to crawl under the stem in a space that stands only three feet high, and look up.

A small part of the stern is intact. Like the bow, it lies nearly on its port side. The propeller is buried deep in the sand, but a spare propeller lies exposed a few feet forward and to port. The propeller shaft extends forward from the stern with an agonizing twist for the first ten feet or so, then proceeds straight for a couple of dozen feet until it enters the existing portion of the shaft alley. The shaft alley is connected to the after end of a triple expansion engine. The engine is the highest part of the wreck, towering some twenty feet above the surrounding debris. The sizes of the cylinders of the *Runa's* triple expansion were 21 inches, 34 inches, and 60 inches, each having a stroke of 39 inches.

Two Scotch boilers are situated forward of the engine. The starboard boiler stands on its end like a fruit can, while the port boiler lies on its side. I did not measure these boilers with a tape measure, but by using my rather unscientific method of spreading my arms and eyeballing the dimensions, I estimated that the encrusted boilers were about 15 feet in diameter and 12 feet in length. The *Runa's* Scotch boilers were 14 feet in diameter and 11 1/2 in length.

The wreckage of the wheel house lies along the outer edge of the debris field forward of the port boiler. What appears to be copper ore is concentrated in mounds in the cargo portions of the hull. The wreck is surrounded by white, highly reflective sand.

Visibility generally exceeds fifty feet, and often reaches seventy-five feet or better. The marine life is spectacular. Schools of baitfish congregate in such density that they often obscure the sun, like a lone dark cloud on a clear sunny day. Amberjack abound, as do barracuda and toad fish. Turtles sometimes take residence in the broken down hull: they lodge themselves under convenient hull plates or I-beams to take a snooze, so they will not float away during their slumbers. Be careful of the brightly colored but venomous lionfish: they are as deadly as they are beautiful.

At nighttime the wreck takes on a completely different aspect. Shovel-nosed lobsters come out in droves in order to feed. They are so plentiful that I once caught one in each hand at the same time. Fifteen-inch-long morays, whose bodies are covered with greenish speckles, fly majestically over the hull. I even spotted a rare - and, so far as I know, unidentified - lobster; it measured six inches in length and was painted fire-engine red, with a white swirled pattern on its carapace and white dots elsewhere; its claw tips and walking legs had distinctive white bands.

I will not go as far as to state categorically that the Ore Freighter is the *Runa*, as Pete Manchee speculates, because it is possible that another wreck nearby, known as the Rosin Wreck, could be the *Runa*. See the section on Unidentified Wrecks for a description of the Rosin Wreck.

As the *Runa*. (From the collection of Pete Manchee.)

From *Harper's Weekly*.

SANDUSKY

Built: 1849
Previous names: None
Gross tonnage: 1,018
Type of vessel: Three-masted full-rigged ship
Builder: Newcastle, Maine
Owner: A.K. Miller & Company, New Orleans, Louisiana
Port of registry: New Orleans, Louisiana
Cause of sinking: Foundered
Location: 135 miles east of Myrtle Beach

Sunk: August 28, 1881
Depth: Unknown
Dimensions: 162' x 35' x 23'
Power: Sail

The hurricane that swept northward along the eastern seaboard in late August 1881 did a considerable amount of damage to the maritime industry along the coast of South Carolina. At least a dozen sailing vessels were driven ashore and came to rest high and dry more than three hundred yards from the water. Six additional sailing vessels were stranded on various beaches. *Pilot Boat No. 3* was driven ashore at Beaufort. "The abandoned lighthouse on Combahee Bank, St. Helena Sound, was blown over to the northward, and the northern half was carried away by the sea. The floor of that side is level with the water."

The tugboat *Canoochee* was dragged four miles over the marshes. The schooner *Daisy*, which was tied to her wharf, "was broken to pieces by driftwood and logs." Two runaway schooners and a sloop crashed into the steamer *Howland Drake*, which was securely docked at Beaufort. The damage to the steamer was slight, but the schooner *Mary Scheper* "lost her sail and bowsprit and cut her sides against the *Howard Drake*."

The steamer *Saragossa* was weathering the storm splendidly when she came upon the dismasted bark *Traveler*, which was flying a signal of distress. "After a trial of two hours and a half, during a strong gale and heavy sea, the *Saragossa* succeeded in getting a hawser to her." The steamer then towed the beleaguered bark into Tybee.

The steamship *Dessoug* was not quite as fortunate. She ran into the storm after departing from Charleston, and was so badly thrashed that she was forced to return, "having had her rudder and tiller broken and her machinery slightly damaged." While the *Dessoug* was limping back to port, her captain spotted two windjammers that were in need of assistance which, due to the steamer's mechanical malfunctions, he could not render. One was a schooner with one mast gone; the other was a square-rigged vessel of which he could see only the upper deck and cabin.

The storm was equally as devastating to seaside facilities. Waterfront bulkheads were battered down. Wharfs were damaged by wind and floating debris; piles were snapped off at the waterline. Several warehouses were unroofed. Fences were "prostrated, and the tin roofing rolled up as a scroll. The trees were also torn up and prostrated." One phosphate washer was sunk; two others and a dredge were blown up into the marsh. Lighters were scattered "in all directions."

Private residences were either destroyed by the wind or swept away by the tumultuous sea. Cellars were flooded. "Mr. and Mrs. Lewis Hay and two little children were in a perilous position all night, in the water up to their waists, in a small house in the Hummocks. The house weathered the storm. A new house near by, which was being built for the superintendent, was blown down. Flats, dredges and boats were sunk and drifted about in the Coosaw and Morgan Rivers." The ferry house was demolished, drowning as many as fifteen people who had taken refuge inside.

Nearly all the rice plantations were submerged by abnormally high tides. Some two-thirds of the crop was ruined by salt water. The number of breaks in the levees was counted by the score.

"Morris Island has been swept clean by the storm, only a small portion of one of the old war batteries remaining above the level of the beach. The island has been so levelled [sic] that an observer on Sullivan's Island can now look uninterruptedly across the island and see the houses at Secessionville."

At Port Royal, "The number actually drowned is uncertain. The reports conflict, varying from twenty to forty. Martin's Industry lightship is gone, and all the bar and harbor buoys have been carried away or shifted."

Into this raging tempest sailed the little schooner *Sandusky*, bound from Pensacola, Florida to Liverpool, England with a cargo of lumber. Captain R.J. Lowden, master, issued the following report of the schooner's travails: "On the 25th [of August] the wind increased to a heavy gale from northeast and the ship commenced leaking badly. On the 26th the gale increased to a hurricane, the leak gaining so fast that both pumps could not keep the vessel free. At 6 P.M. had ten feet of water in her hold, with both pumps constantly going, but to no purpose.

At 8 P.M. a squall of great violence threw the ship on her beam ends, when the masts were cut away. At the same time everything was swept from the deck, including both houses, with all the stores of fresh water. All the officers and crew reached the weather mizzen rigging except two seamen and the cook, who were never after seen, and must have been swept away when the deck load went over. The ship slowly righted after the loss of her top hamper, but was a complete waterlogged wreck.

"The crew remained on the mizzen rigging until daybreak, the sea continually sweeping over them and threatening to carry them off every moment. At daybreak was enabled to better our position somewhat, but as the ship was constantly breaking up it was a day of terror. About 4 P.M. we saw a brig steering nearly for us, but she passed us by without noticing us, though her people were plainly visible to us, the wind still blowing a heavy gale and tremendous seas breaking over the ship. When nearly dark the whole stern frame broke and was swept away with the after part of the main deck; and the timber commenced coming out from between decks. We were obliged to abandon our position aft, and after great risk got forward and into the foretop, where the night of the 27th was passed. The next day was fine, but with heavy seas constantly deluging the ship. At 5:30 P.M. we saw a vessel, which proved to be the steamship *Hudson*, from New Orleans to New York. The crew and officers were taken off after being seventy-eight hours on the wreck without food or water. Every kindness was shown us by Capt. Freeman, his officers and passengers, the latter making up a purse which greatly gladdened the hearts of the destitute mariners."

The *Hudson* landed the fourteen survivors of the schooner at New York.

Although the *Sandusky* was abandoned in the track of northbound vessels, Captain Lowden thought that the hulk would not long exist as a hazard to navigation because the hull was "fast breaking up." When last seen, the partially submerged schooner was located at 33° 25' north latitude, 76° 25' west longitude - about 135 miles east of Myrtle Beach.

The schooner *Lucie Wheatley* was abandoned on the same day off the coast of Georgia. Her survivors were rescued by the steamer *Chalmette*.

This turtle was snoozing contentedly until I pulled it out of its hideaway in order to obtain a photograph of its entire body. A turtle often lodges itself under a piece of wreckage so it will not drift away during its slumber, and so it can sleep without being jostled by surge or current. Tell-tale turtle "rubs" are clean spots found underneath steel beams and hull plates, where constant abrasion caused by the hard shell material over a number of years keeps the metal surface clear of marine fouling organisms.

SHERMAN

Built: 1861   Sunk: January 10, 1874
Previous names: *Princess Royal*, USS *Princess Royal*   Depth: 55 feet
Gross tonnage: 973   Dimensions: 196' x 27' x 16'
Type of vessel: Wooden-hulled screw steamer   Power: Coal-fired steam
Builder: Tod & McGregor, Glasgow, Scotland
Owners: George Weld, Richard Baker, and William Weld (of Boston, Massachu-
    setts), and Frederick Baker (of New York State)
Port of registry: Boston, Massachusetts
Cause of sinking: Foundered
Loran 45413.3 / 59455.7   GPS 33-43.710 / 78-32.495

According to *Early American Steamers*, by Erik Heyl, "Ostensibly the *Princess Royal* was build for the Glasgow & Liverpool Steam Packet Co., in 1861. Her general appearance was much more that of a blockade runner than an Irish Channel steamer, and it is more than probable that she was built for blockade running purposes. The profits were so fantastically large that one or two successful trips more than repaid the speculators all their costs and expenses. The *Princess Royal* was sold to Liverpool owners, who immediately began running the Federal blockade with her."

Heyl's suspicions are born out by the fact that the *Princess Royal* was caught trying to run the blockade off Charleston, South Carolina on January 29, 1863. She carried a cargo of shoes, small arms, armor plates, rifled Whitworth guns, hospital provisions, and marine engines intended for several Confederate rams then abuilding. The USS *Unadilla* forced the *Princess Royal* ashore and placed a prize crew aboard. The Confederates tried desperately to recapture the blockade runner and her valuable cargo, but were unsuccessful. The *Princess Royal* was refloated, taken to Philadelphia, and sold in prize court. In accordance with official procedure, the realized profit of $342,000 was distributed among the officers and crew of the *Unadilla*: a custom that encouraged audacity and a strong fighting spirit among the sailors of the blockading fleet.

Federal records indicate that one of the engines originally destined for the Confederate Navy was instead installed on the USS *Kansas*, already under construction. To add to the irony of the blockade runner, the *Princess Royal* was purchased by the U.S. Navy for $112,000 and commissioned as a blockader. She was armed with "two 30-pound Parrott rifles, one 11-inch Dahlgren gun and four 24-pound howitzers." In her new capacity she served in the Gulf of Mexico theater, where she captured quite a few Confederate blockade runners during the next two years.

After the cessation of hostilities she was sold at public auction in Philadelphia - on August 17, 1865 - bringing into the treasury $54,175 from Samuel C.

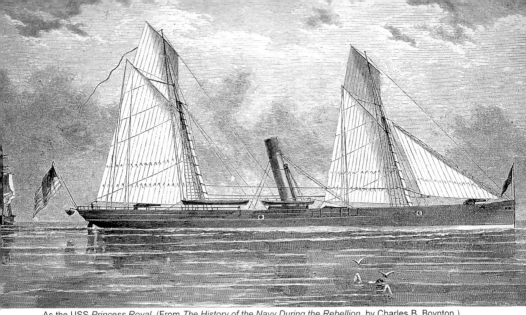

As the USS *Princess Royal*. (From *The History of the Navy During the Rebellion*, by Charles B. Boynton.)

Cook. Mr. Cook operated the *Princess Royal* until 1868, when he sold her to the William F. Weld Company. Her new owners renamed her *Sherman*. Some historians have posted the vessel's name as "General Sherman," but she never received such a designation; all her documentation papers list her simply as the *Sherman*. For most of the rest of her career the *Sherman* ran passengers and freight between New York and New Orleans. However, for a short while in 1873 she returned to her previous occupation as a blockade runner, this time running guns and ammunition to Cuba for the insurrectionists against Spanish rule.

On her final passage to New Orleans the *Sherman* carried four passengers and a crew of either thirty-four, thirty-eight, or forty-two (reports are contradictory). At two in the morning of January 6, 1874 the ship sprang a leak that sent the men racing to the pumps. After eighteen hours of hard labor "the leak was found to be increasing so rapidly that the steamer was headed for the land." It must have been slow going, for all day during the seventh and eighth she slogged toward shore, experiencing "very heavy weather."

By the morning of the ninth the men were completely exhausted. Neither the officers nor crew "had been able to snatch a moment's sleep or rest, the latter being constantly employed at the pumps and the former in endeavoring to devise ways and means for the safety of the vessel." At 5 a.m. the water in the hull rose so high that it put out the fires under the boilers. Now the ship was helpless and at the mercy of the sea. Captain Thomas Haulsey, master, ordered the anchors dropped in order to keep the vessel from rolling in the troughs. The stalwart crew had managed to get the ship to within twelve miles from land.

A boat was lowered and sent to Little River for assistance, but not until 3:30 the next morning did help arrive. It came in the form of the schooner *Spray*, under the command of Captain Morgan and two able bodied seamen. The *Spray* took off the *Sherman's* first mate (William Moan), five crew members, and some of the cargo. Then another schooner, the *Florence*, arrived, and with her standing by the stricken steamer the *Spray* proceeded to Wilmington.

Captain Hill, master of the *Florence*, tied his ship to the *Sherman's* stern. "As much of the cargo as possible was removed and placed on the Schr. *Florence*, together with the passengers and crew, after which a raft was constructed and a quantity of goods removed to that." At 2 p.m. the steam tug *Brandt* arrived from Wilmington and took both the *Sherman* and the raft in tow. With the *Sherman* now the responsibility of the tug's salvage crew, the *Florence* departed for Wilmington. "All the baggage and effects of the passengers, officers and crew were saved."

The raft soon broke loose and was later picked up by a pilot boat. It was slow hauling for the *Brandt*, struggling every inch of the way with so much dead weight in tow. She managed to get her charge fifteen miles closer to Wilmington when "the mate of the *Brandt*, who was acting as helmsman of the doomed vessel, hailed the tug and stated that the ship was about to sink. This was near 7 o'clock in the evening. A boat was immediately sent for the mate and soon after he reached the deck of the *Brandt*, or in the space of about 20 minutes, the *Sherman* made a lunge head foremost and disappeared beneath the waves."

At the time of her loss, the *Sherman* was valued at $90,000, and her cargo at $100,000. Within days of the steamer's demise, the wreck was marked with a buoy as a hazard to navigation.

The wreck was positively identified in 1977 when Wayne Strickland recovered the pitometer (or pitt log, an engine revolution counter) with the ship's name inscribed on the face plate. This helped to ease my confusion when I later found the capstan cover on which was embossed the manufacturer's name: American Steam Windlass Company, Providence, Rhode Island. That plus the fact that I knew of two other divers who had recovered engine parts stamped by U.S. manufacturers would otherwise have led me to believe that the vessel, had its identity not been previously established, had been built domestically. The truth of the matter is that the *Sherman* had been extensively overhauled in New England. That must have been when the original pitometer was replaced with one that was inscribed "Sherman." Shipwreck historians: beware of the obvious moral to this story.

The hull is completely broken down except for the tip of the bow and the extreme end of the stern, each of which rises some eight feet off the bottom. Oddly enough, the bow is heeled about 60° to starboard while the stern is heeled about 30° to port, with the area in between, including the engine and boilers, sitting upright: a strange "twist" of events despite the fact that the bottom of the hull is contiguous. The average depth is 50 feet, although a maximum depth of 55 feet may be found in washouts and scours. Most of the site consists of collapsed and spread out hull plates amid flat patches of sand. Low-lying debris stretches more than 30 feet off the port side of the wreck's centerline, but only about 15 feet to the starboard side of the centerline, giving the wreck a one-sided appearance.

At the aftermost part of the wreck the rudder stands upright with the 30° tilt to port noted above, and turned hard aport at a near right angle to the fore and aft line. Immediately in front of the rudder the large, four-bladed iron propeller is still connected to the shaft; the blades have squared-off ends with rounded corners, with one blade bluntly pointing upward, two pointing to opposite sides, and the bottom blade mostly buried in the sand. The propeller shaft is thirty to forty feet long; it is not a single length of iron but three separate sections that are connected by two shaft couplings which are supported by bearing blocks, the aftermost of which has been almost completely knocked out from under the coupling. An anchor chain made of figure-eight links is draped across the shaft, looking strangely out of place; it is probably the chain that once held a buoy over the wreck to mark the site as a menace to navigation.

The forward end of the propeller shaft is connected to a flywheel that abuts the after end of the engine. The engine rises majestically more than 20 feet off the bottom; the base of the engine is approximately square, with four legs made of thick iron beams that curve gently inward and upward like an underwater Eiffel Tower, in the middle of which is a single tubular cylinder looking like the pipe in the center of an oil rig or the vertical ram of a pile driver. This cylinder is the piston. Adjacent to the engine on the port side is the steam reservoir.

Immediately forward of the engine are two rectangular boilers, side by side, which rise 15 feet off the bottom. Forward of the boilers are areas where the deck planks are exposed; despite some teredo damage they are in remarkably good condition. Lying about midships are cylindrical chunks of white, chalky matter about the diameter of a telephone pole and perhaps fifteen inches in length, as if three-gallon metal pails had rusted away leaving behind their solidified contents. These objects are remains of the cargo.

The keelson is exposed almost all the way to the bow. Lying atop rusted beams is a windlass and a mass of anchor chain, some of which extends into the chain locker inside the partially intact forward compartment, which a diver can enter and have enough space in which to turn around. The capstan lies on its side to starboard, and about fifteen feet away I found the cover lying upside down and partially buried in the sand. I dug it out and flipped it over, chagrined to find that it was not bronze but very brittle ferrous; it broke it two when I moved it. The larger piece was at least 80% of the whole. Embossed on the center was an anchor surrounded by a floral design, and around the top and bottom were patent dates and the manufacturers name and location.

Many artifacts are recovered by patient divers who are willing to dig in or fan away the sand. Tiny lead pellets, or shot, are found under the propeller shaft close to the forward end. The broad expanse forward of the boilers is where the cargo holds were located, and it is here that divers find chinaware, clear glass medicine bottles, blue glass telegraph insulators, and brass items such as harness tackle (those were the pre-motorized days of cavalry and equestrian transportation), luggage tags bearing the letters "US", and belt buckles.

Visibility averages 20 feet but sometimes exceeds 50. I've "seen" the wreck when the visibility was zero, but this eventuality occurs only after a storm; it takes several days of calm seas for clarity to return.

SOUTHERN DISTRICTS

Built: 1944   Sunk: December 6, 1954
Previous names: USS *LST No. 500*   Depth: Unknown
Gross tonnage: 3,337   Dimensions: 314' x 50' x 24'
Type of vessel: LST converted to bulk carrier   Power: Twin diesels
Builder: Missouri Valley Bridge & Iron Company, Evansville, Indiana
Owner: Philadelphia & Norfolk Steamship Company, Wilmington, Delaware
Port of registry: Wilmington, Delaware
Cause of sinking: Unknown
Location: 150 miles east of Charleston

Despite the fact that the *Southern Districts* was built at a different yard from the one at which the *Southern Isles* was built, the two vessels were sister ships in every particular. The reader is advised to peruse the chapter on the *Southern Isles* before reading this one, in order to obtain background material and for reasons of chronology. Both vessels began their careers as LST's (the military abbreviation for Landing Ship, Tank).

According to the Lloyd's Register, *LST No. 500* was fabricated in 1944 in Evansville, Indiana, whereas the List of Merchant Vessels of the United States gives Leavenworth, Kansas as her birthing place. I have no explanation for this disparity. LST's were constructed to identical specifications by companies all over the country. Many of these companies had never built a ship before.

LST No. 500 crossed the Atlantic Ocean and docked in Plymouth, England. There she took on a load of Army personnel and vehicles, and sailed in convoy in support of the Normandy invasion. She disembarked her passengers and freight onto Utah Beach on June 7. She returned to England with Navy casualties, then transported another cargo to Utah Beach. This time her cargo consisted principally of DUKW's (amphibious troop vehicles).

In 1949, *LST No. 500* was purchased by the Philadelphia & Norfolk Steamship Company for its wholly owned subsidiary, the Southern Trading Company. The LST was converted for service in the merchant marine as a bulk carrier, at which time her name was changed to *Southern Districts*. She served in that capacity for the next five years.

As a result of the loss of the *Southern Isles*, the Coast Guard revised its regulations with respect to converted LST's. The hull of the *Southern Districts* was strengthened in order to comply with these stricter regulations.

On November 19, 1954, the *Southern Districts* ran aground in Hillsboro Bay, near Tampa, Florida. She was refloated the same day with the assistance of a tug. Subsequently, she spent over a week in New Orleans undergoing repairs and having her hull examined by a variety of inspectors, including one for the American Bureau of Ships. These inspectors determined that the hull was sound

and fit for service.

On December 2, the *Southern Districts* departed from Port Sulphur, Louisiana. She was bound for Bucksport, Maine with a cargo of sulfur. On board were twenty-four (or twenty-three) officers and men, including Captain Ernest Rowe, master. Irregularly spaced radio messages traced her route across the Gulf of Mexico, around the Florida Keys, and northward toward her intended port of call. Her last radio contact with her owners occurred on December 4, at which time she was in the vicinity of Key West, Florida. She was supposed to report her estimated time of arrival when she was seventy-two hours from port. No such transmission was received. This was not considered a reason for undue alarm, however, because more often than not, the failure to report was the result of malfunctioning radio equipment.

The *Southern Districts* was due to dock at Bucksport on December 10. When she failed to report to the company by December 8 - one day later than she was supposed to report - the company alerted the Coast Guard "to ascertain some tidings of the vessel." The record is unclear as to what, if anything, was actually done to "ascertain some tidings." When the ship did not arrive in port on her appointed date, she was officially classified as "overdue." For the next two days the Coast Guard conducted a "communications search" - an obfuscatory term which meant that they tried to contact the vessel by radio, and that they transmitted a general warning to all vessels to be on the lookout and to report anything suspicious.

It soon developed that on December 5, the U.S. Navy fleet oiler *Anacostia* (T-AO-94) sighted a vessel answering her description at about 33° north, 76.8° west (roughly 150 miles east of Charleston). At the time there were gale force winds and towering seas, but there was no indication of distress. The severity of the storm increased on the following day.

According to a Coast Guard memo, "Commanding Officer of ARSD type vessel reports midnight position for vessel on 6 December as in the general area of the *Southern Districts* at that time. ARSD reports mountainous seas worse than any sea experienced in two recent hurricanes. Vessel had to be held into sea at 2/3 speed. He believes that vessel would have capsized if not held so. All persons remained alert and donned life jackets due to perilous position. ARSD has excellent stability and believed only reason did not founder." (ARSD was the official Navy designation for a salvage lifting vessel.)

From these reports, there was strong reason to believe that the *Southern Districts* foundered in the storm off South Carolina on December 6.

On December 13 - one full week after the *Southern Districts* was believed to have gone down - Coast Guard aircraft searched 26,500 square miles of ocean between Cape Henry, Virginia and Miami, Florida. No sign of the *Southern Districts* was found. Search planes were grounded on December 14 due to adverse weather conditions. With improvement in the weather on the following day, rescue craft scoured the ocean from both the air and the sea, with three Coast Guard planes, four Navy planes, the cutter *Chincoteague* and the buoy tender *Conifer*. "Results negative. Probability of detection, 95% for vessel; 50% for life rafts; 25% for life jackets." Formal search operations were secured at sunset. Four aircraft resumed searching at dawn on December 16. Again, "Results negative."

The *Southern Districts* was given up for lost. She had vanished off the surface of the sea. Her final port of call was oblivion. Her twenty-four crew members were listed as missing, presumed dead. The owners of the Southern State informed the relatives of the crew members, "the vessel, master and all members of the crew . . . must be presumed to be lost."

Under normal circumstances, search operations would have been terminated permanently at this point. But relatives of crew members appealed to their Congressional representatives and wrote directly to the President of the United States, Dwight Eisenhower. They wanted the search resumed because they hoped that survivors were still alive on life rafts that had been swept outside of the search grid.

Olive Downing, wife of the second officer, wrote, "While my husband's head is above water, he will bring that ship to land."

Allie Bargeron, mother of a crewman, pleaded, "I implore you to give them every possible chance for rescue. I am sure loved ones of other crew members join with me and look to you as our last hope in our desperation. May God bless you in your efforts."

As a result of these pleas, and by direct orders from the White House, search operations were resumed after a one-day hiatus. The search area was extended farther eastward, as far as two hundred miles offshore. For the next two days, a combination of Coast Guard and Navy aircraft spent hundreds of hours in the air and flew over more than one-quarter million miles of ocean - without finding any sign of the missing vessel.

Search operations were called off once again, this time permanently.

Mrs. Downing now came to accept her husband's fate. She made a wreath "from greens sent her by a sea captain in Seattle. On the wreath were three red bows." On Christmas day, she and her six-year-old daughter Joan carried this wreath to the dunes in Virginia Beach, not far from their home. There they were met by a Coast Guard contingent in a DUKW, which transported them through the surf zone to sea, where a small but touching ceremony was performed. The wreath was bequeathed to the ocean with a note, which read: "Capt. J.B. Downing - M/V *Southern Districts*. At sea? Christmas, 1954. A merry Christmas from Joan and I who love you so much. May God keep you wherever you are. All our love."

For the Downings, and for the loved ones of the other crew members, that Christmas was anything but merry.

Foremost in the minds of many maritime authorities was the comparison to the loss of the *Southern Isles* three years earlier, under nearly identical conditions. Since the *Southern Isles* broke in two, and sank so fast that there was no time to transmit an SOS, speculation ran rampant that the same thing might have happened to the *Southern Districts*. As a result of this coincidence, on December 31 the U.S. Coast Guard issued orders to its district commandants "to board all LST vessels arriving in any port and cancel all certificates permitting this type of ship to engage in ocean and coastwise traffic."

Converted LST's were grounded, with the exception of those that were employed as unmanned barges. A barge is an unpowered vessel. Thus, LST's that had been converted for service in the merchant marine by having their engines removed, were not de-certified. (As a point of interest, the Coast Guard order applied only to *converted* LST's, not to Navy LST's that were employed in accordance with their military design.)

On January 3, Captain R.F. Rowe, master of the SS *Tullahoma*, sighted a floating plank, a water-soaked gray life jacket, and a life ring bearing the name *Southern Districts* (which he read through his binoculars). The location of the sighting was eight miles east of Sand Key, Florida. The Coast Guard immediately scrambled two aircraft from Miami to search the area for additional evidence, but none was found. It was assumed that the flotsam had either drifted southward with the current, or had been blown in that direction by the wind.

On January 4, the Coast Guard convened a Marine Board of Investigation in New Orleans, Louisiana. The purpose of the investigation was to determine if there was "any deficiency in the ship's makeup" that could explain the vessel's disappearance. The Board consisted of three senior Coast Guard officers. The Board called witnesses to testify, and reviewed documentary evidence that was submitted to support such testimony.

One witness, Charles Collins, sailed on the *Southern Districts* on the three voyages prior to her loss, but left the ship a week before her final departure. He would have left earlier, "but all the crewmen and the skipper were such a swell bunch." He testified, "The vessel groaned and creaked whenever there were rough seas. It was the worst steering ship I ever rode in. I remember the chief mate told me he was always catching the devil about the cargo being wet." The latter statement was hearsay, but Marine Boards of Investigation accept hearsay evidence for what it may be worth. Collins also testified that the vessel was "just one big bucket of rust," and "the first ship that I'd ever been afraid to ride on."

Ex-crew member John Flanagan confirmed Collins' allegations, adding that there were makeshift wooden plugs in line leaks, and that on one trip the bilge pumps "were operated 24 hours a day." Flanagan recalled how "the ship had been repaired twice at sea, once when the engines broke down and a second time when the steering gear went out of commission."

Charles Johnsen, another ex-crew member, made essentially the same allegations as Collins and Flanagan, stating that the decks were covered with "a half inch of rust," and that "she was rusty all over." He also mentioned several cracks. He added hearsay evidence that the third mate told him that he once dropped a sounding rod on the deck and "it fell clean through the deck into the hold."

A number of marine surveyors inspected the *Southern Districts* in dry-dock after the grounding incident. They were called upon to testify.

Marine surveyor J.B. Richardson conducted an inspection to determine why the cargo was wet. He was an independent surveyor working on behalf of the owners of the cargo and the underwriters who insured the cargo. He found rust holes in the tank top that in his opinion were caused by "old age, wear and tear." When he examined the hull he found "a number of holes in the bottom of the ship under the No. 1 and 2 holds and generally observed some cracks and holes on parts of the tank tops." Elsewhere it was reported that he found "several holes and some wooden plugs adjacent to the holes."

Lieutenant Walton Alley, of the Office of Marine Inspection, confirmed Richardson's observations, adding that the holes were the size of a dime. He did not note any excessive amount of rust. He told the Board that every repair that was ordered was made and tested. He also stated that, as far as he knew, the engines were in operating order.

John Bachrach was a marine surveyor for the United States Salvage Association. He found "some rust and scattered areas of light scale," and metal fractures under the engine and under the circulating tank. He observed that "repairs to the damaged sections were satisfactory." When he examined the vessel's log, he "could not find where the ship had encountered heavy weather, any entries of machinery breakdowns or delays at sea." This latter finding could be interpreted two ways: either the ex-employees had lied or the log had been falsified.

Employees of Todd-Johnson Dry Docks, who worked on repairs to the *Southern Districts* after her grounding, contradicted the three ex- crew members. Engineer Walker Coleman testified, "The *Southern Districts* seemed to be in the same condition as all the other LSTs I had seen. I did not see glaringly at fault anything that should have been taken care of that wasn't." Shipfitter George Dubret did not notice any "outstanding signs of deterioration." He stated that the work was tested after completion, and that the Southern States appeared "in as good condition as other ships."

W. Paul Leonard, an ironworker foreman, found the bottom of the ship in good condition and, judging from the condition of the hull, "if I had been a seaman I would have been willing to go out on it." Any deficiencies were corrected. Some welding was done around the rudder and rudder post, but the damage that was repaired was due to the churning of the propellers, not rust or deterioration. When the *Southern Districts* left dry-dock, there were no holes in the bottom and all "good sound metal" was used in repairs. He added that the repairs were permanent, not temporary.

Loading foreman V.J. Matukas testified that he supervised the loading of approximately 3,900 tons of sulfur, and that the load was "sufficiently solid not to shift in rough weather."

James Robertson, a Coast Guard naval architect, studied the vessel's loading report, which "indicated she was loaded just about to the load line, but she didn't appear overloaded." He could calculate "no undue stress" that might have been placed on any part of the vessel.

Captain Jens Jensen, a surveyor for the National Cargo Bureau, inspected the cargo holds for "cleanliness" and found the ship "fit to go to sea." Jensen also measured the vessel's freeboard and draft prior to departure on her final journey. As far as he could determine, given the choppy water in which he made his measurements, the load complied with regulations.

Two river pilots agreed that the ship showed no signs of instability. Paul Cucullu said that the *Southern Districts* was "sluggish and slow like all LSTs." Henry Voge observed, "This particular ship didn't make as many revolutions as the Navy LSTs and there was a slight list to starboard. I noticed it when the water was flowing to starboard as some sulphur was being washed down." Voge added that a slight list was normal. Other witnesses observed no list at all.

The impartiality of the Marine Board of Investigation was hampered somewhat by the presence of attorneys who represented relatives of lost crew members. To a certain extent, the Coast Guard investigators and the attorneys were working at cross purposes. The Coast Guard investigators wanted to ascertain the cause of the vessel's loss, in order to learn what improvements could be made for the overall safety of life at sea, and to implement changes in the standards for construction, maintenance, inspection, repair, and management of merchant vessels. The attorneys wanted to assign blame in order to bolster their forthcoming civil suits. Board members permitted the attorneys to question the witnesses, but balked at filing subpoenas on past masters of the *Southern Districts* at the cost of taxpayers' dollars. The attorneys tried to manipulate the official investigation in order to obtain damning information, or to imply that damning information existed when the witnesses had none to offer.

One attorney submitted as evidence a letter that purported to have been written by a crew member to his grandmother, one week prior to the vessel's departure. Oiler William Cooper reportedly wrote, "After we arrived in New Orleans we found out we have a hole in the bottom of the ship. The chief is in a sweat because the inspectors will be in the engine room and they will find all the salt water and bilge lines full of patches which is not going to go over big with the Coast Guard so all of those lines will more than likely have to be replaced and they will find lots of other things that will not come up to requirements."

Yet Lieutenant Alley testified that there were no complaints from any crew members when he conducted his inspection on November 26 - three days before the date on the letter. The Board must have been suspicious of the letter, because they sent it to experts for handwriting analysis. No other references to this letter were made.

At first blush, the uninitiated might be led to believe that the *Southern Districts* was a leaky sieve. The ship was rusty, the hull had holes, and some of the plates were cracked or fractured. Yet these imperfections were not extraordinary; they were slight and common among ocean-going vessels. Only in hindsight - in light of the vessel's loss - do they seem to have any bearing, and then only one of conjecture. A host of disinterested experts disavowed the incriminating allegations of the ex-crew members who may have been disgruntled with their lot.

One cannot help but speculate that the *Southern Districts* suffered the same fate as the *Southern Isles*: that she broke in two in the storm. But the Board members did not speculate. The *Southern Districts* sank "for cause or causes unknown." They found no one at fault, and noted that no punitive action would be taken against anyone.

More than one editorial proposed a policy of making it mandatory for merchant vessels to transmit a daily report by radio. It is unlikely that this action would have helped the men on the *Southern Districts*, but it could mean the difference between life and death under different circumstances.

Legal proceedings commenced even before the search for survivors was terminated. What follows is a thumbnail sketch of the complicated lawsuits. (I realized that "complicated lawsuits" is redundant.)

On December 17, after accepting the fact that there was no reasonable hope of locating the *Southern Districts* afloat, and in anticipation of subsequent legal action, the owners filed a petition for "limitation of liability" in federal court. This petition was pursuant to the Limitation Act that was passed by Congress on March 3, 1851. This pernicious Act restricts the amount to which a ship owner is liable to the value of the vessel (and its cargo) that is involved in the action. After she was lost, the value of the *Southern Districts* was zero; the cargo of sulfur was worth about $25,000. To put this into perspective, if the Act applied to automobiles accidents, then a vehicle owner who totaled his car when he crashed into another car and killed all its occupants, would not have to pay any more than the value of the luggage in his trunk!

On January 3, Corinne Hudson, wife of Third Officer Dwight Hudson, filed a lawsuit in the amount of $150,000 against the owner and the operator of the *Southern Districts*. Her attorney then had the company vessel *Southern Cities* "arrested." "Arrested" in this case means that a sheriff attached arrest papers to the helm, claiming his jurisdiction over the vessel and thus preventing her from departing. In essence, the *Southern Cities* became a hostage until the owners posted a bond of equivalent value. This attachment carried little weight since the Coast Guard had already decertified her as a converted LST, and she was no longer permitted to ply her trade.

The courts were flooded with more than twenty claims. The only claims that were not settled out of court - and whose records are public documents - were those of Hudson and Marinos Gelardos (wife of seamen Sotirios Gelardos). By invoking the Jones Act (which relates to dependants of deceased employees) attorneys for these wives held out for the judgments of higher courts. Hudson and her two children received $32,500 in compensation, Gelardos received $7,500.

SOUTHERN ISLES

Built: 1943
Previous names: USS *LST No. 76*
Gross tonnage: 3,325
Type of vessel: LST converted to bulk carrier
Builder: Jefferson Boat & Machine Company, Jeffersonville, Indiana
Owner: Philadelphia & Norfolk Steamship Company, Wilmington, Delaware
Port of registry: Wilmington, Delaware
Cause of sinking: Broke in two
Location: 32-30 North

Sunk: October 5, 1951
Depth: Unknown
Dimensions: 314' x 50' x 24'
Power: Twin diesels

73-00 West

The *Southern Isles* began her career as an LST - the naval abbreviation for Landing Ship, Tank. LST's had a curious design - one that was unique in the construction of ocean-going vessels. The stem of the blunt bow was split vertically and could be opened to the sides like a pair of giant garage doors. This permitted vehicles - specifically armored combat vehicles - to drive into the huge interior space from the loading dock. The flat bottom forward allowed the LST to approach gently sloping shores and embankments. When the doors were opened and the ramp was extended, tanks could be driven onto a beachhead in support of military operations. Once the tanks were offloaded and the weight in the forepart of the vessel was removed, the weight of the machinery aft cantilevered the draft toward the stern, allowing the vessel to be reversed off the beach.

LST No. 76 was commissioned in 1943. She was a twin-screw vessel, and fitted with diesel engines that could propel the ship at 10.8 knots. She crossed the

Sister ship *Southern Districts*. (Courtesy of the National Archives.)

Atlantic Ocean in convoy, then operated in the African and European theaters. She first saw action in Algeria, in April 1944, when her anti-aircraft guns fired a barrage in defense of an aerial attack. For much of the war she supported operations in the Mediterranean. She assisted the landings in Italy, and conducted amphibious assaults in southern France. In addition to tanks she carried various military cargoes, including LST parts, ammunition, food supplies, mail, troops, and, on one occasion, eleven DUKW's (amphibious troop vehicles).

LST's were mass produced for one specific purpose. After the war ended, that purpose evaporated. The U.S. Navy was left with a surplus of over one thousand LST's - most of them essentially useless in terms of military applications. They were laid up by the hundreds. But, the Navy brass reasoned, since LST's were basically cargo vessels, there was no reason why they could not be employed in the merchant marine service. Thus a great number of LST's were converted for use in the transportation of bulk cargoes.

The Philadelphia & Norfolk Steamship Company purchased *LST No. 76* in 1950. In April, the vessel was converted for commercial service by the Norfolk Shipbuilding and Drydock Company, in Norfolk Virginia. LST conversions consisted primarily of welding the bow doors shut as a means of ensuring the watertight integrity of the hull in rough seas, and of dividing the interior space into cargo holds that were accessed by overhead hatches. The installation of three crossthwart watertight bulkheads divided the cargo holds into four watertight compartments. The tank decks were either lowered or removed. *LST No. 76* was fitted with two cylindrical aluminum tanks for the transportation of liquid cargoes. The former LST was then renamed MV *Southern Isles*.

On September 12, 1951, after more than a year in service, the *Southern Isles* was dry-docked for examination at the yard that performed the conversion. The hull was found fit, and the *Southern Isles* was duly issued a certificate of inspection.

The *Southern Isles* was chartered to the Southern Trading Company on a bare boat arrangement. Southern Trading Company was a subsidiary of the Philadelphia & Norfolk Steamship Company. Essentially, then, the P & N was chartering the vessel to itself under a different name. The Southern Trading Company also chartered the *Southern Counties* and *Southern Districts* (q.v.) from the P & N, all for the purpose of transporting ammonium sulphate, bauxite, iron ore, phosphate rock, and sulfur.

The *Southern Isles* departed San Juan, Puerto Rico on September 30, 1951, with 4,000 tons of iron ore destined for Chester, Pennsylvania. This was her fourth voyage in her capacity as an ore carrier. The load she carried was no different in weight from the loads that she had carried on her previous voyages. Nor did the load differ substantially from the loads that were carried by her running mates, which were also converted LST's.

On October 3 she ran into a fierce tropical hurricane. Captain George Sadler, master, deemed it prudent to alter course and reduce speed. He turned the *Southern Isles* southward - opposite to the direction in which he wanted to go, but safer with regard to the high wind and breaking seas that he now had on his fantail.

The *Southern Isles* as an LST. (Courtesy of the National Archives.)

For two days the *Southern Isles* rode out the storm. When the worst of the tempest passed, the *Southern Isles* resumed her course against a force 5 wind that was blowing from the west-northwest. The seas were described as "moderate rough, with heavy, confused, long swells of 4 to 6 feet in height." The *Southern Isles* proceeded at nine knots on a course of 335 degrees true, buffeting the waves without difficulty.

The general alarm sounded at 3:51 on the morning of October 5. Immediately thereafter, the hull broke in two amidships. According to deck mechanic Samuel Lynn, "The ship felt like it hit a brick wall. She stopped dead in her tracks." Raymond Holton, a cook and baker, said, "The ship was broken in the middle. The center went down and the ends came up."

So quickly did the *Southern Isles* dive for the seabed that there was insufficient time to launch lifeboats. Many of the crew members drowned in their bunks. Those who managed to survive the sinking found themselves swimming in total darkness.

James Childress, an able bodied seaman, had a narrow escape: "I was swept down between the two pieces of the ship. I owe my life to a miracle and to the help of Lynn and Holton. They took hold of me and held me up."

At that moment, the *Charlotte Lykes* was plying a course of 50 degrees true. Her watch officers observed "the lights of a vessel which suddenly disappeared" four miles directly ahead. Twenty-eight minutes later, the *Charlotte Lykes* arrived alongside a ring buoy that was equipped with a burning water light. Shortly thereafter, the watch officers heard cries for help from the water. The captain of the *Charlotte Lykes* ordered a lifeboat prepared for launching. Fifteen minutes after hearing the first cries for help, survivors were spotted in the bright beam of the searchlight.

Despite the tremendous seas running, crew members of the *Charlotte Lykes* lowered a lifeboat and proceeded to rescue the men who were floundering. The first to be picked up was Wilson Deal, chief cook and steward. Next to be rescued was First Mate James Midgette. Midgette's leg was horribly mangled, and he had been clinging precariously to an overturned lifeboat for nearly an hour. In short order the lifeboat picked up five more survivors and two dead bodies.

The *Charlotte Lykes* also transmitted a call for help. The merchant vessel *Florence Luckenbach* was in the area, and responded by radio that she was on her way. The Coast Guard redirected the cutter *Cherokee*, which was already at sea, to the site of the catastrophe. The Navy ordered three destroyers, which were returning from Europe to their base in Charleston, to proceed at once to the scene. The merchant vessel *Warrior* assisted in the search operations, as well as two Coast Guard planes, three Air Force planes, four Navy planes, and two Navy blimps. This massive array of vessels and aircraft spent the entire day combing an area that was more than one hundred miles across.

All these efforts came to naught. The *Florence Luckenbach* recovered one body, but no more survivors were found. The survivors and the bodies were transferred to the *Cherokee*. The merchant vessels then proceeded on their journeys, and the military craft returned to their ports.

Midgette died aboard the *Charlotte Lykes* four hours after he was rescued. Of the total complement of twenty-three officers and men, seventeen died in the awful tragedy. The body of Captain Sadler was never found.

The Coast Guard conducted a Marine Board of Investigation into the loss of the *Southern Isles*. There was no doubt as to how the vessel sank. In the terminology of marine engineering, she "sagged." That is, her ends were lifted momentarily on two tall waves while leaving her middle unsupported. The heavily laden hull could not withstand the temporary strain. But were there pre-existing conditions that contributed to the hull's structural fatigue?

The Board calculated that on her previous three voyages in the ore trade, the *Southern Isles* was overloaded by 374.96 tons, 223.75 tons, and 386.59 tons respectively. On her final voyage she was overloaded by an amount that was less than the overload of any of these three previous voyages. Additionally, on her final voyage her draft exceeded by 3-3/8 inches the draft that was allowed by her International Load Line Certificate.

Let me put these numbers into perspective. The deadweight tonnage of the *Southern Isles* was 3,950. Deadweight tonnage is defined as the number of tons of cargo that a merchant ship can safely carry. Thus the largest amount of overloading was less than 10% more than her allowable tonnage. Her permissible draft was 15 feet 3/8 inch. Therefore, her overdraft was less than 2% more than her allowable draft.

As a result of these calculations and the loss of the vessel in a hurricane, the Coast Guard determined "That the *Southern Isles* was not a suitable type of vessel for service as a bulk carrier or iron ore or similarly dense cargoes. . . . That the abnormal strains produced in loading and unloading in her three previous voyages carrying iron ore weakened the structure of the *Southern Isles*. . . . That at the time of foundering the *Southern Isles* (with a blunt bow) was being operated at too great a speed in a nearly head sea. . . . That the causes of the breaking of the *Southern Isles* were a weakening of the hull structure by overloading and by unequal distribution of weights during loading of and discharge of iron ore cargoes and the driving of the vessel during heavy weather encountered on her final voyage."

Furthermore, the Board made the following recommendations: "That converted landing ships of construction similar to the *Southern Isles* not be authorized to carry bulk cargoes of densities approximating those of iron ore. . . . That all converted landing ships and craft certificated for oceans or coastwise waters be re-inspected to determine condition of hull structures and that reports of these conditions be forwarded to the Commandant for review. . . . That the Commandant direct that the Merchant Marine Technical Division make a study of the structural strength and weakness of converted LSTs and recommend improvements for LSTs certified for ocean or coastwise waters. . . . That the case be referred to the Department of Justice recommending prosecution of Milton P. Jackson, president of the Southern Trading Company."

The latter recommendation was based upon the finding that the company had issued instructions to its masters to carry 100 tons of cargo more than the vessels' deadweight tonnage (an overage of about 2-1/2%). This recommendation was overruled on the basis of insufficient evidence.

The Board allowed that overloading may *not* have contributed to the vessel's loss, "all other conditions being the same." In other words, the *Southern Isles* may have broken in two even if loaded according to accepted load limits. The Board issued the following remarks in this regard: "Following World War II and in anticipation of conversion of surplus Naval vessels for service as merchant vessels, serious consideration was given to the standard of safety which such vessels would have to meet for the various services in which such vessels might be employed on the different classes of waters. As a result of studies, standards were developed and instructions issued for compliance with necessary safety requirements as a condition to the issuance of certificates of inspection to such vessels. The *Southern Isles* . . . was originally constructed as an LST, a combatant vessel, and accordingly not in conformance with established principles and requirements for the construction of merchant vessels. In her conversion, however, known experience with respect to any inherent deficiencies was considered and corrective measures taken to insure that the vessel could be operated in her proposed service with safety."

"Inherent deficiencies" referred to the known structural weakness that had been observed in combat operations: a tendency of the hull to break in the middle. The Coast Guard was charged with making recommendations. It was not authorized to enact law. Now turn to the chapter on the sister ship of the *Southern Isles*: the *Southern Districts*.

ST. CATHAN

Built: 1936
Previous names: None
Gross tonnage: 565
Type of vessel: Armed trawler
Builder: Cook, Wellington, & Gemmell, Beverly, England
Armament: One 3-inch, 23 caliber deck gun, depth charges, machine guns
Owner: British Navy
Cause of sinking: Collision with SS *Hebe*
Loran 45238.1 / 59616.6

Sunk: April 11, 1942
Depth: 105 feet
Dimensions: 172' x 29' x 14'
Power: Coal-fired steam

Official designation: FY 234

GPS 33-08.303 / 78-20.789

The *St. Cathan* began her career as a fishing trawler working for T. Hamling & Company. She was one of a number of sister ships that were designed to work in the North Sea. Almost immediately following Germany's invasion of Poland - on September 1, 1939 - most of these trawlers (including the *St. Cathan*) were chartered by the Royal Navy for anti-submarine duty. Each one was fitted with a gun that was mounted on a platform above the foredeck, with a pair of depth-charge racks on the fantail, and with machine guns on the bridge deck. The refrigerated holds became magazines.

Drafting and arming these erstwhile trawlers helped to protect the British Isles from marauding U-boats, but still more ships were needed. Politically, the United States maintained a surface show of neutrality in the European conflict. But in actuality, the U.S. sided with the Allies against German aggression. As a consequence, the United States agree to lend to England fifty obsolete World-War-One destroyers and ten Lake-class Coast Guard cutters in exchange for ninety-nine-year leases on sites in the Bahamas, Antigue, Jamaica, St. Lucia, Trinidad, and British Guiana, for the establishment of U.S. military bases. This trade deal was known on the books as Lend-Lease.

Wise heads in the U.S. Navy knew that war could not be avoided forever. They wanted to initiate a massive ship building program. But their hands (and the purse strings) were tied by the American populace. Since they had last fought "over there," most U.S. citizens did not want to engage in what they perceived (or rationalized) was a European war that did not materially affect the comforts of peace that they had grown to take for granted. Thus, when the Japanese forced the issue by bombing Pearl Harbor - on December 7, 1941 - the U.S. Navy found its fleet woefully inadequate to fight a two-ocean war: a Pacific war against Japan, and an Atlantic war against Nazi Germany.

The Nazis wasted no time in making an offensive against the American homeland. Within a month of the declaration of war, Germany sent its first barrage of U-boats to the U.S. eastern seaboard, in an offensive known as Operation Drumbeat. The first U-boat struck in mid-January. Within days, ships were being

Before the armament was installed. (From the collection of Pete Manchee.)

torpedoed all along the coast. A convoy system could not be established immediately due to the lack of escort vessels. Nor could the beleaguered British Isles afford to return the aged destroyers. Instead, the Brits sent two dozen armed trawlers to take up the slack until the U.S. Navy could stand on its own keels.

The *St. Cathan* was officially transferred to the U.S. Navy in February 1942. Along with the trawlers came their British officers and crews. The resulting command structure was somewhat nebulous. The trawlers remained under titular British control, and were operated in accordance with British naval procedure, but they operated under orders from the U.S. Navy. In essence, these trawlers became autonomous vessels whose allegiance was clearly defined, but whose day-to-day activities went unrecorded because neither naval command accepted responsibility for maintaining them. Thus a great deal of important archival documentation was never kept by either navy.

The story of the loss of the *St. Cathan* can be found in the chapter on the *Hebe*, the ship with which she collided, and which also sank: a double tragedy.

Today, the wreck of the *St. Cathan* lies in 105 feet of water. The hull is intact and contiguous. The wreck came to rest with a list to starboard. The port side rises some ten feet or so above the seabed, while the starboard side gunwale disappears beneath the sand. The starboard anchor is firmly secured in its hawse pipe. The windlass stands high on the small portion of the forecastle deck that is recognizable.

Immediately abaft the forecastle, much of the wreck is broken down to the level of the sand. The deck gun stood proudly on its mount in the 1980's. Since then there has been considerable collapse. Deep ocean swells generated by Hurricane Hugo - which swept through the area on September 22, 1989 - caused the gun mount to collapse. Subsequently, the breech and barrel were nearly buried under the sand, and now it takes a sharp eye to distinguish the barrel from the surrounding I-beams. Hugo also destroyed most of the forecastle, which used to be penetrable but which is now an open sore that is hardly recognizable.

The single boiler lies exposed amidships, dominating the wreck by its comparatively monstrous size. Immediately abaft the boiler lies the small triple expansion reciprocating steam engine. Close to the starboard hull and adjacent to the after end of the boiler sits the degaussing generator. Thick cables lead from the generator to the hull. These cables then go around the perimeter of the hull under the gunwale. The purpose of the degaussing system was to demagnetize the steel hull; that is, to neutralize its magnetic field so that it would not detonate German magnetic mines. In 2001, the degaussing generator was no longer exposed.

Abaft the engine the hull is broken down on both sides. The stern and the fantail are intact. The steering rudder is visible on the stern, as well as a couple of depth charges. Most of the metal canisters have rusted away, revealing the deadly explosive material. Although they are probably inert, it is best not to beat on these depth charges with hard metal objects.

Top: Crystallized depth-charge explosive material.
Middle: Depth-charge detonator.
Bottom: End of the detonator, showing the depth settings.
Note that the actuating handle is set on "SAFE."

SUWANEE

Built: 1850
Previous names: *Pampero*
Gross tonnage: 666
Type of vessel: Wooden-hulled side wheeler
Builder: J.S. Brown, Baltimore, Maryland
Owner: Simons, Cattell, Carey, and Hopewell
Port of registry: New York, NY
Cause of sinking: Foundered
Loran 45333.6 / 59483.4

Sunk: December 4, 1866
Depth: 75 feet
Dimensions: 189' x 27' x 10'
Power: Coal-fired steam

GPS 33-29.510 / 78-24.624

When the *Suwanee* was launched she was christened as the *Pampero*. She carried freight under this name for the first six years of her life. In 1856 she was rebuilt to such an extent that she came out of the yard a completely different vessel, and was given the name by which she was thereafter known. Her hull was lengthened by forty-four feet, which not only gave her a new length of 189 feet, but which increased her tonnage (and thus her cargo carrying capacity) from 494 to 666. In addition to the propulsion provided by her inclined, single-piston engine, the *Suwanee* was fitted with three masts which were schooner rigged. Her boiler was replaced in 1858.

On May 14, 1861 (shortly after the onset of the Civil War), the *Suwanee* was bound for New Orleans when she was denied permission by the Union blockader USS *Crusader* to enter any port belonging to "seceded States." As Louisiana had joined the Confederacy, the *Suwanee* was given a choice to either clear for New York or to surrender to Union forces. The captain of the *Suwanee* chose to relinquish his command rather than to yield to Union prerogative. The side-wheeler was detained "for the use of the Government," and saw some service under the command of Lieutenant Duncan. However, the *Suwanee* must have been released from impounded service, because later Union dispatches refer to her as a "chartered steamer." Whether she was originally chartered from the Southern Steamship Company, of New Orleans - the owner of the vessel at the time of her capture - was not mentioned. More likely than not, the *Suwanee* was "liberated" from her legitimate owners in favor of Union prosecution of the war.

Speculation aside, according to her certificate of enrollment for November 12, 1863, the *Suwanee* was owned by four individuals: Henry Simons (1/2 share), Alexander G Cattell (1/4 share), R D Carey (1/8 share), and John C Hopewell (1/8 share). (Periods were not placed after the initials.) A new certificate was issued three years later - on November 24, 1866 - in which Cattell's name was given as Alician du G Cattell, and Carey's name was given as I. Carey. *Suwanee* was also misspelled as *Suwannee* (two n's). The port of registry was changed from Philadelphia to New York. Some of the owner's names that were given in subsequent newspaper accounts differ slightly.

Three days after her final certificate was issued, the *Suwanee* departed New York on a passage for Brazos Santiago, a Texas port at the mouth of the Rio Grande. Under the command of Captain Joseph Catherine, she was carrying "a cargo of arms and ammunition for the Republic of Mexico." The bars at the mouth of the Rio Grande were too shallow for ocean-going vessels to cross. Trade goods destined for Matamoras and the interior of Mexico were offloaded at Brazos Santiago, then transported overland or by shallow draft steamship.

The *Suwanee* encountered difficulties almost immediately. Supercargo J. Fred Schultz stated that the load of freight was so heavy that the vessel's guards were under water. He gave the following account:

"The weather was moderate until after passing Absecom light, when the wind freshened from the south and west, with a head sea. While standing down for Cape Henlopen, bound for the Delaware breakwater, the steamer struck on the Shoal off Hereford Inlet. Finding it impossible to get her off without lightening, we threw over about 200 cases of heavy goods, when she floated off; we then run for the breakwater and anchored. After taking in some freight there, we put to sea on the 30th, with a strong westerly wind. Nothing occurred up to the night of the 3d December. When off the South Carolina coast, running down for Cape Romain light, a heavy gale set in from the South and east, the wind and sea increasing, until at midnight it blew a hurricane; the ship laboring heavily, frequently falling off into the trough of the sea, taking in water over the hurricane deck. From this time up to 5 A.M, the water gained rapidly; the steam and hand pumps were kept a going, and efforts made to lighter her by throwing over cargo. At 5 A.M., the water was within twelve inches of the fires, and the firemen up to their waists in water, trying to keep the fires a going. At 6 o'clock, finding the ship must go down, got out the boats and launched them safely, although the sea was running very heavy; all the ship's company left her in safety, and about an hour after we saw her go down.

"After leaving, the boats, three in number, steered to the north and west, the captain's boat containing 15 persons being ahead, the other two boats, in charge of the chief mate and 1st engineer, keeping company. About 9 A..M. we lost sight of the captain's boat, and having no compass in either of our boats, we shaped our course by the sun; trying to make the land about meridian we made a sail to the eastward, the 1 mate made a signal of distress and both boats kept away from the friendly ship. It proved to be the brig *Potomac* of Bucksport (Me.), J.T. Snow, master, 60 hours from Charleston for Georgetown (S.C.). The captain took us on board and did everything in his power to meet our necessities, none of us having anything but the clothes we had on. He landed us safely at Georgetown (S.C.), and under the providence of God we are indebted to him for our lives. We are under a lasting obligation also to Captain Davis, of the steamer *Fannie*, for a free passage to this port [Charleston] and his kindness to us while on board."

Meanwhile, the captain's lifeboat was still at sea. On board were the captain's wife and two children, two passengers, and nine crew members. The occupants rowed northward and arrived at Wilmington, North Carolina that afternoon. Not a soul was lost.

According to the Steamboat Inspection Service, "On an investigation it appeared in evidence that the ship was too heavily laden, and that was the sole cause of her foundering."

Where does the *Suwanee* lie today? In June 1989, commercial fisherman Billy Long and firefighter Blaine Garren put a diver on the wreck of a paddle-wheel steamer off Myrtle Beach. This was a site that Billy Long had fished for years. Very little of the hull was exposed, but the site was littered with munitions and Civil War relics. They believed that it was the remains of a Confederate blockade runner, perhaps lost during a passage from Nassau, the Bahamas, to the Southern port of Wilmington. They immediately made plans to salvage the wreck for profit.

About a month after the discovery, Long claimed that he had "been given exclusive rights to the wreck by a federal court judge." The claim appears to have been a gross exaggeration, if not a wholesale fabrication. This author has been unable to locate any court records to substantiate his claim. Nevertheless, the bluff and the fear of legal repercussions kept most divers off the site for several years. Long never commenced his proposed plans for salvage, and divers who later visited the site encountered no interference from the Long arm of the law. Today the wreck is dived openly by the public.

Recreational divers soon began to recover items that clearly established that the wreck could not have been a Confederate blockade runner. Brass belt buckles stamped "SNY" were obviously from the State of New York. This led to the belief that the wreck was the *Governor* (q.v.). Then George Purifoy recovered nearly seven tons of lead (ninety ingots each weighing 150 pounds, stacked like cordwood) and a 1,200-pound cannon. The cannon was a 20-pounder Parrott rifle dated 1863. This cannon dispelled any notion of the wreck being the *Governor* because it postdated the *Governor's* loss (November 20, 1861). Nonetheless, so firmly entrenched is the belief (or the optimistic hope) that the wreck is the *Governor*, that still today the site is mistakenly called the *Governor* by the vast majority. More open-minded divers and historians refer to the site as the Civil War Wreck.

Although no positive identification has yet been made, I strongly suspect that the wreck is that of the *Suwanee* - which at the time of her demise was carrying leftover Civil War materiel to freedom fighters in Mexico - what would today be called "military surplus." Pete Manchee reached this same conclusion independently.

As can be imagined by the cargo she was carrying, the *Suwanee* is a fascinating dive for the souvenir hunter. When first discovered, her cargo was strewn about the sea bed like overstocked items in a department store garage sale.

Most of the wooden hull and deck planking has been eaten away by teredoes; squiggly white tubes, which are the shells of these destructive wood boring mollusks, lie scattered about because the wood in which they were once encased has completely rotted away. Occasionally the shifting sand will expose relatively intact beams, timbers, and the boards from wooden packing crates.

Where portions of the lower hull are uncovered, the copper sheathing, which was fastened to the outside of the hull below the waterline in order to prevent teredoes and barnacles from getting a grip, is readily apparent; small pieces of this sheathing stick up out of the sand or are strewn about the site.

Nearly all of the wreck is buried, with a relief that rarely exceeds six inches. Waves of sand like miniature dunes wash across the site as if it were a desert oasis, which in many respects it is, since it provides a substrate for the lowest forms of marine life with which the food chain begins. The biggest mass of wreckage is the machinery. The engine appears to have toppled over backward, but in actuality it is an inclined engine instead of the more common vertical engine which powered most sidewheel steamers. Barely a foot or two separates the engine from the boiler abaft. The engine rises about eight feet off the bottom, and the boiler about six feet. At the forward end of the engine and on both sides of it are the shafts, which are disconnected from the engine and which extend at right angles to the paddle wheels. The remains of the paddle wheels lie in arcs across the bottom.

A few feet forward of the engine and toward the port side is a badly corroded condenser, with its tubes exposed. A few feet farther to port is a large cylindrical structure lying on its side, with a central tube which is big enough to swim through. Around the perimeter of the central tube is a fluted lining.

The tip of the bow rests one hundred feet from the shafts. Most of the intervening space is comprised of wavy sand with occasional bits of wreckage protruding, but there are enough pieces to make a path that is traversable in all but the worst visibility. There are no discernible edges of the wreck; rather, the debris thins out until little or nothing remains exposed. The bow consists of a concreted clump about six feet by eight with a couple of feet of relief; the most recognizable feature in this clump is a pile of anchor chain. The starboard anchor lies flat and is completely exposed; the port anchor lies with almost completely buried with only fluke sticking up about three feet out of the sand. However, on occasion, sand is deposited to such an extent that it can cover this bow wreckage almost completely.

Abaft the boiler is very little wreckage. A crate of Parrott shells is partially exposed on the starboard side (unless they have since been recovered). Several brass spikes which appear to be driven into the buried keel point the way to the stern. Beyond that the wreck lies completely under the sand, so there is no way of knowing where the hull ends.

In addition to "SNY" buckles (which, by the way, is the only known source for this particular type of buckle), the wreck has yielded Federal buckles stamped "US" and officers buckles, which portray an eagle. Other recovered items are sword hilts (or hand guards) for U.S. Cavalry sabers, Parrott rounds (artillery shells), cannon balls ranging in diameter from 3-inch to 8-inch, Enfield rifles (usually just the wooden stocks, as the iron barrels have long since turned to mush), leather knapsacks, a ceramic spittoon, a ceramic wash basin and pitcher, and large quantities of Enfield rifle bullets as well as bullets of other calibers, and a second smoothbore cannon (or Parrott rifle). There are still some lead ingots left. Each ingot is stamped "SAN ANDREAS".

The *Suwanee* is very much a digger's wreck. If you want to find anything, be prepared to spend your time fanning the sand with your hand or, perhaps, with a Ping-Pong paddle. Better yet, use a scooter. There are undoubtedly many crates of Civil War relics lying beneath the thin layer of sand, waiting to be retrieved by the patient and enterprising diver.

Artifacts recovered by Pete Manchee.

TENNESSEE

Built: 1864

Previous names: *Muscoota*

Gross tonnage: 1.033

Type of vessel: Iron-hulled side wheeler

Builder: Continental Iron Works, Greenpoint, New York

Owner: Thomas Clyde, Portsmouth, New Hampshire

Port of registry: New York

Cause of sinking: Fire

Location: On the beach some 30 miles south of the Cape Fear bar

Sunk: June 29, 1870

Depth: 10 feet

Dimensions: 255' x 35' x 21'

Power: Coal-fired steam

The *Tennessee* began her career as the USS *Muscoota*. The iron-hulled side-wheel steamer cost the government $275,000. She was delivered to the U.S. Navy on December 7, 1864, and was commissioned on January 5, 1865. Her propulsion machinery consisted of a single inclined, direct-acting engine whose cylinder had a diameter of 58 inches, and whose piston had a stroke of 8 feet 9 inches. She was fitted with four boilers, each with a single furnace; of these there were two horizontal tubular boilers, and two were superheating boilers. This machinery could propel the sidewheeler at a maximum speed of 13 3/4 knots, but her cruising speed was 8 knots. Cruising speed was normal operational speed; it was based upon economy of fuel and minimum stress on machinery. The *Muscoota* was fitted with two masts that were schooner rigged.

The Navy rated the *Muscoota* as a second class steamship. She carried a battery of ten guns and a compliment of 154 men. During her short stint in the Civil War she served in the East Coast Blockading Squadron. "Cost of repairs while in naval service was $32,102.05." Right down to the penny!

On June 17, 1869, the Navy sold the *Muscoota* to Thomas Clyde for $50,000 - certainly one of the greatest bargains of the century! Clyde owned the New York & South Carolina Steamship Company. He retired the military moniker *Muscoota* and renamed the vessel *Tennessee*. Unfortunately for Clyde, he got only one year's service out of his incredible bargain.

The *Tennessee* departed from Charleston on June 28, 1870, with Captain Chichester in command. Bound for the markets in New York City was a typical Southern cargo consisting of 748 bales of Upland cotton, 20 bales of Sea Island cotton, 67 casks of clay, 81 tierces of rice, 88 bales of domestics, 490 barrels of rosin, 4 bales of wool, 550 boxes of vegetables, and 377 barrels of potatoes. The *Tennessee* had not gone far when fire broke out "in the pressed cotton stowed in the forward hold."

The time was one hour after midnight on the 29th. The *Tennessee* was then about forty miles north of Cape Romain. "Finding it impossible to subdue the flames she was beached at 11 AM, 30 miles south of Cape Fear bar, and scuttled

As the *Muscoota*. (Courtesy of the Naval Photographic Center.)

in ten feet of water. All hands saved."

The fire was not extinguished until the *Tennessee* burned down to the water's edge. "Nothing was saved from the wreck with the exception of such baggage as the passengers had with them at the time in their state rooms, and some few articles of cabin furniture that Capt Chichester managed to secure."

Clyde engaged the services of the Coast Wrecking Company to determine the feasibility of salvage. Travel was slow in those days, so a week or more passed before the salvage outfit arrived on the scene with the wrecking steamer *Empire* (which was dispatched from New York), the salvage tug *Alexander Oldham*, the schooner *Ray*, "extra cables, anchors, steam pumps, divers and engineers." The wreckers hoped to pump the water out of the hull and pull the sidewheeler off the bar, then tow the *Tennessee* to port to be rebuilt. This the wreckers were unable to do.

They managed to save only 27 bales of cotton, which were transported to Wilmington, North Carolina on the sloop *Flash*. Most of the cotton was stowed in the lower hold, which was completely flooded because the hull was so badly battered. Worse yet, the intensity of the heat had warped the machinery. According to the final notice that referred to the *Tennessee*, "The hull and machinery will probably be abandoned as worthless."

At the time of her loss, the *Tennessee* was valued at $200,000; her cargo was worth $85,000.

The actual location of the *Tennessee* is unknown.

UNITED STATES

Built: 1864
Previous names: None
Gross tonnage: 1,289
Type of vessel: Wooden-hulled screw steamer
Builder: S. Gildersleeve, Portland, Connecticut
Owner: F.W. Nickerson and Company, Boston, Massachusetts
Port of registry: Boston, Massachusetts
Cause of sinking: Ran aground
Location: Off Cape Romain light, six miles from the lighthouse

Sunk: April 3, 1881
Depth: 12 feet
Dimensions: 197' x 36' x 24'
Power: Coal-fired steam

    Had it not been for the mitigating circumstances of hazy atmosphere and strong southwest winds, Captain S.H. Mathewes might well be accused of the mariner's cardinal sin of permitting his vessel to run aground after losing his way along a regularly plied route. The *United States* was bound from Boston, Massachusetts to Savannah, Georgia with passengers and a cargo of general merchandise when adverse wind and sea conditions drove the screw steamer far enough off her course to strike a sandy shoal in twelve feet of water, "in the vicinity of Cape Romain, a little to the northward and about halfway between Georgetown and Charleston. . . . . Crew and passengers saved." The date was April 3, 1881.

    Because the wreck lay in an exposed position, it was imperative that she be hauled off the bar before the arrival of a tempest. A passing steamship, the *Planter*, observed the plight of the *United States*. The *Planter* ducked into

From *Early American Steamers*, by Erik Heyl.

Georgetown with word of the catastrophe, then returned to the *United States* along with the steamer *Louisa*. The combined efforts of the two steamships were not strong enough to pull the stranded steamer off the sand bank.

Captain Mathewes dispatched his first officer to engage wrecking tugs to come to the steamer's aid. The *Wade Hampton* and the *Republic* raced to the site with salvage pumps and towing gear. By the time of their arrival, however, the hull of the *United States* had been bilged by the savage surf, and her lower cargo hold was filled with water. "The sea was too heavy for the tugs to work alongside, and at 2 P.M. the captain determined to abandon her. A portion of the cargo and tackle was secured and placed on board a pilot boat from Georgetown, and the crew, number twenty-seven persons, was transferred to the tug *Forest City*, which had arrived at the scene of the wreck with the agent of the vessel from Savannah. When the vessel was abandoned there was fourteen feet of water in her hold, and the wreck was fast going to pieces."

Since the depth of water in the hold was two feet deeper than the depth of water that passed over the bar on which the *United States* lay aground, the hull must have sunk at least two feet into the sand. "The steam wrecking flat *Uncle Sam*, under the command of Capt. Smith, was left alongside with a view to save whatever could be secured from the wreck."

The wreck was breaking up even as the Uncle Sam offloaded "shoes, some musical instruments, and other merchandise" from the "between decks."

On April 11, the insurance underwriters put up the remains of the *United States* for auction. "The vessel was knocked down at $1,050 cash, the purchaser pledging himself to remove all the cargo possible on salvage. The ship was valued at about $60,000, and was partially insured. She belonged to F. W. Nickerson & Co., Boston, who spent $20,000 on her last summer putting in new boilers and refitting the vessel. The cargo, which was valued at about $25,000, was insured in Northern companies."

On April 20, it was reported, "Most of the cargo that was saved from the *United States* arrived on the steamer *St. John's* from Charleston on Saturday night. It consisted principally of furniture."

There were no further mentions of the *United States*. The location of the wreck, and even her name, has long since been lost in the sands of time. Researchers should note that the vessel was equipped with a two-cylinder, vertical direct-acting engine. Each cylinder measured 40 inches in diameter and had a stroke of 3 feet 4 inches. According to the Steamboat Inspection Service, the *United States* was lost "on the shoals off Cape Romain light, six miles from the light-house."

WILLIAM LAWRENCE

Built: 1869
Previous names: None
Gross tonnage: 1,049
Type of vessel: Iron-hulled screw steamer
Builder: Atlantic Works, Boston, Massachusetts
Owner: Merchants and Miners Transportation Company, Baltimore, Maryland
Port of registry: Baltimore, Maryland
Cause of sinking: Ran aground
Loran 45596.9 / 61103.8

Sunk: February 11, 1899
Depth: 30 feet
Dimensions: 207' x 35' x 20'
Power: Coal-fired steam

GPS 32-11.658 / 80-35.024

The *William Lawrence* is a prime example of the work-a-day steamships that operated along the eastern seaboard in the latter part of the nineteenth century. She was one of the numberless and inglorious merchant vessels that transported passengers and freight at a time when long-distance overland travel was either unduly expensive or too uncomfortable to contemplate.

The *William Lawrence* was constructed with the benefit of the technological advances made during the American Civil War. She was fitted with a single piston engine that generated 138 nominal horsepower. A four-bladed iron propeller pushed the iron hull through the water at a moderate speed of 12 knots. The vessel sported two masts from which canvas could be hung. However, it is unlikely that the vessel was ever propelled by means of sail. In early steamship days, sails were carried more as a backup than as an alternative means of propulsion. Sometimes, sails were rigged in order to stabilize a vessel in a crosswind.

The *William Lawrence* completed more than one thousand voyages during a career that spanned thirty years.

On what proved to be her final passage, the *William Lawrence* departed from Baltimore, Maryland on February 8, 1899. She steamed south along the Chesapeake Bay, turned east, rounded Cape Henry, then proceeded south along the coast toward her ultimate destination of Savannah, Georgia. On board was a cargo of general merchandise that was estimated to be worth some $30,000. This cargo consisted of bolts of cloth, clothing, leather shoes, toys (particularly dolls), jars of pickles and preserves, and empty medicine bottles. Captain A.L. Willis was the master.

Shortly after entering the ocean, the *William Lawrence* encountered a fierce winter storm that struck the entire east coast. Gale force winds blew out of the northwest, bringing with them severe cold and precipitation in the form of snow. Land travel was disrupted and telegraph lines were blown down by what was described in Georgia as "seventy-two hours of the worst weather ever known on the coast."

According to one correspondent, who interviewed the second officer, Robert

From the collection of the South Carolina Institute of Archaeology and Anthropology.

Beale, "The fog was so thick that one could hardly see across the deck and there was a heavy gale blowing. The weather was intensely cold. The ship's compass was evidently not in proper working order, and something seemed to be wrong with the machinery of the ship. Some time before she struck it was realized that she was off her course, and soundings were taken. These showed that the vessel was in shallow water and she was ordered slowed down. Before the proper course could be ascertained the vessel struck hard upon a reef or shoal.

"Every effort was made to get the vessel off, but without avail. A considerable portion of the cargo was thrown overboard in the effort to lighten the ship. The men remained by until Sunday morning [February 12], when it was seen that she was breaking up. Capt. Willis then ordered the men to leave. There were four boats and the disembarkation was performed in an orderly manner under the direction of Capt. Willis and the other officers. Capt. Willis remained to the last, and it is said took the poorest boat for himself and companions."

The four lifeboats were soon separated by the vagaries of the wind, and most lost sight of each other in the fog and blasting snow. They were in the vicinity of Hilton Head.

In one boat were six men, of whom A.J. Morrisell, the second assistant engineer, was the highest ranking officer. Morrisell assumed command, and directed the men to row in the direction of Port Royal. With great good fortune, the boat managed to locate the entrance to the sound despite the near-blinding snow and fog. From there the men proceeded to the naval base at Parris Island, which they reached at 4:30 that afternoon, after suffering great torment from the cold. Naval personnel "rendered valuable assistance" to the shipwrecked mariners.

Three lifeboats were still unaccounted for. Morrisell immediately sought to telegraph a report of the melancholy circumstances to John Carolan, the Savannah agent for the Merchants and Miners Line. A tug transported the men to the telegraph office at Port Royal. Word of the catastrophe could not be sent right away, however, because of the disruption in communications brought about by the storm. Thus an entire day passed before anyone outside of Port Royal learned about the loss of the *William Lawrence*, and about the lifeboats that yet were missing.

Another boat contained seven men, with Second Officer Beale in charge. The men pulled the oars with a will. "Having some idea of the lay of the land they endeavored to make Port Royal harbor, but their frail craft was buffeted by the icy blasts for many hours. They finally made buoy No. 3 at the mouth of Port Royal harbor. Their strength was exhausted, and they could go no further. They managed to tie up to the buoy, where they remained about two hours hoping that a boat would rescue them. The sea was so rough, however, that it was dangerous to remain at the buoy and they were compelled to cut loose. Helpless now, they drifted back towards the scene of the wreck and the boat soon ran aground. An oar was jammed into the mud and the boat made fast. The seven men made their way ashore so exhausted and benumbed that they could hardly totter to a place of safety when they fell exhausted. Here their situation was but little better. The prospect of immediate death had merely been exchanged for that of a lingering one. They were without food or shelter and exposed to the icy blasts of the storm which raged over the island. Their only hope was to wait until the storm had subsided when they might be seen by some passing boat. Their situation was so desperate that some of the party talked of suicide, and threatened to throw themselves into the sea from which they had recently escaped, to end their sufferings.

"There was one hero who sustained the failing spirits of his companions, a tall, rawboned Irishman, John Montgomery by name. He alone of all the crowd never lost heart. When others cried Montgomery laughed. He told stories and jokes to keep his companions awake when sleep would have meant death. When despair had settled over some, and they wished for death to end their sufferings, Montgomery claimed to see a light in the distance, and predicted the approach of boats for their rescue. He had that indispensable companion of the soldier and sailor, a pipe, whether of the dhudeen [sic] variety is not known, and a supply of tobacco. With his pipe between his teeth, he walked the beach, defying the elements, and constantly on the lookout for a sail."

Two full days passed while the castaways suffered horribly from exposure, thirst, and hunger. By then, "two of the best tugs in the service of the Savannah Towboat Company, the *Cynthia No. 2* and the *McCauley*," had been scouring the barrier islands for signs of survivors. The *Cynthia No. 2* located the wreck on a submerged shoal, "in the north breakers off Port Royal bar. . . . Her hull is broken in half and only her smokestack and a portion of the deck work are showing above water." The tug retrieved the Merchant and Miners banner from the sunken steamer, and returned to port with the flag secured to her staff, flying at half mast.

The barren sand spit, on which Beale and the others huddled, was devoid of shelter. Not even the rise of a low dune offered protection from the incessant wind. Finally, forty-eight hours after wrecking, *Pilot Boat No. 2*, of Port Royal, hove into view of the men on the island. "It was Montgomery who saw the pilot boat and signaled her to come to the assistance of himself and companions. Some of the men had to be lifted bodily and carried to the boat."

The pilot boat transported the men to Port Royal. There they were reunited with their comrades from the other lifeboat. However, their agony was not yet at an end. Second Officer Beale, Chief Engineer Edward Roach, and steward Frank Tindle (whose family name was sometimes given as Dingle) had badly frozen feet and legs. Chief cook Harvey Kelley "was also suffering severely with his feet." Oscar Bowler, the quartermaster, had badly frostbitten hands.

The passenger steamer *Clifton* was riding at her dock, and was even then preparing for her departure for Savannah. The thirteen survivors boarded the steamship. Some of the men from Beale's boat had to be carried up the gang-plank because of their injuries. "They were made as comfortable as possible in the cabin of the *Clifton*, until their arrival at Savannah, when they were trans-ferred to St. Joseph's Infirmary."

The thirteen crew members rejoiced at their survival. "Some of the men, who had suffered most, were well known to the employes [sic] and other ship-ping people, who met them, and there were some affecting scenes as the hands of those who were supposed to have been lost were grasped by their friends from on shore. About half the men, who had been rescued, looked well and hearty. The other half had evidently experienced severe suffering."

(In another account, *Pilot Boat No. 2* met the *Clifton* on her way to Savan-nah, and the men were transferred to the passenger steamer at sea.)

Despite the fortuitous rescue of thirteen men, their number comprised only half the crew. Another thirteen crew members were among the missing, includ-ing the captain. Michael Jenkins, president of the Merchants and Miners Line, issued orders that no expense was to be spared in continuing the search for the rest of the survivors. The *Cynthia No. 2* explored the coastline while the tug *Cambria*, with Carolan aboard, searched the islands.

"As the *Cambria* neared the military reservation at Hilton Head about 9 o'clock, a small party of men was seen on the beach making signals to the tug. It was soon realized that these were the missing men, of whom the tug was in search. They did not wait for the tug to come to land, but came out in their boat. They were soon aboard, and were given a warm reception. Agent Carolan was delighted to find that there was not a man missing, and that furthermore they were all in good condition, not being in need of medical assistance.

"Their story was soon told. The two boats left the ship together, Capt. Willis being the last man to leave. The captain was in charge of one boat and First Offi-cer Hooper of the other. By orders of the captain, the two boats were kept togeth-er. The effort was made to reach Port Royal harbor, but with little success. After being at sea for over twelve hours, the boats were finally beached through the breakers. It was a dangerous attempt. The party got through safely, but both the boats were stove in. The land which they had made they afterwards learned to be Capers Island, a small bare sand spit off the Carolina coast, some distance from Port Royal. Here they remained until Tuesday morning. Their situation was not

the pleasantest in the world. They were without food and water, the small stock
of crackers and the keg of water which they brought with him from the ship having been ruined by the salt spray. The lack of food was not their worst incon-
venience. The island afforded no shelter, and they were forced to remain exposed
to all the bitter weather of Sunday night and Monday and Monday night, their
only protection being a low sand spit, which only partially shielded them from
the wind, and not at all from the sleet and snow. They were fortunate in having
a supply of matches, and by the aid of these a fire was made from the wooden
seats of the lifeboats, which was kept up by such driftwood as could be gathered.
There was little comfort in a fire under such disadvantages, but it kept them from
freezing and saved them from the sufferings which befell Second Officer Beale
and his party in boat number 2.

"Tuesday morning, the weather having moderated, one of the boats which
was less damaged than the other was patched up and in this the party made its
way to the military camp on Hunting Island, a distance of some eight or nine
miles. Here they were warmly received by the soldiers who extended them the
most generous hospitality and showed them every kindness. Sergt. Smith, who is
in charge of the station, was very kind to the shipwrecked mariners. Tuesday
night was the first they had spent in comfort since the ship struck ground Saturday morning. Having been so kindly treated at the post they were naturally in
much better condition than they would have been had they awaited the rescuing
party on Capers Island."

The *Cynthia No. 2* was detailed to retrieve the belongings of the crew of the
William Lawrence. "Nearly every man aboard the *Lawrence* took with him his
bag containing his clothing and other personal possessions when the ship was
abandoned. Some of the bags were lost, however, and all the others were left
behind." Four crew members were left at Hilton Head "to look after the effects
of members of the crew."

The *Cambria* proceeded to Savannah with the remainder of the rescued men
safely aboard. When the tug passed Tybee Island, Captain Van Avery, master of
the *Cambria*, signaled to the telephone station that he had the crew of the *William
Lawrence* aboard. This joyous news spread quickly to Savannah. "As the tug was
sighted coming up the river crowds gathered on the balconies of the business
houses on the Bay, and hats and handkerchiefs were waved at rescuers and rescued. Every vessel along the river saluted as the *Cambria* passed, and Capt.
Avery responded vigorously to the salutes with the siren of the *Almirante Oquen-
do*, which he brought back with him from Santiago Bay." (This was the year following the Spanish American War.)

"The tug stopped at the Baltimore steamship wharf, where the party speed-
ily disembarked. The other seamen of the *Lawrence's* crew, with the exception of
those in the hospital, were at the Wharf, and there were some warm handclasps
as they exchanged greetings. The first man of the rescued party to leave the wharf
was Louis Vleeschouwer, a stowaway, whose presence on the boat was discovered shortly before the wreck. Capt. Willis knew nothing of the presence of the
man with the unpronounceable name until the wreck occurred."

Captain Willis was reticent about discussing the circumstances leading up to the grounding. He was insistent, however, that there had been no mechanical malfunctions and that the "compass was evidently out of order." He attributed the wreck to the stress of the weather. "It was the worst weather I have ever experienced. There was a heavy gale, but the worst feature was the very heavy mist which made it impossible to see anything twenty or thirty feet away. The cold was very severe. . . . We made efforts to get the vessel off, and with this in view began heaving the cargo overboard Saturday night. We continued this until the steam pipes of the engine broke and then we were helpless. It was evident by morning that the vessel was going to pieces, so I ordered the men to the boats. The ship's crew was divided into two parties of thirteen each, with two boats to each party. Each party was directed to keep together."

One newspaper reported, "Capt. Willis spoke highly of Sergt. Smith and also of Dr. Edwin P. Shattuck, the government surgeon at Hilton Head, who spent some time attending to the wants of the men. One of the men, Frank Fuller, had his ears badly frostbitten, and it is probably due to the attention given him by Dr. Shattuck that he still has those useful members in their natural form.

"The heroic measures which Capt. Willis adopted in the treatment of his men on the island explains how it is that they are now but little the worse for their experience. In talking of the matter last night Capt. Willis said, 'I made them keep moving. Had they been allowed to lie still they would have been as badly frozen as the men who were in the second officer's boat. When the men wanted to give up and cease their efforts I urged them on with language that I would never have used to them under other circumstances. The only way to keep from freezing under such circumstances is to keep the blood in circulation, and, to do this you must keep moving. That is all that saved us, in my opinion.'

" 'There is Grundgreen,' said Capt. Willis, pointing to one of his men. 'He is the only man of the second officer's party who is not in the hospital, and he does not appear to be at all hurt. He kept moving all the time, and urged the others to do the same thing. He sung them songs and stories, and did everything he could to keep their courage up.'

"Grundgreen is a short, stout man with a red mustache. He is a German, but the imperfect manner in which he speaks is due to a difficulty of utterance and not to his German birth. 'Stuttering Jack,' the other men called him.

" 'I keep moving,' said Grundgreen when asked how it was that he had escaped when others of his party had suffered so severely. 'I would sleep a little when I got tired, but as soon as I began to feel cold I would get up and run along the beach.' "

The astute reader will have noticed that a previous report credits the life-saving qualities of the German-born Grundgreen to the Irishman John Montgomery.

It would be nice to end this story of hardship with "All's well that ends well." However, this is reality and not a fairytale, and all did not end well. The men in the hospital were suffering from the aftereffects of frostbite. Doctors contemplated that amputation might be the only way to save their lives. At first it was feared that "Chief Engineer Roach would lose one foot and all of the toes on the other; that Steward Dingle [or Tinkle] would lose both feet, and that two seamen would lose one foot each. They were frozen in Officer Beale's boat. Several of the men may lose one or both ears."

Contrary to initial diagnoses, the condition of the hospitalized men improved. On February 20 it was reported, "Quartermaster Bowler, Cook Kelly, and Sailor Montgomery are reported to be rapidly improving and are expected to soon be able to leave the hospital. While the condition of Chief Engineer Roach, Second Officer Beale and Steward Tindle [or Dingle] is much improved, the outcome of their cases is still uncertain. While no fatal results are anticipated it may be that some of them will be maimed for life as the result of their injuries, and it is very much feared that such will be the case."

Edward Roach died the following day.

The last report on the condition of the other patients was printed in the local newspaper on February 23. According to that account, Robert Beale "has been taken North to Baltimore for treatment, his sufferings having affected his mind. . . . John Montgomery, a sailor, is the only one of the six men of the crew sent to the hospital, who has recovered sufficiently to be discharged. Steward Frank Dingle [or Tindle], Quartermaster Oscar Bowler and Cook Harvey Kelly are still at the hospital."

Meanwhile, Carolan examined the wreck from aboard the *McCauley*. He quickly determined that the cargo was "so badly damaged that the salvage would not pay the expenses of getting it out. The wreckers had been at work, however, and several boat loads of stuff were seen being taken away from the wreck. The boats visited the wreck at low tide and were able to get hold of a good deal of stuff which had been loosened from the cargo in the breaking up of the vessel."

There was no further mention of salvage.

Over the years the wreck gradually fell apart. The natural rate of deterioration was accelerated by the tremendous forces of nature. Because of the shallow depth, the hull lay at the mercy of the waves, which battered the iron plates continuously. Hurricanes, and the fierce ground swells that they generated, added their own brand of annihilation. The same mechanism that sucks a beachcomber's feet into the sand acted upon the hull, with the result that the hull sank into the substrate until the lowest cargo level was completely buried. The upper portions of the hull were both encrusted with marine fouling organisms, and sandblasted horribly whenever the seabed was churned up by ordinary wave action and by extraordinary storm effects. Tides that raced as fast as five knots pummeled the wreck twice daily from opposite directions. The *William Lawrence* lies in an area that is highly dynamic and incredibly destructive.

The resting place of the *William Lawrence* was largely ignored until the advent of scuba. Until then it was little more than an obstruction noted on the nautical charts as the "Lawrence Wreck Boiler." This annotation was made because the boiler stood up so high that it protruded above the surface, and was considered a hazard to navigation. In 1931, the wreck showed five feet at mean low water. In 1973, it showed three feet at mean low water. The *William Lawrence* became a popular spearfishing site in the 1960's, with snapper, grouper, and black sea bass being the primary targets. The site was known locally as the Boiler Wreck. At high tide, the boiler presented more of a hazard to safe navigation because it lurked barely beneath the surface. In a running tide a "boil" showed over the boiler when it was submerged, but when the tide turned slack, the boil disappeared. Yet the site was never marked by a warning buoy. Nor is the wreck marked today, although a channel marker is moored nearby.

In the 1980's, the *William Lawrence* was rescued from obscurity by recreational divers who spent their spare time exploring the wreck in the search for nineteenth century relics. Divers routinely recovered shoes and shoe soles, mirrors, clocks, portholes, pins, pencils, toys, novelty items, ordnance, and a wide variety of bottles (for relish, ketchup, perfume, and medicine). Even socks and jeans have been recovered - and worn by those who recovered them after laundering them in a washing machine! One diver recovered a comic book that was still substantially legible.

The process of erosion and deposition is ongoing, with the result that some areas on and around the wreck may be swept clear of sand, while other areas become buried. The site is forever changing in appearance. Thus a spot that produced dispensary bottles one day might be completely covered with sand several months later; and vice versa.

Howard Tower published a description of the wreck in 1986: "Seventy-five feet of the forward hull is in good shape, and the bow rises 20 feet above the ocean floor. From the front it looks like the edge of a great knife. The midships lay flat and is largely covered in sand. At the stern a great iron screw and shaft are visible." The seabed consists of compacted sand and gravel.

While the site and its cargo was being obliterated slowly by the unrelenting forces of nature, three enterprising divers decided to accelerate the rate of recreational recovery efforts by concentrating their energies on "working" the wreck assiduously. These three people were Frank Chance, Paul Chance, and David Topper: the same threesome who did such excellent work on the Confederate steamship *Nashville*. (See the Suggested Reading list for the book they produced on the *Nashville*.) Their serious salvage initiative commenced in 1984.

Tower was invited to accompany them on one of their early trips to the wreck. In addition to bolts of black cloth and clear strap-sided flasks, he found "buttons, shoes, pencils, antique glassware, marble casters, and some green perfume bottles shaped like rifle cartridges." He also uncovered "100,000 straight pins. The container had long since crumbled. And while madly fanning the sand with my hand, I received dozens of punctures in a split second." Tower estimated that "hundreds of tons of general stores still remain encased within this encrusted steamer."

Meanwhile, the Chance Brothers and Topper were trying to "blast the bow anchor loose from its chain and sea floor encrustation." To accomplish this they used primacord and small explosive charges. They did not succeed in recovering the anchor that day, but they returned at a later date and were successful in raising it and towing it to shore. They also found and recovered another anchor that lay away from the hull. Using an airlift, they uncovered more than one hundred

South Carolina dispensary bottles of the palmetto tree type, as well as a number of other relics that dated from the turn of the century, including novelties, metal toys, costume jewelry, the remains of clocks, and marble casters.

Tower wrote: "The wreck is not archaeologically significant because there is nothing entombed which cannot be found on display in antique shops across the nation. Nautical technology of the post-Civil war period is, also, well documented. Divers are doing society a favor by recovering antiquities from the wreck so the items may be enjoyed by the public."

The first that most South Carolina state representatives knew of the existence of the *William Lawrence* was two years later, when they read Tower's article that described the bygone salvage operations. State reps took exception to Tower's presumption of insignificance, noting in response to his published pronouncements that the cargo might "provide significant data about the way cargo was stowed. Furthermore, the *Lawrence* is important because the vessel, launched in 1869, had a screw propellor [sic] and represents an early form of advanced technology in steamship propulsion." With respect to the dispensary bottles, State reps deplored the absence of "archaeological data on methods of packaging or stowing this glassware." They wanted answers to questions such as, "What states were these products shipped from? Where were they made? Where were products going? What was the quality of workmanship for various items?"

Divergent points of view reflect the backbone of a democratic society.

There are no records extant in State archaeology department files to indicate that two years after the explosive event, the Chance brothers and Topper were still working the *William Lawrence*. The State's primary source of information was Tower's article, which was published two years after the fact. In January 1986, Alan Albright, then underwater archaeologist for the State, contacted Tower and asked him to elaborate on certain points. Howard explained that explosives were used only to free the anchors. Despite Tower's assurances, and

Side-scan sonar image provided by the South Carolina Institute of Archaeology and Anthropology.

absent any contradictory evidence, internal State reports misrepresented the facts, contending that the use of explosives had "mutilated the hull to expose more of the cargo." This misinformation was distributed to State officials who professed a sudden interest in "protecting" the wreck from commercial salvage.

The distinction between the recreational recovery of relics and the commercial salvage of those very same relics is gray and ill-defined. The two primary differences are motive and method (but not opportunity). "Recreational" implies fun, while "commercial" infers profit. In general, recreational divers recover collectibles for their own satisfaction, while commercial salvors recover valuables in order to return them to the stream of commerce. Furthermore, recreational divers usually recover only those items that are exposed; or perhaps they expose a few items by fanning off sand with their hands. Commercial salvors use more sophisticated tools such as airlifts, water jets, and prop wash deflectors.

Once State reps became aware of the trove of trinkets that divers had been recovering from the wreck for decades, they sought to prohibit such wholesale recovery. But the State did not have jurisdiction over the site.

Salvors, State reps, and recreational divers all agreed that the wreck lay "approximately 4.3 nautical miles from Bay Point Island and 4.6 miles from Hilton Head Island at the entrance to Port Royal Sound." Since a State's jurisdiction extends only three nautical miles from shore (one marine league), the wreck was located outside the territorial borders of the United States, in international waters. This made it difficult for the State to stop ongoing salvage operations (if, in fact, such operations were still ongoing).

As a consequence, the State took another tack on the situation: it sought to file criminal charges against the Chance brothers and Topper, "relative to unauthorized use of explosives . . . and unlicensed salvage operation . . ., both carrying maximum sentences of $10,000 or two years [imprisonment]. It also seems prudent only to seek charges [probably no pun intended] against Mr. Topper who

Layout provided by the South Carolina Institute of Archaeology and Anthropology.

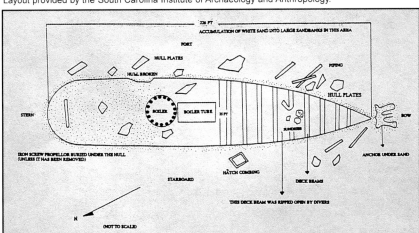

resides within the state, and leave the Chance brothers to another day as they reside in another state."

Salvage operations that are conducted in international waters do not need to be licensed. Yet some State reps wanted fervently to believe that the *William Lawrence* should be under their control, and that the commercially salvaged artifacts should be turned over to the State. They wanted to make a test case. But legal counsel advised them to reconsider their ambition because the jurisdictional dispute "would likely be an insurmountable stumbling block in the prosecution." Due to the State's uncertain grounds (or waters) in this regard, counsel suggested that the State might achieve at least part of its avowed goal by "requesting such return [of artifacts], and civil court processes as a final resort."

The civil process could be a double-edged sword, however, because the State might lose the case - and the wreck - irrevocably. In the end, the best advice was: do not start a fight that you might not win, especially when the loss would prove to be worse than the status quo.

Alternatively, some State reps considered informing the ATF (Bureau of Alcohol, Tobacco, and Firearms) about the unauthorized use of explosives. Even if the "charges" could not be supported, the allegations carried considerable threat value. Any legal defense is costly to a defendant who has limited financial resources. The government's financial resources are essentially infinite.

However, other State reps speculated that the explosives might have been furnished by James Cooler, thought to be an associate of the Chance brothers and Topper. Cooler owned a construction company called Cooler Construction, and therefore might have been authorized to possess explosives. This put the State in a quandary about making unsubstantiated allegations. To complicate the issue, when Albright asked Tower about Cooler's participation, Tower stated that Cooler was not on board on the day on which Tower dived the wreck (when explosives were used to free the anchor), so that a connection between Cooler and the Chance brothers and Topper could not be firmly established from the only witness available to the State.

State reps equivocated on how best to proceed - and on whether to proceed at all.

Coincidentally, on May 14, 1986, Lee Spence applied to the State for a license to salvage the wreck. In light of the legal fireworks that were exploding at the time, and because the site was the subject of a so-called "criminal investigation," Spence's request was denied pending a resolution of the "current legal proceedings."

The spurious legal proceedings languished. In fact, no legal proceedings even existed - just the thought of potential legal proceedings.

A year and a half later (on October 26, 1987) while the State's imaginary attack plan was still focused on the Chance brothers and Topper, commercial diver Jeremiah Shastid made an out-of-the-blue flanking maneuver: he applied to the Federal Admiralty Court in Charleston for exclusive rights to salvage the *William Lawrence*. There are no documents in the public record to indicate that Shastid knew anything about the prior salvage operations or about the State's disinclination to permit commercial salvage. Neither the State nor anyone else submitted objections to the Court. Therefore, on December 29, Judge Falcon Hawkins ruled that the wreck did indeed lie "within the Admiralty and Maritime jurisdiction of this Court." Shastid was appointed Substitute Custodian of the *William Lawrence*. This judgment enabled Shastid to salvage the wreck without interference. Shastid incorporated a salvage outfit under the name Sea Dweller Diving Company (to which was appended the name James Shastid).

Corporate records are not available to the public, so that follow-up salvage operations must be pieced together from recorded court proceedings. It appears that Shastid rented equipment from Donald Bracey and James Montgomery, in order to proceed with the salvage of the wreck. Apparently, some recoveries were made before Shastid ran out of money. Bracey then paid Shastid $5,000 for a 25% interest in the claim. In March 1988, Shastid defaulted on his responsibilities as Substitute Custodian by not commencing full-scale salvage operations by the deadline imposed by the Court. Shastid claimed that he was suffering from lack of funds.

On March 31, Bracey and J & W Investments (a partnership consisting of James Montgomery and his wife) filed a complaint against Shastid. They requested a restraining order because they believed that the wreck was more valuable than they at first supposed. Shastid maintained his status as Substitute Custodian, but had to pay $5,000 to Bracey and Montgomery.

On April 5, Shastid was dismissed as Substitute Custodian and was temporarily enjoined from conducting further salvage operations. He was also enjoined from interfering with the salvage operations conducted by Bracey and Montgomery. Shastid had to return any recovered artifacts and borrowed salvage equipment to Bracey and Montgomery, who jointly were the Court's new Substitute Custodians.

On April 7, Shastid stated that he was no longer associated with the *William Lawrence*, and that he was effectively "out of it."

Bracey and Montgomery commenced full-scale salvage operations. It appears, however, that not everyone wished for their salvage efforts to succeed. Competitors and disgruntled recreational divers contacted State authorities about their enterprise. Within days, and after a flurry of phone calls, the State created a task force to deal with this new situation. Whereas before, in the case against the Chance brothers and Topper, the State had everything to lose, now circumstances were reversed. Bracey and Montgomery were armed with a court injunction that protected their exclusive right to salvage the wreck without interference. Now the State had nothing to lose by tackling the Court.

On April 14, State reps boarded the salvage vessel that was moored over the *William Lawrence*. They ignored the court order that they were shown, and seized all the artifacts that had been recovered that day. They also demanded an inventory and the location of any artifacts that had been recovered previously, so that they could be seized at a later time. The salvors undoubtedly perceived these seizures to be a blatant case of piracy, while State officials considered it their duty to protect the wreck from gross commercial salvage. State reps tagged each artifact, and wrote a receipt for their seizure. When the salvors demurred about the inventory and location of other artifacts, State reps intimated that arrests might be forthcoming - this despite the fact that Bracey and Montgomery had complete lawful sanction from the Federal Court, and were acting within their legitimate rights as Substitute Custodians for a federal judge!

The State filed a Motion to Intervene with the Federal Court. The State cited the South Carolina Antiquities Act as its justification for seizing the recovered artifacts, and for claiming ownership of the *William Lawrence.*

Gordon Schreck was the attorney retained by Bracey and Montgomery. To obtain the court's endorsement, he submitted evidence that showed that the *William Lawrence* was located more than "one marine league" from the State's Atlantic shoreline, and that "reference to charts and aerial photographs indicate that there appear to be no land masses which could be reasonably construed as part of the 'Atlantic seashore', so as to bring this wreck within the State's territorial limit as defined in the Underwater Antiquities Act. . . . The State of Carolina appears to take for granted, without any support in fact, that the shipwreck which is the subject of this action 'is located within the territorial waters of the State of South Carolina', and that 'title to the land on which the *Lawrence* sits is vested in the State of South Carolina.'" Judge Hawkins agreed.

To contest this point, the State solicited assistance from the National Oceanic and Atmospheric Administration and from the Wildlife and Marine Resources Department. They dispatched a bevy of surveyors to locate any spit of sand that might exist closer to the wreck site than the seashore or coastline: the commonly accepted point from which the distance offshore is measured. They located what they described as a "land mass" that lay seaward of the Port Royal area, and which protruded "above the tidal plane at mean low tide." This putative "land mass" was submerged at high tide.

Schreck took exception to the use of this newly discovered "land mass" as a coastal baseline. "It cannot be reasonably maintained that a shifting sandbar almost a mile off the mainland qualifies as a 'beach' or 'coastline' in common parlance. . . . The State's contention that a small, isolated and submerged sandbar, complete[ly] surrounded by the ocean and subject to the vicissitudes of the sea, can constitute the 'Atlantic seashore' for purposes of measuring the State's territorial limits, is a strained and uncommon interpretation which goes contrary to any reasonable or established definition."

Schreck's argument may have been valid with respect to reason, common sense, and U.S. federal law. But in rendering his opinion, Judge Hawkins relied upon Article Eleven of the Geneva Convention (to which the United States subscribed). This Article stated (in part): "A low-tide elevation is a naturally-formed area of land which is surrounded by and above water at low-tide but submerged at high-tide. Where a low-tide elevation is situated wholly or partly at a distance not exceeding the breadth of the territorial sea from the mainland or an island, the low-water line of that elevation may be used as the baseline for measuring the breadth of the territorial sea."

While the court deliberated on these fine legal arguments, Hurricane Hugo swept through the area. The September hurricane rated a category 4. In addition to causing forty-nine to eighty-six fatalities (statistics differ) and seven to nine billion dollars worth of destruction, waves and ground swells did considerable damage to the *William Lawrence*. Much of the upper part of the hull was knocked down, reducing the height of relief from twenty feet to ten. The propeller and shaft were no longer exposed, either because the fantail collapsed on top of them or because they settled into the sand enough to become covered. The boiler barely protruded above the surface at extreme low tide.

On December 20, 1989, Judge Hawkins reversed his earlier decisions (first rendered in the Shastid case, then reiterated in the case concerning Bracey and Montgomery) and sided instead with the political pressures that were brought to bear by the State. The *William Lawrence* and "her tackle, apparel, equipment and cargo," became a ward of South Carolina. On such a slender strand as a transitory sandbar were Bracey and Montgomery forced to give their hard-earned relics to the State.

Wrote Bruce Rippeteau, Director of the South Carolina Institute of Archaeology and Anthropology (SCIAA): "The judgement [sic] is a major victory for sport divers and archaeologists - it serves to support our position that certain wrecksites [sic] should be set aside and protected from exploitation by a few so that the majority can enjoy them." He also wrote, "This represents an important win for the State, but also for our many divers and fishermen who practice their recreational pursuits in South Carolina waters. . . . The ruling has, once again, opened the wrecksite [sic] to the dive community and to fishermen, both of whom were restricted from entering the area of the wreck while the federal admirality [sic] award *et al.* on the site was in effect."

Christopher Amer, the current State underwater archaeologist, concurred with Rippeteau's sentiments when he wrote that the State's success in the legal battle would "ensure that the wreck would not be destroyed by commercial salvors - so that it could remain as a popular dive spot for sport divers."

One cannot help but speculate about the future legal position of the *William Lawrence* when the ephemeral sandbar that proved crucial to determining the most recent outcome of the case, is washed away by the natural migration of sand, or is obliterated overnight by storm-tossed seas.

Archaeology department files do not record what happened to the "case" against the Chance brothers and Topper. In any event, the State never carried out any of its dire threats. According to Amer, the "case" simply petered out due to the lack of pursuit. What happened to the items that the threesome recovered is anyone's guess.

Subsequent State memoranda denounced these various commercial salvage operations as illegal. In actuality, the recovery activities were not illegal when they were conducted. They can be construed as illegal only in retrospect, when a different interpretation of the State's coastal baseline was accepted in the third opinion of a federal court judge. In American jurisprudence, previous violations of newly adopted penal codes cannot be prosecuted retroactively. Salvors who acted in full compliance with the law - when that law was the accepted law of the land - should not be viewed as wrongdoers or offenders. Nor is it in the American spirit to castigate people of different persuasions.

Memoranda further distorted the facts and cast aspersions by claiming that "a group of divers contested the state's claim to the site." In actual fact it was the other way around: the State contested the salvor's claim to the site: a claim which those divers had firmly established in Federal court. Another memoranda declared that "professional salvors sought to destroy the remains" of the wreck. These and other slurs serve only to contribute to the false perception that commercial salvors work illegitimately.

In October 1990, "the South Carolina Underwater Archaeology Division staff visited the site of the SS *William Lawrence* to conduct an initial reconnaissance of the site and to return confiscated artifacts." A "portion of these items were retained for exhibit purposes and show and tell sessions for school groups. Selected pieces also form a part of our comparative type collection for future research. Items which SCIAA felt they did not need for any of these purposes were catalogued and then returned to the site. . . .

"In November 1990, the Underwater Archaeology Division staff returned to the site again. The objective of this trip was to attempt to protect the vulnerable forward hold area. A large blanket of geo-fabric was used to cover the hold. It was weighted down by sand bags. The fabric allows water to circulate but hopefully will trap sand particles and protect exposed cultural material beneath."

Alas, within months this fabric washed up on the beach. No other attempt has been made to either stabilize the wreck or protect its contents. Quite the contrary, the contents may be recovered by anyone with a South Carolina hobby license - presumably, even those commercial salvors who recovered the relics the first time.

The hobby license rules and regulations were revamped as a result of the *William Lawrence* litigation. Anyone can apply for such a license, and the process of application is simple, painless, and inexpensive: much like applying for a hunting or fishing license. The license comes complete with a 28-page copy of the South Carolina Underwater Antiquities Act, with which the recreational diver should become familiar. For more information in this regard, see the Fossil Hunting section in the Introduction.

Of particular importance here is the stipulation that "no more than ten artifacts a day may be recovered from a shipwreck site. Divers may not destroy the integrity of the ships' structure by removing or moving timbers, fittings, fastenings, or machinery." Also, items may be recovered only by hand. "All powered mechanical dredging and lifting devices and buoyancy equipment except a personal flotation device of any sort are prohibited including, but not limited to, prop wash, air lift, water dredge, and pneumatically operated lift bags."

Divers should note that a license is required only to *collect* artifacts, not to "inspect, study, explore, photograph, measure etc."

In 1991, the SCIAA considered designating the *William Lawrence* as a Heritage Preserve. This status would enable the State to exercise strict control and authority over the site, and would have made the site "off-limits for collecting and spear-fishing," in contradiction of the State's avowed purpose for obtaining jurisdiction over the wreck.

Amer held a public hearing at which the majority of attendees were either professional archaeologists or recreational divers. He wanted to get both camp's feelings and opinions on the matter. The divers presented a strong argument for leaving the wreck without official recognition, claiming that it was already well protected by the hostility of the environment in which it resided. Unpredictable weather prevented most charter boats from reaching the wreck. Once on site,

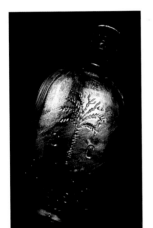

exceptionally strong currents often kept divers out of the water. Those divers who managed on occasion to get down to the bottom, frequently found the visibility so poor that they could hardly see anything more than a few feet away.

Amer adopted an enlightened stance that was atypical for a bureaucrat, especially in this age of over-regulation. He let the elements of nature protect the wreck from excessive access.

In 1998, the *William Lawrence* was nominated for inclusion on the National Register of Historic Places. This recognition does not preclude spearfishing or artifact collecting.

When I dived on the wreck in October 2002, visibility measured in inches - perhaps between six

and twelve. Despite these conditions, Andy Ogburn found and recovered a palmetto type dispensary flask, a delicate stemware drinking glass, and five china saucers. Although this was the off-season, two fishing boats were already anchored on the site when we arrived. They were pulling in black sea bass as fast as they could reel in their lines - as well as a host of undesirable species which they released. Both boats were anchored in the wreck, and one had its chain so fouled that the operator asked Pete Manchee to free it for him (which he did). This led me to wonder how many thousands of times, in the past decade, anchors had been tossed indiscriminately into the rusting hull and onto the cargo of brittle glassware: to rip, rend, and smash the "protected" wreck and its cargo.

A permanent mooring established over the wreck could prevent a lot of breakage and inadvertent demolition.

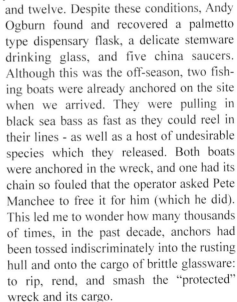

Shipwrecks of Georgia

Visions of salvage. (From *Gleason's Pictorial*.)

As the *Gettysburg*. (Courtesy of the Institute for Great Lakes Research.)

BARNSTABLE

Built: 1887
Previous names: *Gettysburg*
Gross tonnage: 1,210
Type of vessel: Wooden-hulled bulk cargo carrier
Builder: John Craig & Son, Trenton, Michigan
Owner: Barnstable Company, New York, NY
Port of registry: San Juan, Puerto Rico
Cause of sinking: Foundered
Loran 45520.5 / 61320.4

Sunk: September 13, 1919
Depth: 50 feet
Dimensions: 208' x 35' x 17'
Power: Coal-fired steam

The *Barnstable* was built in 1887 as a bulk cargo carrier. For thirty years she plied the fresh waters of the Great Lakes under the name *Gettysburg*. Her primary cargoes were lumber, iron ore, and coal. She could carry as much as 800,000 board feet of lumber. When she was not transporting lumber between various lake ports, she carried iron ore downbound and coal upbound. She was sold to the *Barnstable* Company on March 13, 1916, was renamed *Barnstable*, and left the Great Lakes to become a "saltie." For the next three years she worked the coastwise trade along the eastern seaboard.

On September 13, 1919, the *Barnstable* steamed out of Savannah harbor on a passage to Havana, Cuba. Her cargo consisted of 1,223 tons of coal that was insured for $17,000. Including Captain R.E. Moon, master, she carried a total complement of twenty-eight. No sooner did she poke her stem into the open sea than she ran into a moderate gale. There was no reason for Captain Moon to think that his vessel could not handle to stress of the weather. Yet, with the wooden hull "working" in the growing waves, the *Barnstable* soon began to leak. The crew operated the pumps for four hours before giving up their attempt to save the ship.

Captain Moon's report of subsequent events was all too brief, and other accounts - both official and unofficial - were amazingly contradictory. By extracting the slender truth from the overabundance of fiction, it appears that the *Barnstable* went down close to midnight on September 13, and fairly close to shore. One account states that she was lost "off St. Catherine's Light." According to another account she went down "off Tybee Light." Captain Moon wrote "14 miles S x E 1/2 E from Tybee L.H." "L.H." undoubtedly stood for lighthouse. By a broad interpretation, Captain Moon's position could be construed to be off St. Catherine's Island - but farther from St. Catherine's Island than from Tybee Island.

From official published accounts, it appears that the crew put to sea in two lifeboats, with fourteen men in each. It also appears that the boats became separated, and that neither boat reached land in very short order. One boat landed on St. Catherine's Island on - as near as I can determine - September 15 "after an all-night battle with rough seas." These men brought word of the catastrophe to civilization. The other boat, containing Captain Moon, the chief officer, and twelve crew members, was blown farther south, and did not make landfall until much later - perhaps not until the following day. By the time the captain's boat was beached on Sapelo Island, four of the crew members had died from exposure.

One reliable unpublished account provides some additional information. According to the deck log of the Revenue Cutter *Itasca*, on September 15 she received word of the catastrophe while moored in Savannah, and immediately put to sea "at full speed under forced draft" in order to search for survivors. She located the submerged wreck at 5:30 that afternoon. As the *Itasca* maneuvered close aboard, lookouts spotted a man clinging to the mainmast. A surf boat was lowered and the man was duly rescued. He was found to be "nearly exhausted from exposure and lack of food." His name was Joe Hendricks. He informed his rescuers that the *Barnstable* "sprung a leak and sank while at anchor, Saturday night September 13th, about 9:00 P.M."

Hendricks verified that two boats had gotten away from the wreck. "One, however, having half filled with water as it cleared the side, the crew making frantic efforts to bail it out as it drifted southwestward with the wind and sea, and that he was the only person left aboard the ship."

The log of the *Itasca* noted that the depth around the steamer was eight fathoms, with five fathoms of water over the deck, and that both masts were standing. Another entry gave the position of the wreck as 31° 46' 30" north latitude, 80° 41' 00" west longitude. After rescuing Hendricks, the *Itasca* spent two hours searching in the vicinity, but found no other survivors. She then hove to and dropped anchor for the night.

Although I have been unable to obtain the loran or GPS coordinates, the site of the *Barnstable* is known. Henry Ansley, Georgia's Artificial Reef coordinator, has dived on the wreck. He provided the following description: "What remained was essentially the wooden ribs (heavy timbers) and keel. The ribs were basically just laid out and lying in the sand - not buried, although it appeared they could easily be sanded over. Except for some short (3') pieces (timbers) at one end of the ribs, there appeared to [be] very little relief or structure left at all. I also remember scattered, small pieces of coal here and there. I don't remember any boilers or machinery.

"The growth on the timbers was also limited and there were few bottom fish around, although there were several schools of "baitfish" well up in the water column above the remains (which helped us locate it on our fathometer/fish finder).

"Whether the boilers or other pieces of the wreck were beyond our visibility (I seem to remember horizontal water visibilities at around 30-35'), I don't know. The remains were in about 50' of water."

Researchers should note that the *Barnstable* was propelled by a compound engine that was built by S.F. Hodge & Company of Detroit, Michigan. The cylinders were 26 inches and 44 inches in diameter, with a stroke of 40 inches. Her original fire box boiler was built by Thomas McGregor, also of Detroit. It measured 10 feet 6 inches by 16 feet. I found no mention that the boiler had been replaced.

Both the Lloyd's Register and the Record of the American Bureau of Ships gave the *Barnstable's* port of registry as New York City. Captain Moon wrote in his wreck report that the vessel was registered in San Juan, Puerto Rico. Perhaps her registration was changed after the Register and Record were published.

Heavily laden with a deck cargo. Note the steering ball on the end of the bowsprit - a common feature on Great Lakes steamships. (Courtesy of the Institute for Great Lakes Research.)

BAVARIA

Built: 1857
Previous names: None
Gross tonnage: 2,273
Type of vessel: Iron-hulled screw steamer
Builder: Caird & Company, Greenock, Scotland
Owner: Mississippi & Dominion Steam Ship Company, Liverpool, England
Port of registry: Liverpool, England
Cause of sinking: Fire
Location: Off the Georgia coast, 130 miles east-southeast of Port Royal

Sunk: February 7, 1877
Depth: Unknown
Dimensions: 296' x 39' x 25'
Power: Coal-fired steam

The *Bavaria* was originally constructed for the Hamburg American Steamship Company, in 1857. She was fitted with a compound engine whose cylinders measured 45 inches and 80 inches in diameter, with a stroke of 42 inches. This engine could generate 300 horsepower. Her masts were bark-rigged as an auxiliary means of propulsion in case of a machinery breakdown. For most of her career the *Bavaria* transported passengers and freight between New York and Hamburg, Germany. After she was sold to the Mississippi & Dominion Steam Ship Company, she was rebuilt, in Southampton, England, in 1873. She continued her employment on the New York-Hamburg route until 1877. The company then dispatched the passenger-freighter on her first voyage from Liverpool, England to New Orleans, Louisiana.

The cargo she carried on her return passage to Liverpool was valuable: 4,356 bales of cotton, 1,000 barrels of rosin, 55 bags of cottonseed, and 239,000 Mexican dollars.

Captain H.C. Williams, "who is as courteous as he is brave and determined," issued the following statement concerning the loss of the SS *Bavaria*:

"The steamship *Bavaria* left New Orleans on Saturday morning, February 3, passed to sea the same day, and had favorable weather to February 6. When the ship was in latitude 31 14 north, longitude 78 42 west, at 7 P.M., the ship was examined by Capt. Williams and the chief engineer, when all things were found in proper condition. About ten minutes after this examination the cargo of cotton was reported on fire, burning down through the steerage deck; commenced working all hands with the fire hose and fire buckets, but notwithstanding these efforts the flames spread rapidly. At 8 P.M. the fire had taken possession of the ship to such an extent as to render the saving her hopeless. The officers and crew were then divided off, the sailing staff being sent to the boats, and the engineer staff continuing to work the fire hose. At 10.30 P.M. expecting the flames to break out each minute on deck, manned all the boats, getting some of the sea boats away with difficulty in consequence of the intense smoke. About this time the crew embarked in the boats but remained by the steamer until 1.30 A.M., when the

From the author's collection.

ship being a mass of flames fore and aft, ordered all the boats to follow the captain's boat on a west northwest course for shore, distant about 130 miles, Port Royal being about west northwest. At 2.30 A.M., Capt. Frostick, of the bark *Dorothy Thompson*, of Sunderland, for Bull River, saw the burning ship at a distance of 20 miles, getting up with the wreck about 6 A.M. The flames had then considerably subsided, everything being burnt except the after part of the poop; the ship was red hot fore and aft, for and mainmast burnt away, and mizzenmast burning. Seeing the davits swinging out Capt. Frostick decided that the crew had not been taken off, but had left the ship in the boats. The *D. Thompson* was then steered for the shore. At 10 A.M., February 7, fell in with boats Nos. 2 and 3, and from them learned that the other boats were steering west northwest. Following on at 2 P.M. boats 4 and 6 were fallen in with, and all hands taken on the bark. The wind increasing to a number 8 gale, with rain, Capt. Frostick continued on, and at 4 P.M. sight boat No. 1, containing Capt. Williams and crew and Mr. O'Neill, wife and three children. This finished the rescuing of the entire officers, crew and passengers of the *Bavaria*, which had no sooner been accomplished than the bark had to be hove to in a furious number 9 gale. On the 9th instant the crew safely reached port and were landed at Beaufort."

Thanks to Captain Frostick's persistence, which was clearly above and beyond the call of duty - even the exceptional duty of mariners toward their companions in distress - no lives were lost in what could have developed into a terrible human tragedy. Captain Williams, in accord with wishes of the *Bavaria's* survivors, wrote a formal letter of gratitude which he presented to Captain Frostick. It read:

"We, the captain, officers, engineers, crew and passengers of the screw steamship *Bavaria*, desire hereby to express our deep gratitude to Capt. Frostick, officers and crew of the bark Dorothy Thompson, for their great humanity in rescuing us from six ship's boats, in a northwest gale, on the axis line of the Gulf Stream. We feel assured that the remarkable judgment that enabled Capt. Frostick to take in at a glance of the burning ruins an exact apprehension of the catastrophe, and our subsequent movements, whereby he was enabled to pick up boat after boat, the last one at a distance of thirty miles from the wreck, will alone suffice to ensure his future career as one of usefulness and prosperity. Nevertheless, we would add our heartfelt wishes for his future welfare, assuring him that his kindness, care and hospitality in ministering to our necessities will never be forgotten by the sixty-four souls he has rescued from what must have been during the ensuing night certain death."

Estimates of the *Bavaria's* value differed. According to one source, the hull was worth 50,000 British pounds. According to another source, "The value of vessel and cargo is $500,000." And according to a third source, "The ship and cargo was worth about $700,000." It is safe to assume that, today, whatever is left of the iron hull and machinery is totally worthless. Not so her cargo.

Almost as an afterthought the following sentence was appended to the official account of the *Bavaria's* loss: "No specie saved." Specie is gold, not paper money. Specie could be gold bars, minted coinage, or a combination of both. A treasure consisting of 239,000 Mexican dollars worth of gold - at 1877 prices - lies somewhere off the coast of Georgia awaiting discovery.

During peacetime. (Courtesy of the Steamship Historical Society of America.)

ESPARTA

Built: 1904
Previous names: None
Gross tonnage: 3,365
Type of vessel: Freighter
Builder: Workman, Clark & Company, Belfast, Ireland
Owner: United Fruit Steam Ship Company, New York, NY
Port of registry: New York, NY
Cause of sinking: Torpedoed by *U-123* (Kapitanleutnant Reinhard Hardegen)
Looran 45375.3 / 61832.2

Sunk: April 9, 1942
Depth: 50 feet
Dimensions: 330' x 44' 28'
Power: Oil-fired steam

GPS 30-50.850 / 81-10.155

The *Esparta* was a standard, unglamorous workhorse that carried cargoes for the United Fruit Company for thirty-eight years. She was fitted with refrigeration machinery to keep produce fresh. Refrigeration was especially necessary for the *Esparta*, not only because of the perishable quality of the agricultural products that she transported, but because she had to traverse the hot equatorial ocean in order to deliver her South and Central American freights to New York markets. For obvious reasons, the *Esparta* and her sister ships were disparagingly referred to as "banana boats."

In early April 1942, the *Esparta* departed from Puerto Cortez, Honduras on a routine passage to New York. Her holds were filled with bananas, coffee, and miscellaneous cargo. Her intended route was the same as the one she had taken on her previous passage - and the one previous to that, and the one previous to that . . . There was one significant difference, however - since January, when the first German U-boat arrived off the North American coast, each succeeding voy-

During wartime. (Official U.S. Coast Guard photo.)

age had become more dangerous. The eastern seaboard had become a shooting gallery, with the merchant fleet furnishing targets for the submarine arm of the Nazi war machine. Scores of innocent tankers and freighters were sent to the bottom by overzealous U-boat commanders in their eagerness to raise Hitler's bid for world domination.

At first this intense U-boat activity was confined to the northern states. Gradually, newly-arriving U-boats spread their reign of mad destruction to the southern states and into the Caribbean. The U.S. responded to this growing deadly menace by formulating the convoy system, by providing armed escorts for coastwise traffic, by equipping merchant vessels with emergency life rafts, and by emplacing guns on merchant ships - guns that were manned by naval gun crews. Ships that were routed independently were cautioned to hug the shore and to proceed "blacked out" at night: that is, without showing navigation lights and with portholes covered so that interior lights did not give away the ship's position. Men were not even permitted to smoke on deck because the glow on the tip of a cigarette would be seen in the dark for several miles.

The *Esparta* ran this harrowing gauntlet alone - and got caught. The *U-123* was lurking off the Georgia coast when the *Esparta* hove into view, after midnight on April 9. Hardegen fired a torpedo that struck the freighter on the starboard side in the way of number four hatch. The inrush of water created an immediate 15° list. The detonation started a small fire that the able crew might have controlled, had it not been for the rupture it caused in the tubing of the refrigeration system. Twelve hundred pounds of ammonia gas was released in a sudden burst. The toxic fumes forced some of the men to leap overboard.

With the ship settling fast and with the fumes and flames spreading, the captain gave the order to abandon ship. The radio operator remained at his post long enough to tap out an SOS. The crew launched lifeboats no. 1 and no. 3, as well as one of the rafts. So quickly did the crew depart that the captain and the radio operator were left without means of escape. They jumped overboard. After a few minutes in the water they were picked up by the men on the raft. Then they were transferred to one of the lifeboats. One seaman drowned when he became panic stricken. The other thirty-nine crew members huddled in the darkness.

The U-boat surfaced some fifteen minutes after the attack, one quarter mile from the still floating wreck. It blinked a light, then submerged. Later, the men reported this strange behavior to interrogators from the Office of Naval Intelligence.

Dawn found the men adrift and the *Esparta* still afloat. After seven hours in the open, a "Navy Crash boat" arrived on the scene and picked up the beleaguered seamen. (In the official report, the name of this vessel was given as USS Tyrer, but no such name exists on the Navy register.)

The *Esparta* settled deeper in the water until her stern came to rest on the bottom. The starboard list increased to 35° as the hull continued to flood. Because of the shallow depth, the bow and the top of the bridge protruded well above the surface. The ship remained in this position long enough for reconnaissance aircraft to photograph the wreck during the day. The time of its total submergence went unrecorded.

Coincidentally, the *Esparta's* sister ship *San Jose* had been sunk only three month earlier - on January 17, 1942 - after a collision with the *Santa Elisa*. Ironically, and despite overwhelming evidence to the contrary - including the testimony of survivors from both colliding vessels - Hardegen took credit for loss of the *San Jose* with the claim that he had sunk her with a torpedo. Recent research has shown that Hardegen had a history of falsifying his log (called KTB in German) as well as his war diary, in order to increase his tonnage record. (For full details, see *Shipwrecks of New Jersey: South*, by this author.)

Reinhard Hardegen survived the war. On June 5, 1942, command of the *U-123* passed to Oberleutnant zur See Horst von Schoeter. According to the log of the *U-123*, it was decommissioned at Lorient, France on August 19, 1944.

On February 8, 1944, the 6th Naval District reported the results of an examination of the site. They found the wreck lying on its side with a least depth of 36 feet over top of it. They gave the location as 30-50-45 north and 81-09-58 west.

At some time the wreck must have been demolished by explosives as a hazard to navigation. Today, the site can best be described as "blown to smithereens." The wreckage consists of a huge debris field that is full of twisted beams and bent hull plates, appearing much like a Cyclopean version of Pick-up Sticks. Near the stern, three lengths of propeller shaft are identifiable: two lengths that are flanged together and lying athwartships; and, forward of that, a single length that lies longitudinally and which is offset to starboard. About one hundred feet forward of the shaft sections lie the wreck's most distinctive features: three huge boilers that are partially buried in the sand. Two boilers lie side by side in what might have been their original position. Another boiler lies forward of the starboard boiler.

The wreckage appears to terminate forward of the boilers. But in actuality, more wreckage appears about seventy-five feet farther forward. Most of this wreck is unidentifiable. The exception is a section of what appears to be the lower portion of the stem, which is twisted to the side and facing to port. This bow section is about forty feet in length.

Marine life on the wreck is effulgent. Large coral heads and beautiful sponges blanket most of the metal surfaces with a colorful array of shapes. Small tropical fish abound. Numerous flounder scoot along the bottom. Game fish such as cobia may be seen in schools of ten or more. While exploring in the sand in search of isolated pieces of wreckage away from the main wreck, I noticed one massive section in the distance that I was at first unable to approach - the harder I kicked, the more it seemed to recede. Finally, I got close enough to observe that the dark brown shape that I mistook for a chunk of rusted hull plate was instead a giant stingray more than twelve feet across!

Although I gave the depth in the sidebar as 50 feet, washouts can be found that go as deep as 54 feet.

The *Esparta* is an excellent spearfishing site.

Partially submerged. (Courtesy of the National Archives.)

ESSO GETTYSBURG

Built: 1942
Previous names: *Gettysburg*
Gross tonnage: 10,173
Type of vessel: Tanker
Builder: Sun Ship Building & Dry Dock Company, Chester, Pennsylvania
Owner: Standard Oil Company of New Jersey, New York, NY
Port of registry: Wilmington, Delaware
Cause of sinking: Torpedoed by *U-66* (Kapitanleutnant Markworth)
Location: 31° 02' North

Sunk: June 10, 1943
Depth: Unknown
Dimensions: 503' x 68' x 39'
Power: Oil-fired steam

79° 17' West

The *Esso Gettysburg* was the first T-2 tanker that Sun Ship built for the U.S. Maritime Commission. Immediately upon completion, in 1942, she made a couple of coastwise voyages. Then she was requisitioned by the War Shipping Administration, which needed tankers to carry cargoes primarily to overseas destinations. She made a number of trips to Gibraltar and one to Oran - in heavily guarded convoys - as well as some to ports within the continental United States. In sixteen successful voyages she delivered more than one and a half million barrels (over 70 million gallons) of fuel oil, mainly for the fighting fronts. She then returned to the United States and was sold to the Standard Oil Company for domestic service. By that time in the war, Standard Oil had already lost twenty-six tankers: all to enemy action, eleven to U-boat attacks.

June 1943 found the *Esso Gettysburg* en route from Port Arthur, Texas to Philadelphia, Pennsylvania with a cargo of 120,000 barrels of crude oil. Her total complement consisted of seventy-two officers and men, of whom twenty-seven were armed guardsmen in charge of the tanker's impressive armament: one 3-inch gun mounted on the forecastle, one 4-inch gun mounted on the poop deck, and four 20-mm anti-aircraft guns mounted abaft the wheel house.

Captain Peder Johnson, master, proceeded with caution across the Gulf of Mexico. The tanker was traveling independently. Off the Florida coast, the *Esso Gettysburg* picked up an aerial escort consisting of a blimp and several airplanes. These aircraft did not fly directly overhead, but patrolled the general vicinity and were sometimes out of sight. On June 10 the tanker crossed the southern boundary of the Eastern Sea Frontier, off Jacksonville. Shortly thereafter she passed along the Georgia coast some ninety miles from shore, east of St. Simon's Island. "The weather was clear, the sea calm with a moderate swell, and the visibility unlimited." Captain Johnson maintained a speed of 16 knots.

Death announced its arrival at 2 p.m. Without warning, a torpedo struck the port side in the vicinity of Nos. 6 and 7 tanks, between the midship house and the mainmast. The explosion was so violent that it ruptured twenty-five feet of deck and hull near the sheer strake, sent a geyser of oil and water spray a hundred feet

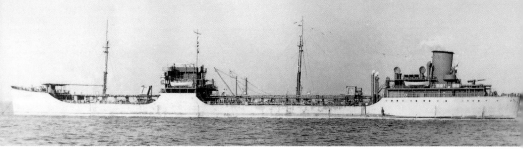

into the air, tore up the deck over the port wing tanks, knocked down the longitudinal bulkhead, and disabled the steering apparatus.

Four seconds later, while oil and water were still falling from overhead, a second torpedo struck on the port side of the engine room. The force of the explosion blew four ventilators on the after deck house higher than the masts. The electrical system was put out of commission, and the gyrocompass and revolution indicator were rendered inoperative. Flames erupted immediately, and in the blink of an eye the after part of the vessel became engulfed in flames. Within seconds the fire spread toward the midship house. And while the flames swept forward, water flooding into the engine room caused the tanker to settle by the stern.

Many off duty personnel were trapped below decks. Chief Mate Kastberg was asleep when the first torpedo struck. He got out of his bunk and got fully dressed, "shoes, cap, and life jacket included. I had a flashlight and a knife on a table in my room. I broad daylight I grabbed the flashlight. It ran through my mind that I might need it for signaling. I tried to use the regular passageway from my room, but saw a mass of flames. Then I went up to the boat deck by the inside stairway and came out by the radio room. Seeing fire and smoke near my lifeboat, No. 2, I crossed over to the starboard side, where I saw the captain and a number of men gathered around No. 1."

Steward Isaac Weissman was in his quarters. "I knew immediately what had happened because I was aboard the Panamanian flag tanker MS *Heinrich v. Riedemann* when that vessel was torpedoed off the Venezuelan coast, April 16, 1942. I grabbed my kapok life preserver, put on pants and shoes, and went to the port alleyway, where I observed a sheet of flame sweeping rapidly forward. Then I went back towards the starboard alleyway and up through the captain's quarters to the forward part of the vessel and No. 1 lifeboat."

Ensign John Arnold, the commanding officer of the armed guard, "was seriously burned about the hands, arms, shoulders, and face, after the second explosion. His clothes were set afire and after he had put out the flames by rolling on the deck, he proceeded immediately to the forward gun, ordered it to be manned and directed the firing of one round, notwithstanding great pain, spreading fire, and sinking condition of [the] ship. Although [the] sub was not sighted, the gun was fired to deter it from surfacing."

The conflagration was not confined to the vessel. The sea itself was burning. Flames spread across the water as far as one hundred feet from the hull. A thick cloud of black smoke rose a quarter mile into the air. Those who survived the initial detonations and managed to make it topside, were faced with a choice of ways to die: they could burn to death on the ship, or they could burn to death in the water. Between the fire and the flames, drowning might have been a painless luxury.

According to Acting Able Seaman James Lane, "When the first torpedo struck there was just a loud crash with oil and debris scattered and sprayed all about the ship; the second torpedo seemed to give rise to the flames which shot high in the air and enveloped the whole stern end of the ship. . . . I saw groups of men running back and forth on the stern of the vessel and heard Bos'n Albion K. Shaw holler 'Jump!' The flames and the heat were becoming so severe that I dived over the stern into the water and was followed by one of the Navy gunners, Sherman L. Doucette. Neither of us had time to get life preservers. . . . About five minutes after Doucette and I had dived into the water and got out of the oil, we saw about 15 to 20 sharks constantly circling around us, at times disappearing and then reappearing; they kept with us all the while we were in the water."

Second Mate Thomas Chapman "launched Nos. 1 and 2 life rafts and proceeded toward No. 1 lifeboat, which was being lowered into the water with the assistance of Chief Mate Kastberg and Third Mate Crescenzo. The second mate joined them to lend a hand and the boat was about a foot above the water when the falls suddenly jammed and the heat and flames became so intense that the men in this group were forced to leave and run forward. They dived from the bow into the water."

The burning hull listed 20° to port and settled slowly, almost imperceptibly, until the water reached the main deck at the midship house. The tanker then began sliding backward under the surface. The angle of the plunge increased until the hull was nearly vertical. When last seen, "only about 10 to 15 feet of the bow projected from the water and this was gradually settling down as darkness fell."

Kastberg was among those who abandoned ship from the bow. "While swimming away from the ship, six of us got together. . . . Suddenly a shark was among us. As I had previously got rid of my shoes, I felt him brush past my bare feet. Only three of us had life jackets, and we were supporting the other men. The shark circled off toward the ship, but came back again and charged. Chapman grabbed a knife, but we cautioned him against using it except as a last resort. We all kicked and splashed and the shark again swerved away, but a few minutes later he made a second charge. We repeated the kicking and thrashing in the water and he went off.

"When well clear of the flames we saw some other men swimming to the north of us; we hailed them and told them to join us so that we could all keep together. Soon afterward we saw Third Mate Crescenzo towing Ensign Arnold. Finally several other men joined us. We decided to swim closer to the burned out area, figuring that the oil would keep the sharks away.

"This decision was fortunate, as it resulted in our finding two lifeboats that had drifted clear of the flames. Chapman and I swam toward the boat which seemed usable - lifeboat No. 3. On the way I picked up a Navy issue first-aid kit; it belonged in the flare box and had apparently been blown overboard. The metal lifeboat was so hot that we had to splash water on it to cool it off. In reality it was just a burned-out hull and it had shipped a considerable quantity of water. The water saved submerged material from the flames."

The charred remains of three of their shipmates lay inside the lifeboat. By this time the men had been afloat for three hours.

Kastberg: "Largely untouched by the fire were three tanks of water and, in the gear box, a compass and a waterproof case containing a flare pistol and three flares. There was also a piece of tarpaulin. We got in, put the bodies overboard, and started to bail the boat out so that she would ride higher in the water. Then other survivors joined us and got into the boat. Soon afterward, we saw two men approaching; they were Able Seaman Lane and Navy gunner Doucette. The Navy man was blinded by oil and we guided him by our voices. This was about 4 1/2 hours after the torpedoing. There were then fourteen men in the boat.

"Half an hour later we picked up another Navy man, Gunner's Mate Third Class Edward S. Graves. He was hanging on to a fog buoy which had drifted away from the ship. His chest hurt him painfully; he had three fractured ribs. This was about 7 p.m., five hours after the disaster.

"From available pieces of gratings we started to cut crude paddles. We organized ourselves and decided to stay near the scene of the attack until daylight. The bow of the *Esso Gettysburg* was still above the surface. Her tanks were exploding under water. Then the ammunition magazines exploded.

"We decided that if help did not come by daybreak, we would start for shore. Believing we were 100 miles off the coast, we figured it would take us 15 days of paddling to reach land and that by rationing the drinking water we would have enough for 30 days.

"We feared sharks and set watches for the night. Each man was given a drink of water and told he could not have another until daylight. We were drifting in the Gulf Stream faster than the wreck of the *Esso Gettysburg*.

"Navy gunner Oliver G. Lepscier kept the time with his shockproof, waterproof watch. We made a bed for Ensign Arnold to keep him as comfortable as possible. He was stoical and uncomplaining, waiting until daybreak for treatment of his burns. When there was light enough for me to see clearly, he asked me to cut some of the hanging flesh away from the burns. I did this carefully and applied a dressing from the first-aid kit. I also applied it to two other men.

"We continued to make paddles, finally finished them, and set off in a westerly direction. Allowing for a known error of the compass, we laid out a course that would land us at Point Lookout.

"About 8:30 a.m., we sighted a plane. It was flying as if to make a grid search, about 15 miles away. We tried a flare, but it was not usable. We succeeded in firing a second flare, but the plane did not see it and disappeared.

"Continuing to paddle, we sighted a ship on the horizon, about 8 miles away. Then we saw another plane and fired our third and last flare. The plane saw us and approached." The plane was a B-25 Army bomber that was flying a routine patrol. "We waved everything we could and I blinked my flashlight. The plane's lights blinked in recognition and flew on to report to the ship - the SS *George Washington* - which turned toward us.

When the *George Washington* came within hailing distance, we were asked what ship we were from and where she was attacked. The skipper did not want to risk stopping and told us to come over, but I called out that it would take us too long to paddle that far. The *George Washington* then stopped, lowered a boat, and picked us up.

"The doctor on board treated the injured men and saved those who were burned from having severe scars. The skipper, Captain [T.H.] Park, asked us whether we wanted to be taken to the nearest port or to the ship's destination, New York. I told him we wanted to be landed as soon as possible on account of the injured men. The *George Washington* put us ashore on Charleston, S.C., that night. The Navy took care of the seven survivors of the gun crew and the United Seamen's Service took charge of the eight survivors of the *Gettysburg*; they were fine, giving each of us a complete new outfit and a free telephone call to his home. In the morning the Company agent arrived and took care of us."

These fifteen men - human jetsam from the *Esso Gettysburg* - were the only survivors. Fifty-seven men perished, including Captain Peder Johnson. In addition to Weissman, two other crew members had survived earlier U-boat attacks. Able Seaman Jessie McDonald was another two-time survivor, having previously survived the loss of the *Wm. Rockefeller* on June 28, 1942. (For details, see *Shipwrecks of North Carolina: from the Diamond Shoals North*, by this author.) First Assistant Engineer Tenant L. Fleming, who lost his life on the *Esso Gettysburg*, had survived the sinking of the *R.W. Gallagher* on July 13, 1942.

With respect to Ensign Arnold, "All survivors reported that the Officer's conduct was extraordinarily courageous at all times until rescue was effected, he exhibited great selflessness and fortitude. His deportment was said to be inspiring to all hands." The Navy took such a bold view of his valor under painful and trying circumstances that it awarded him the Navy Cross.

Two months after sinking the *Esso Gettysburg*, on August 3, the U-66 was caught in a devastating Allied air attack. Three men were killed and eight were wounded, including Friedrich Markworth. Command of the U-boat was given temporarily to Oberleutnant zur See Frerks. Later, he relinquished command to Kapitanleutnant Gerhard Seehausen. On May 6, 1944, while operating off Madeira (west of the Straits of Gibraltar), the *U-66* was sunk by the destroyer escort *Buckley* (DE-51). Thirty-six Germans were captured, while twenty-four perished, including the captain.

The actual location of the *Esso Gettysburg* has not been firmly established. However, for what it is worth, the NOAA obstruction database lists the wreck at 31° 00' 00.83" / 79° 14' 59.12".

EVENING STAR

Built: 1863   Sunk: October 3, 1866
Previous names: None   Depth: Unknown
Gross tonnage: 2,014   Dimensions: 288' x 39' x 23'
Type of vessel: Wooden-hulled side wheeler   Power: Coal-fired steam
Builder: Roosevelt, Joyce, and Waterbury, New York, NY
Owner: New York Mail Steam Ship Company, New York, NY
Port of registry: New York, NY
Cause of sinking: Foundered in a "cyclone"
Location: 180 miles east of (or off) Tybee Island

With regard to the number of lives lost, the wreck of the *Evening Star* was the greatest maritime tragedy ever to occur off the Georgia coast. Only a handful survived to tell the sordid tale. So high was the loss of life, and so rampant were allegations of malfeasance, that the House of Representatives ordered an investigation into the casualty. Investigators examined the vessel's construction, management, and history, to determine if pre-existing conditions may have contributed to the vessel's demise.

The *Evening Star* was built in 1863 at the cost of $100,000 (another source states $500,000). Her hull was constructed of live-oak, white oak, and hackmatack (also known as balsam poplar). The outside planking was five inches thick. For additional strengthening, the hull was diagonally strapped with iron. These iron straps were 4 inches wide and 5/8 inch thick, and were spaced 4 1/2 feet apart. "From this it will be seen that the ship was thoroughly well built, and that so much of current report to the contrary is manifestly erroneous."

"The ship was square rigged forward, and fore-and-aft rigged on her mainmast. All her spars, sails, and rigging were new and in excellent condition." Independent of this auxiliary means of propulsion, the *Evening Star* was propelled primarily by a single beam engine that was built in 1853 for the Lake Erie steamer *Queen of the West*. The *Queen of the West* was laid up in 1857, when a "panic brought lake traffic to a virtual standstill." She lay idle until 1862 (or 1863), at which time her engine was removed and shipped to New York, and the hull was dismantled and scrapped.

According to one source, the engine was built by the Morgan Iron Works. According to another source, the engine was built by Henry R. Dunham & Sons of New York City. Both sources agree that the cylinder diameter was 80 inches and the piston stroke was 12 feet. The two tubular boilers were built by the Allaire Works of New York. These boilers were fitted with blowers, which forced air over the coal "when an increased supply of steam was required. There were also two engines used for hoisting cargo, and an independent boiler to supply this engine with steam, and at the same time to work two powerful steam-pumps with which she was furnished. . . . The space occupied by the engine, boilers and coal-bunkers, below the main deck, was inclosed [sic] by watertight bulkheads, running from the floor of the ship to the top of the main deck beams."

The paddle wheels measured thirty-three feet across.

"The ship's company was composed of captain, first and second officers, boatswain, and ten seamen. The engine department was composed of one chief engineer, two assistants, three water-tenders, six firemen, and eight coal-passers." This list did not include those crew members whose responsibilities catered to the well-being of the passengers: cooks, messmen, stewards, one stewardess, pantrymen, porters, waiters, a storekeeper, and a butcher. This brought the ship's company to fifty-nine.

"The ship was provided with all the life-boats required by law, six in number, besides one wooden 20-feet boat additional."

On May 31, 1866, while on a passage from New York to New Orleans, Louisiana, the *Evening Star* ran aground on Pickle Reef, Florida. She remained on the reef for more than fifty hours. Despite a slight southeasterly swell, the vessel rested easily. After coming off the reef, she continued her passage to New Orleans without further incident. Investigators learned "that she made another

Courtesy of the National Archives.

trip after that accident, in which she encountered a heavy gale of wind from the north in the Gulf of Mexico, and behaved well in it; that she made no more water after going on the reef than before, which was evidence that she had not been seriously damaged while ashore. It was, however, thought best to give her an overhauling, and she was put upon the ways on the 13th of July, when it was discovered that her garboard was very slightly scratched, and her keel split in places extending from about midships to thirty feet aft, but it was not started in any way in the seams. This portion of her keel was removed and a new piece put on, and secured by 6-feet scarfs and fastened into the inner keelsons through with three hundred and thirty pounds of copper bolts one and one-eighth inch in diameter. She was then thoroughly caulked and payed with pitch and composition.

"Before leaving the ways she was examined to ascertain whether there was any evidence of damage by the opening of the butts in water-ways, plank-shear, or clamps. She was, also, completely overhauled by the local inspectors in New York, and it was found that she was in as good condition as ever."

The results of the investigation found the *Evening Star* a "good, serviceable, seaworthy vessel."

The side wheeler departed from New York on September 29, 1866, under the new command of Captain William Knapp, "a gentleman of acknowledged ability and much experience afloat." She carried a general cargo in her holds. On board were passengers estimated to number 219, of whom 166 were traveling cabin class and 53 were traveling steerage. Among them were 59 members of Paul Alhazia's French opera troupe, 30 performers from Dr. Spaulding's Circus Company, and "seventy-five to a hundred prostitutes, who annually migrate from New York to Southern cities, remaining in the North during the hot weather, and regularly returning to the warmer climates in the Winter." Prominent among the prostitutes on board was one Mrs. King, of New Orleans notoriety. She owned a mansion on Basin Street that was valued at $75,000. She was obviously very successful in her chosen profession.

With all sails set and the engines operating at optimum efficiency, the vessel sped along the Atlantic sea lanes at the rate of eleven knots. For three days nothing untoward occurred.

Around three o'clock in the afternoon of October 2, the wind commenced to freshen and the barometer to fall. Within two hours it was blowing a "whole gale." Because the *Evening Star* was laboring heavily, the canvas was stowed and the vessel was steered into the sea (south-southeast). She shipped a wave over her top-gallant forecastle, "which did no damage." The buffeting of the oncoming waves reduced her headway to four to five knots.

"About 10 p.m. on the 2d she was struck by a very heavy sea on her port quarter, knocking one of the seamen over the quadrant, breaking his arm, and causing the rudder-chain to slip out of the groove. The ship immediately fell off into the trough of the sea, and commenced shipping very heavy water over midships. Much time seems to have been consumed in securing the rudder, which, after an hour had elapsed, was finally secured to windward, the helm hard down. This, however, failed to bring her up by reason of the heavy sea which was then running. The engines, meanwhile, were in good condition, making three or four revolutions per minute." (This meant that the paddle wheels were revolving at the rate of three to four turns per minute.)

At this time there was no evidence of leakage through the hull, "the bilge injection keeping her free and frequently sucking." (When the pumps sucked air, it meant that there was no more water to suck.) The upper works were continually slammed by walls of green water. Then, around 11 o'clock, the forward gangway on the starboard side was stove in by a wave that was more violent than its predecessors. "Water came pouring through in immense volumes."

Every able-bodied passenger was drafted to assist crew members in sealing the breach in the hull. "Pantry-room, bulkheads, doors, mattresses, and every available article were brought into requisition, but to no purpose, and their efforts to prevent the ingress of the sea were finally abandoned as futile, in order that their energies might be directed to bailing as the only effectual means left to keep the water under."

The mass of water that flowed through the breach in the hull found its way into the engine room through a doorway and a ventilator. Water washed over combings, through openings in the deck, and between the panels of the deck houses, "which had been broken by the sea." All available hands took turns at the pumps, fighting desperately to keep the boiler fires from being extinguished. "In this they succeeded for a considerable time, but owing to the excessive rolling of the ship, increased no doubt by the weight of water in the ship and the shifting of the cargo, their efforts were destined to be unavailing. At about three o'clock the steam-pipe gave way, but the engines were kept working by the engineer for two hours after, and, indeed, until the fires were put out, about five a.m. This break of the steam-pipe was caused by the straining of the ship."

One of the surviving passengers, W.H. Harris, praised the crew: "They worked quietly in all that terrible storm without a murmur."

The donkey engine and boiler gave out at about the same time that the steam pipe broke. "The leak in the pipe increased to such an extent that the men were unable to go into the fire-room, save at intervals. In consequence of this accident the quantity of steam was necessarily diminished, but the loss of the ship can in no wise be attributed to this circumstance, for she was certainly a doomed vessel before this occurred. The energy and perseverance of the engineer were most praiseworthy. He was at his post endeavoring to keep the machinery in motion with the bar and hand-gear until the engines stopped altogether. By this time the ship was given up for lost, and preparations were made to leave the ship, as she was discovered to be settling."

Chief Engineer Robert Finger spoke for himself, stating that the hurricane carried away "both wheel-houses, leaving nothing but the 'A' braces and guards." Harris described it differently: "The whole of the paddle boxes had been carried away, nothing but the fans being left. The pilot-house was gone, and the guards also." (By "guards" he meant the paddle guards: the encompassing wooden frame that protected the paddle wheels from damage, and prevented people from falling into them.)

From *Harper's Weekly*.

The passengers were gathered in the social hall at one end of the saloon, the floor of which was covered with sea water. At 6 a.m., October 3, Captain Knapp announced that he and his men had done all they could to save the ship, but that there was no longer any hope of keeping her afloat. He had no choice but to order abandon ship. Now came a horrible truth: while the *Evening Star* "had all the boats which the law requires, seven in all, she had not half enough to save the number of persons on board; nor were the boats fitted with the detaching apparatus required by law."

Ellery Allen, the purser, assisted in freeing the metallic lifeboats from their fastenings. When the boats were free and ready, he opened the upper saloon door, "which had been previously kept closed on account of the heavy weather, and to keep out the water," at which time, "There was a wild rush on deck, and madness and confusion followed. It was now about daybreak, and the hurricane was at its worst. The ship had a long time lain helpless in the hollow of the sea, which dashed on and over her."

Most of the passengers did not have life preservers. Allen placed a group of ladies of the night in one of the lifeboats, but the lifeboat capsized as soon as it touched the water, and all the women drowned.

Chief Engineer Finger stated, "None of the officers of the ship were in the boats, all of them remaining on deck till she sunk beneath the waves."

According to an account that Allen gave to a correspondent, "At last she gave one fearful lurch, which was followed by the crashing upon her decks of the sea to which she thus exposed herself, and she went down. At this moment Purser Allen states he was standing upon the deck with two women clinging to him. The ship, the women and he went down together. The Purser's next recollections are his coming up amid floating driftwood, with which he was tossed from wave to wave. Buoying himself up as best he could, now losing this support and battling with the sea for another one, he managed to cling to life in this critical way for three hours. During this time his limbs were beaten and chafed by the floating driftwood, one sharp piece of which pierced his cheek, and another almost severed his upper lip. Dead, almost, he somehow reached one of the ship's lifeboats. Into this boat he succeeded in getting."

Harris had a similar experience: "In an instant the sea swept me clear of the deck, and carried me down some twenty-five feet, I thought. When I came to the surface I found myself in the midst of the wreck of the vessel, surrounded by floating spars and drift wood. Men and women were floating all about, clinging to anything they could lay hold of. All shouts for aid were drowned by the fury of the hurricane. I secured a piece of the wreck with which to support myself, but I had to abandon this owing to the danger I was in of being struck by pieces of the flying wreck, which were being hurled about in all directions by the wind and the waves. I then got hold of a piece of the fragments of the saloon, upon which I pulled myself, but was thrown off again and again by the violence of the waves, in each new effort to regain my position, lacerating my hands and limbs on the nails and splinters in the pieces of the wreck. In this way I clung to life for two or three hours. While drifting about in this way I could see the whole of the wreck as it lay before me. I saw the hurricane deck, two hundred feet long, crowded with human beings, herded together. Some of these were standing, and some sitting, all helpless and despairing. I now drifted near a life-boat, keel up, for which I abandoned my piece of wreck and swam. When I succeeded in getting in with the others I recognized the Purser, Mr. Allen."

Others managed to reach this capsized lifeboat during the fury of the storm. But their troubles were far from over. By coordinating their efforts they were able to right the boat and get inside. Harris: "There were now ten of us, but . . . we were frequently upset, each time losing one or more of our number, again adding to them by picking up others." The numbers did not change, just the names. Harris recounted the sad story of "a young woman, about 18 years of age, who "caught hold with us and clung on for several hours. She held on while we were capsized three times, but kept growing weaker. At last we were turned over again, and she was lost."

Allen: "We were all thrown out six times by the boats being capsized by the sea, the wind and the drift-wood. During this forenoon the sea run very high, and until the afternoon we were surrounded with immense quantities of drift-wood, the wind still blowing a hurricane. At night the wind moderated very much - the sea also." Although all the lifeboats were provisioned with cans of bread and breakers of water, this simple fare was washed away when the lifeboat capsized. Harris picked up a turnip, "of which we each took a bite, and this was all we ate during the day."

Ten cold survivors spent the stormy night adrift: eight crew members and two passengers. The hurricane passed during the hours of darkness. Dawn appeared "calm and pleasant." Harris: "At daylight we came up to one of the wrecked, who was floating on a piece of the cabin, and had an oar with which to guide his craft. We got alongside and put some of the men on it, after which we upset our boat, thus getting the water out of it. We then got in again, and felt comparatively comfortable, but still suffering for the want of food and water." (This passage sounds confusing, making it seem as if they put some of the men on the cabin and left them there. I think, however, that they merely put the men on the cabin temporarily while they dewatered the lifeboat, then reboarded and took the stranded survivor with them.)

Around eight o'clock in the morning of October 4, "We fell in with the third mate, with nine men in another life-boat, who gave each of us a handful of crackers; but, unfortunately, our throats were so parched with the long thirst, and by drinking sea water, we were unable to swallow this food."

Allen: "We now made two sails from four life preservers, the other boat fixing her own sail. Both boats now stood to the westward for the land. Wind about east-north-east. At dark this night we lost company with the other boat." Thus passed a long and excruciating day in the heat of the sun.

At five o'clock the following morning they spotted a sail on the horizon. The bark *Fleetwing* hove to and picked up the men. The ten survivors had endured two days and nights in an open boat. They revived handily under the attention of the *Fleetwing's* officers and crew. Because the *Fleetwing* was bound for Southampton, England, when they spoke the schooner *S.J. Waring* on the following afternoon, and learned that she had been so damaged by the hurricane that she was proceeding to Savannah for repairs, the men transferred to the Georgia bound vessel.

In Savannah, local resident Captain Dickerson "generously provided for their wants, and everything has been done to secure their comfort. Allen resumed his shipboard duties as purser by obtaining passage for the survivors to New York on the propeller *Virgo*.

Harris: "We were all very much sunburned while in the open boat, and during our passage home the skin has peeled off our faces and hands. I am still lame and sore, but will be all right in a few days." Harris recalled with melancholy how the prostitutes behaved "nobly" and "with great propriety. . . . One of the prostitutes who was the proprietress of an elegant house of ill-fame in New-Orleans, had a beautiful pair of ponies on board and a fine new carriage. They were all anxious to work when danger appeared, and some of them did good service." (By "they" I believe that Harris was referring to the prostitutes, not the ponies. And by "good service" I believe he meant that the prostitutes worked toward the saving of the ship, not in their usual capacity of employment.)

The lifeboat in charge of Third Mate Thomas Fitzpatrick rowed all the way to shore - nearly two hundred miles - arriving at Fernandina, Florida on October 7, after four exhausting days at sea. On board were six survivors and two dead bodies. The travails that were suffered by the purser's lifeboat were paralleled on the third mate's boat in every detail, including periodic capsizings and the subsequent loss of occupants. One of the occupants lost was Captain Knapp. When he was thrown out of the boat for the fourth time, he was struck on the forehead by a length of driftwood, and killed. The survivors lost count of the number of times the lifeboat capsized; their best estimate was between twelve and fifteen. They had once had as many as sixteen people on board, but only six survived to tell the tale. Of the six, five were crew members and one was a passenger.

Although hopes were entertained on shore that the other lifeboats might be found, only one other lifeboat survived the savage sea. This boat was picked up by the schooner *Morning Star*, which transported the survivors to Charleston, at which port they arrived on October 9. This lifeboat contained seven souls: three crew members and four passengers, of whom two were females.

Of 278 persons who departed New York aboard the *Evening Star*, 255 perished and 23 survived. Only two of the many women lived through the ordeal, but none of the handful of children.

W.M. Mew, the chief Congressional investigator, determined that the principal cause of the catastrophe was "an error of judgment on the part of the captain." He based this determination on the fact that Captain Knapp did not endeavor to keep the *Evening Star* headed into the wind and the sea when he had the means and the opportunity to do so. Even after the engine was disabled, Mew thought that this "might have been done by means of a drag, assisted by a little show of canvas on her mainmast. Nothing of the sort was even attempted, and from the time she fell off into the trough of the sea no effort seems to have been made to haul her up, after the rudder was secured; and the only means of safety, in the judgment of the captain, seems to have been in keeping the ship free of the water which was shipped, by bailing, &c., in the hope that the storm might abate. It is a wonder that the vessel lived so long under these circumstances."

Mew also made some commonsense recommendations which could have ameliorated, if not averted, future maritime disasters. "The loss of this ship is not without its appropriate lesson to ship-owners; . . . while some of the larger companies furnish exceptions, by the care shown in the equipment of their ships, to the necessity for legislation upon this subject, it is none the less certain that the enactment of stringent laws governing our merchant marine is an absolute necessity. I therefore beg respectfully to call your attention to this matter, in the hope that radical changes in the existing laws may be suggested to Congress."

The lessons learned by the loss of the *Evening Star* were largely ignored, and Mew's hope for radical changes with regard to the safety of life at sea fell on deaf Congressional ears. Indeed, when the Titanic sank nearly half a century later (in 1912), there *still* were not enough lifeboats on board for the entire ship's complement. Civilization rarely benefits from a single note of warning; progress usually requires repetition.

The location at which the *Evening Star* went down cannot be pinpointed. The position was generally estimated to have been 180 miles east of Tybee Island. The position was also reported as 180 miles off Tybee Island. There is a vast amount of difference between "east of" and "off." East is a specific direction - 90° on the compass - whereas "off" can be interpreted as anywhere along an arc that is drawn with Tybee Island as the focal point.

According to Purser Allen, "Captain Knapp informed me at midnight of that day that the ship was about 240 miles northeast of Matanilla Reef, and from that time until the ship went down I should judge she did not change her position much." Matanilla Reef is in the Bahamas, north of Abaco and about 150 miles east of the Florida coast. This statement would place the sinking position east of northern Florida.

By Harris's observation it appears that when the hull sank from sight due to the weight of the machinery, the hurricane deck broke free - as they are wont to do because of the buoyancy characteristics of wood - and continued to float for quite a while, carrying its human flotsam elsewhere to its doom.

MIELERO

Built: 1917
Previous names: None
Gross tonnage: 5,853
Type of vessel: Tanker
Builder: Fore River Ship Building Company, Quincy, Massachusetts
Owner: Cuba Distilling Company, New York, NY
Port of registry: New York, NY
Cause of sinking: Broke in two
Location: 155 miles east of Ossaba Island

Sunk: January 26, 1920
Depth: Unknown
Dimensions: 389' x 54' x 29'
Power: Coal-fired steam

Most people think of tankers in conjunction with petroleum and oil companies. But a tanker may carry any cargo that exists in the liquid state. The *Mielero* was owned by the Cuba Distilling Company. On what proved to be her final voyage, the *Mielero* was transporting 1,600,000 gallons of molasses from Matanzas, Cuba to Philadelphia, Pennsylvania. The tank steamer was only three years old when she broke in two amidship in what was described as "heavy northeast seas."

Forty people were on board at the time. Two lifeboats were launched before the separated halves slipped beneath the tumultuous waves. One lifeboat was occupied by Captain Simmons (master), his wife and two children, and eighteen crew members. The other lifeboat was occupied by Chief Officer L. H. Çrotary, the third mate, four engineers, and twelve crew members. The *Mielero* was equipped with a wireless set, but no transmission for help was intercepted by any vessels at sea or by radio stations ashore. No one but the occupants knew about the lifeboats that were bobbing on the angry Atlantic Ocean.

Not until four days later did the steamer *Ozette* - on a passage from Savannah to Bremen, Germany - come upon one of the lifeboats and its beleaguered, near-dead occupants. It was the third officer's lifeboat. The *Ozette* immediately transmitted her position as well as a succinct account of the circumstances. All vessels were warned to be on the lookout for the missing lifeboat. From Charleston, the U.S. Navy dispatched the destroyer *Belknap* and a naval tug to search the sea for survivors. Both vessels returned to port two days later after a fruitless and unproductive patrol. No sign of the missing lifeboat was ever found.

The *Sucrosa*, another vessel belonging to the Cuba Distilling Company, departed Matanzas on January 27. She rendezvoused with the *Ozette* at sea. The *Mielero's* survivors were transferred to the *Sucrosa*, which transported them to Baltimore, Maryland.

The lifeboat's position that was given by the *Ozette* was "lat 32 10 N, lon 78 30 W," or about one hundred miles east of Hilton Head, South Carolina. What bearing this location may have with respect to the site of the sinking is left to conjecture. In 1957, the U.S. Hydrographic Office placed the *Mielero* at 31° 45' north latitude, 78° 40' west longitude, or about one hundred fifty-five miles east of Ossaba Island, Georgia. A wreck symbol is marked on the chart at that location. I do not know what information was used in order to make such a determination. As with the captain's lifeboat, the wreck of the *Mielero* is still among the missing.

Researchers should note that the *Mielero* was propelled by a steam turbine that was located aft. Steam was generated by three Scotch boilers.

From the author's collection.

HULL 252
FEB. 8, 1917.

NORTH AMERICA

Built: 1864

Previous names: None

Gross tonnage: 1,651

Type of vessel: Wooden-hulled screw steamer

Builder: Philadelphia, Pennsylvania

Owner: ?

Port of registry: Philadelphia, Pennsylvania

Cause of sinking: Foundered

Location: 31° 10' North

Sunk: December 23, 1864

Depth: Unknown

Dimensions: ?

Power: Coal-fired steam

78° 40' West

As soon as the *North America* came off the ways she was chartered for service by the War Department as a troop transport. She operated in that capacity for only a few months when she foundered in a storm while returned invalided soldiers to the north. Captain Charles Marshman, master, survived the tragedy and wrote a clipped, firsthand account of the experience.

"Left New-Orleans on the 16th December, 1864, and Southwest Pass on the 18th, having been detained by fog. Had on board 203 sick soldiers, 12 cabin passengers, and a crew of 44 men. From the time of leaving the bar until the 20th, noon, had fine, pleasant weather. At 4 P.M. of that day commenced blowing heavy from south southwest, with a heavy sea running - vessel laboring and straining greatly. 21st, a continuance of the same weather.

"22d - First part of the day, weather moderating; at noon began blowing; heavy sea getting up. The Engineer reported ship leaking badly. 1 P.M. he reported the water gaining; changed our course to the westward. Took off the fore-hatches, and discovered the water running in forward; cut away the ceiling to try to stop it; but could not; put blankets and a sail over the bow, but all to no purpose; water gaining very fast. At 2 P.M. a vessel hove in sight; bore away for her, and hoisted our colors Union down - we being at the time in lat. 31° 10' N., lon. 75° 40' W. At 2:15 P.M., spoke the bark *Mary E. Libby*, Capt. Libby, from Cardenas, Cuba, for Portland. Informed Capt. Libby of our situation. He replied that he would remain by us, and take all on board, if necessary.

"At 2:20 P.M. the engineer reported that the water had put the fires out. Hailed the bark, and told Capt. Libby of it; he then hove the ship to, and prepared to receive our people on board; at the time we had four feet of water in the hold; commenced clearing away the boats; at 2:30 P.M. started the first boat, with the Chief Engineer in charge and all the lady passengers; we got six boat-loads on board of the bark. The seventh boat left at dark, containing our Purser (Mr. C. Pettit) and eight men, and is supposed to be lost, as they never reached the ship. Night setting in dark and blowing hard, with a high sea running, so that the boats could not get back from the bark to the steamer.

"7 P.M. - Ship settling fast, having 12 feet of water in her hold. Prepared our last boat. 7:30 P.M. - Finding it impossible for any more boats to return to the steamer that night, I left the ship, taking with me my First and Second Officers and eight men. 9 P.M., arrived on board the bark; hoisted the boats on deck for the night; made sail, and proceeded toard [sic] the steamer; her lights all in sight, distance about six miles. One P.M., lights all disappeared suddenly; we suppose the ship to have gone down at that time. At daylight, nothing in sight except a water cask. Made all sail, and cruised all round, but did not see anything of her.

"12 M - Gave up all hopes; the bark made sail and proceeded on her course. Number of passengers saved, 62; lost with the ship, 197. Total 259."

Assistant Surgeon E. McClintock, who bore responsibility for his patients, rendered a more detailed and graphic account. "Never was there a prospect of a fairer voyage. Our vessel was considered, if possible, a little better than first-class; ample provision had been made for the comfort of the sick, furloughed and discharged on board - 203 in number - and the officers having, in addition to the heads of seamen, the hearts of men, bore a willing hand to everything that could alleviate the suffering or increase the comfort of the men. We left New Orleans at 5 P.M., Friday, the 16th, and after being detained twenty-six hours by fog, passed the bar Sunday morning at 7 1/2 A.M., in a calm sea and fine weather.

"We passed Key West at 1 P.M. on the 20th, sea calm and men doing well.

"At 2 P.M. on the 21st, the wind began to raise, and at 4 blew a gale, the sea running high, when more than the usual quantity of water was found in the hold. On the 23d this gradually increased, and at 11 A.M. the pumps failed to keep her clear, and it then first became apparent that the vessel must go down, and her course was changed landward. There was but one sail in sight, about ten miles to leeward. The colors were raised at half-mast, union down, and a sail passed beneath her bows - all to no effect. The leak had now become frightful. At 2 P.M. we reached the vessel in which lay all our hopes, which proved to be the *Mary E. Libby*, of Portland, bound homeward from Cardenas, she having observed our signal and stood by for our relief.

"As if to make our misfortune more complete, the water now reached the fires, extinguishing them and rendering our vessel unmanageable, and the sea still running high the vessels drifted together, and collided, tearing up the cathead of the *Libby*, which then drifted beyond some distance to the seaward. The boats were now our only resource, and were lowered away one by one, seven in number, without accident, except the sixth, in which was purser Charles Pettit, and B.D. Walker, Hospital Steward U.S.A., which did not reach the bark, and was probably lost, as it was only by the greatest skill that any reached the *Libby*, now six miles distant.

"Capt. Marshman, with the first and second officers, were the last to leave the ship at 6 1/2 P.M. His boat was filled and one man lost overboard, but by almost superhuman exertion it was bailed out and the man recovered. The next morning the Libby having in a measure repaired damages wore round to the place of disaster, but naught was seen save a floating boat, telling too plainly of the fate of Purser Pettit and his companions. Her lights went out suddenly at 1

3/4 A.M. of the 23d, at which time she was supposed to have gone down.

"We now had time to review our situation. We were still south of Savannah, and 140 miles east. Capt. Libby at once made a muster of his men and stores, which was found sadly disproportioned, especially in water, and all hands went cheerfully on allowance. On Sunday, Dec. 25, spoke the brig *Ellen P. Stewart*, of and bound to Philadelphia, Capt. Kane, who relieved us of 14 men, and supplied us with a cask of that which was all around, "but not a drop to drink." Thursday, 23d [sic], spoke steamer *Arago*, from Port Royal, on Absecon Light, and all went on board for New-York, which we made at 11 P.M., Dec. 29."

The Steamship Inspection Service noted laconically the tremendous number of fatalities, listing the death toll merely as a statistic, then added, "Loss of property, including ship, estimated at about $300,000."

No one seems to have shown any written remorse over the loss in human terms. One hundred ninety-seven sick and wounded soldiers went to a watery grave without comment. No recriminations were made against Captain Marshman for abandoning his ship with nearly two hundred souls still on board, nor against Assistant Surgeon McClintock for leaving his charges to certain death. Personally, I can find no fault in their actions to save themselves from a similar fate when to remain on board would only have added their lives to the roll of the dead. They made the best of a bad situation. Most of the sick and wounded soldiers, even if they were ambulatory, could not have been transferred safely from ship to ship by means of boats under the conditions then prevailing.

Yet I am amazed that others less forgiving did not call attention to the decided lack of propriety, or castigate the ship builders for constructing an unsound hull. Perhaps in the greater exigencies of a war in which thousands were killed every day, the loss of so comparatively few went without notice. Or, perhaps in those days of social innocence, people accepted the fact that man's puny mechanical achievements were no match against the greater power of nature.

The only published comment was one of praise about a devoted sister who refused to abandon ship without her unwell brother. Millie Fowler traveled to New Orleans to obtain a furlough for Charles Fowler, of the Eleventh New York Cavalry. In this she failed, but she did manage to get him transferred to a New York hospital. They were returning home together aboard the *North America*. In the tradition of the sea, the women were requested to board the first lifeboat to proceed to the *Mary E. Libby*. Miss Fowler refused to go without her brother. "The boats went to the bark and returned, and not until she had succeeded in having her brother safely put into the boat, would she be induced to leave herself."

Let it never be said that uncommon valor in the face of death is an attribute only of the male of the species. Heroes are born, and so are heroines.

Stickler that I am for perfection in detail, I should note that official sources give the night of December 22 as the date of the *North America's* loss. The statistical sidebar that leads this chapter gives the date as December 23. This is because both Captain Marshman and Assistant Surgeon McClintock stated that the steamer's lights disappeared after midnight - a minor correction to the historical record.

As the *Tennessee*. (From *Early American Steamers*, by Erik Heyl.)

REPUBLIC

Built: 1853

Previous names: *Tennessee,* USS *Tennessee,* USS *Mobile*

Gross tonnage: 1,149

Type of vessel: Wooden-hulled side wheel steamer

Builder: John A. Robb, Baltimore, Maryland

Owner: Russell Sturgis, New York, NY

Port of registry: New York, NY

Cause of sinking: Foundered

Location: Off Savannah

Sunk: October 25, 1865

Depth: About 132 feet?

Dimensions: 210' x 34' x 17

Power: Coal-fired steam

The Republic began her career in 1853 as the *Tennessee*. For eight years she operated primarily between east coast ports and the Caribbean. In 1861, she was on the run between New York and New Orleans. She was docked in her berth in New Orleans at the onset of the Civil War. The Confederates seized the ship and planned to convert her to a commerce raider. But within days, before the *Tennessee* could escape, Admiral David Farragut captured New Orleans. The Union navy seized the vessel, installed a five-gun battery, and commissioned her as a warship.

The *Tennessee* led an active naval career. She bombed Confederate forts, captured blockade runners, and maintained a nearly constant patrol in the Gulf of Mexico. In 1864, when Union forces captured the Confederate ironclad ram *Tennessee* and commissioned her in the U.S. Navy, the name of the side wheeler was changed to *Mobile*. Shortly afterward she was heavily damaged in a gale. She was sent to New York for repairs. Navy surveyors condemned the vessel because she was so "severely strained and wrenched." She was laid up for the remainder of the war.

On March 30, 1865, Russell Sturgis bought the *Mobile* on the auction block for $25,000. He refitted her for passenger service and changed her name to *Republic*. Sturgis placed the side wheeler on her pre-war route: New York to New Orleans. Her first few voyages were routine. On what proved to be her final passage, the *Republic* departed New York under the command of Captain Edward Young.

Captain Young survived the catastrophe, and wrote a detailed account of the circumstances of the loss. "We left New York on the 18th October, with a general cargo, $400,000 in specie, and some 20 odd passengers, bound for New-Orleans direct. The ship was staunch and strong, well manned, and provided with everything requisite for the voyage. Nothing worthy of note occurred until the 23d, when the vessel encountered a gale, being off Savannah and in twenty-two fathoms of water. The gale continued to blow very heavily from E.N.E., and it increased to a perfect hurricane before night, and shifting to N.E. with a very heavy sea running. At 6 A.M. on Tuesday, the 24th, it was impossible to turn the engine over by hand, consequently the ship fell off into the trough of the sea, and became unmanageable. After trying for nearly two hours to work the engine by hand, with 31 pounds of steam (six more than was allowed,) we lost all use of the steam pump. At this time the vessel was leaking badly, making water rapidly. The main spencer was blown to pieces, and the paddle-boxes and part of the house were destroyed. Everything on deck was washed overboard and lost. [A spencer is a small sail that was set in heavy weather to help maintain headway.]

"At this time the gale was at its height. We got four pumps from the forward deck and put them to work below, also the donkey engine. However, the water gained on the pumps very fast, and so all hands, with the assistance of the passengers, set to work to bail with the buckets.

"At 11 o'clock the gale still continued, with heavy cross seas, and the ship labored hard, with the water still gaining. We then commenced throwing the cargo overboard, in order to lighten the ship. After clearing the between decks, we found that the water continued to make considerable progress, so everybody was put to work passing buckets to bail the water out.

"On Wednesday, at 9 A.M., the pumps gave out, the ship rolling fearfully. Finding it impossible to save the ship, the crew set to work building a raft, and they also prepared the boats for leaving the ship; the passengers meanwhile busy passing buckets.

"At 1:30 P.M., the water being above the engine-room floor, I called all hands to launch the boats and the raft. At 4 P.M., all but twenty-one passengers were stowed in the boats, the ship suddenly went down, giving the four boats barely time to get clear of the wreck. The remaining twenty-one passengers then jumped into the sea, swimming as best they might for their lives. In a few minutes all but two were safe on board the boats; those two being in the thickest of the debris, it was impossible for the boats to reach them, and night coming on, it is not known whether they were saved or not, although it is hoped that they were, having plenty of floating material.

"Everything on board, except what the passengers stood in, went down with the ship. All the boats got around the raft and tried to make fast. But we found it impossible, as one boat was so strained that it was necessary to let the raft go. A high sea was running when the boats parted company. Three men in my boat were kept bailing all night, the others pulling hard to keep clear of the wreck, and also to keep her head to wind and sea.

"On Thursday, as we were preparing to make sail for the nearest shore, we made a sail to eastward, distant some six or seven miles, for which we pulled, and in doing so passed the floating deck of the *Republic*. We reached the vessel, and found her to be the brig *J.W. Lovitte*, Capt. Thomas F. Gillist, of Yarmouth, Nova Scotia, from St. Johns, N.B., bound for Charleston, S.C. We were very kindly taken on board, and in due time safely arrived at Charleston.

"I desire to say that my crew worked admirably, no disorder or panic occurring. The passengers also behaved nobly, being cool and courageous, the ladies especially distinguishing themselves."

Captain Young's report needs some elucidation. The actual number of passengers on board was between forty-one and forty-four (the records are unclear on that point). In the written account, "20 odd passengers" was probably a typographical error, especially in light of the captain's later statement, "all but twenty-one passengers were stowed in the boats." He must have meant "40 odd passengers." (Unless he meant that twenty of the passengers were odd.)

In his humility, Captain Young neglected to mention that he did not abandon ship and board a lifeboat, but remained on the steamer with the passengers, standing "upon his deck until the vessel sank beneath the waves, leaving him struggling in the debris."

It may not be apparent to the reader that the four lifeboats became separated in the dark, and that the only one to be picked up by the *J.W. Lovitte* was the boat under his command, containing fourteen persons. To learn the fate of the rest of the passengers and crew, we must pick up the thread of the story from other sources.

Another boat was under the command of Chief Officer E.E. (or S.P., or S.E.) Young. If the chief officer was related to the captain, that fact was not mentioned in contemporary accounts. This boat, containing twelve passengers and crew, swamped a few minutes after the *Republic* disappeared from view, "but owing to the energy and coolness of those on board, the boat was cleared of water and kept head on the sea till daylight. Buy a singular good fortune, Capt. Geo. W. McNair, late of the ship Inspector, was on board the boat, and as the chief officer was exhausted by his efforts to save the steamship, Capt. McNair took the management of the boat, so as to give Mr. Young some time to rest; and the passengers kept rowing with a desperation which only the fate before them could inspire. The demijohn containing the only water on board got broken before one drop of it was used - thus thirst, more terrible than anything that can be described, was added to their other calamities.

"The boat had no provisions except salt meat and ship's bread, which got saturated with salt water, with the exception of three cans of preserved fruit. These may be said to have saved the lives of the people on the boat, and were kept to the very last.

"On Thursday, every one having become so much exhausted that it was impossible to make headway by rowing, a table cloth was found in the boat, and they extemporized a sail, and with that the boat was kept on her course to the westward, as well as could be done with nothing but sun and the stars to guide them. Thursday night was one of intense suffering, and insanity, the invariable result of exposure, want of sleep and thirst, began to exhibit itself.

"Friday morning came, and no sail, no land in sight. It was water - water everywhere. The imagination of all on the boat began to conjure up sights and sounds which were only imagination. Insanity was dawning upon every mind. At about 10 in the morning of Friday, a sail in the distance was discovered, and, as the breeze had died away, the sail in the boat was taken down, and the oars again assumed for a pull for life. They kept on for hours, but could not gain on the sail in the distance, and finally gave up.

"Having worked in the sun with all the energy possible so long, and yielding the chase in disappointment at last, the sensation of thirst now seemed, at this time, to be unendurable. Men's throats were swollen, their jaws set, and speech began to be difficult. As a last resort, the whole party jumped into the sea to bathe and absorb moisture externally. It seemed to allay the burning thirst.

"Soon another sail came in sight in the opposite direction, and, as a last effort, the boat was reversed and they began to pull for it. The sail proved to be the barkentine *Horace Beals*, from New-York, commanded by Capt. Joseph Blankenship, who picked them up at 6 o'clock P.M., after they had been in the water for fifty-one hours; and everything the could be done for their comfort was done by Capt. Blankenship. They could not stand when they were hoisted upon his deck, but were soon restored by the use of stimulants and water.

"If ever a man was a nobleman by nature, who held his patent direct from his Maker, that man was Capt. Joseph Blankenship. The survivors cannot say too much in his praise. From the time they were taken on board till Sunday evening, they remained upon his ship, when the steamer *Gen. Hooker* came up and took them off, and brought them" to New York.

A third boat contained twenty-three or twenty-four occupants (the same source contradicts itself). This boat was under the command of a passenger, Captain Hawthorne, "an experienced sailor." Also on board were his wife and two children, two female passengers, a number of male passengers, two of the *Republic's* engineers, and more than a handful of crew members. Particulars of their travails were not forthcoming, other than the fact that they "succeeded in arriving safely at Hilton Head . . . all in good health." How long they spent at sea, and whether they rowed or sailed to land, is left to conjecture.

The fourth boat, containing eleven occupants, was in charge of the second mate, Edward Ryan. This boat was the captain's gig: a four-oared boat that was smaller than the other three. The lifeboats must have been widely dispersed by the storm that raged during the night of October 25, for when the sun rose the following morning, the men in the gig found themselves to be completely alone in the wide, wide sea. At times the boat was half full of water, and "at the mercy of the winds and waves."

The gig drifted for three days and four nights, during which time the men were "without food and water." They spotted two southbound steamers, "but in spite of every effort, displaying their clothes on the end of oars, &c., were unable to attract attention, the vessels being at full speed and a very heavy sea running at the time. They were finally rescued by the schooner *Harper*, Captain Coombs commanding. "They were all taken on board the schooner in an exhausted state, and much swollen."

It was reported on November 4, "By the careful attention of Capt. Coombs and the inhabitants of Hilton Head, they are all doing well." The gig was picked up twenty-five miles from Cape Romain. Apparently, the *Harper* then transported the survivors to Hilton Head.

No mention was made of the raft.

By adding the number of occupants in all four lifeboats - none of whom perished from their various ordeals - we can tabulate that there were sixty-one survivors. According to *Merchant Steam Vessels of the United States*, there were thirty-four fatalities. The combination of these two figures implies that one hundred five persons were on board the Republic at the time of her loss. If we assume that the number of passengers was "40 odd," then we are left to conclude that there must have been "60 odd" crew members. I consider such a large complement unlikely. Thus, how many people - if any - died in the foundering of the *Republic* is open to conjecture.

Six passengers (three men and three women) who were on Captain Young's boat, wrote a letter of praise to the captain: "We, the undersigned, a part of the passengers of the ill-fated *Republic* . . . hereby tender our thanks to you, her late Commander, for your kind care of us all; for your never flinching exertions to save both passengers and ship, and when it came to the worst, and the ship was to be abandoned, we felt that we found in you all the requisites of a sailor and gentleman; that your judgment and coolness saved many lives that would otherwise have been sacrificed; and, being the last man on the ship, was actually carried down with her when she went down from sight forever. Words fail to express the thanks of our hearts. Our prayer is that our Heavenly Father, who watched over us all in this our dire distress, may always watch over you and protect you wherever you may be, by land or sea."

It is interesting to note how much times have changed since 1865. Today, the ecclesiastical cloth has been replaced by the judicial robe, and a prayer to the Heavenly Father is likely to be forsaken for the intersession of a lenient judge. In cases of accidental human tragedy, and situations in which the forces of nature prove stronger than mankind's presumptuous means to resist them, survivors are more likely than not to declare the infliction of post-traumatic stress syndrome, and to exploit the court system in order to obtain vast unearned wealth at another's expense.

The burning question now is: where are the remains of the *Republic* and its $400,000 in specie - whose modern equivalency would be multiple millions? (Or was the value of the specie another typo?)

Captain Young's last reported position was off Savannah where the water depth was 22 fathoms, or 132 feet. "Off" can have many meanings. Along the eastern seaboard, "off" may mean east or close to east of the given landmark. "Off" may also mean "in a direction perpendicular to the coastline," which at that point trends on a bearing of approximately 30°. This position would be farther south than due east of Savannah. With far less precision, "off" is sometimes used as a means of establishing a general area with respect to a landmark with which the lay mind is likely to be familiar, in which case the position could be anywhere along the curved line drawn by a pair of dividers.

To compound the imprecision, Captain Young's final fix was made two days before the *Republic* sank. For part of one day the paddlewheels were still churning the seas, albeit slowly. But then the engine quit turning, and for thirty-four hours the steamer lay to without mechanical means of propulsion. In short, she was adrift. At that place the Gulf Stream current flows approximately northeast. This was evidenced by the fact that two lifeboats were picked up off the coast of South Carolina. At the same time, the wind was blowing first at gale force out of the east-northeast, then at hurricane force out of the northeast. Thus the current and the wind were nearly diametrically opposed to each other. A case could be made for a scenario in which these counteracting forces worked in such a way that the *Republic* remained essentially motionless with respect to the seabed; or, in modern terminology, its ground speed was zero.

I submit that anyone searching for the wreck of the *Republic* should start by looking along the 22 fathom line within the broad parameters deduced above. The 22 fathom line is about fifty miles offshore.

The *Republic's* paddlewheels measured 28 feet in diameter, and were turned by a vertical beam engine whose cylinder measured 72 inches across with a stroke of 9 feet. The propulsion machinery was built by Murray & Hazelhurst of Baltimore, Maryland. Her hull was constructed of the finest oak, and was "copper and iron fastened." She was metalled in 1860 - that is, her hull was sheathed as protection against fouling marine organisms (barnacles and such). The metal was probably sheet copper.

Most of the hull has likely been eaten away. But specie is not biodegradable.

UNIDENTIFIED WRECKS

SOUTH CAROLINA

Anchor Wreck (alias Screw Steamer)

Loran 45314.6 / 60179.0   GPS 32-41.269 / 79-09.280
Metal hull, high relief   Depth: 100 feet

This is the wreck of a large freighter with a ferrous metal hull whose plates are riveted to the beams. The length is in the neighborhood of 250 feet. Much of the hull rises ten feet or more above the seabed. It is called the Anchor Wreck not because of the two stock anchors that grace the bow, but because of the cluster of three anchors abaft the windlass. These extra anchors may have been cargo. In the early 1990's, the bow was in line with the centerline, but now it is sheered off to starboard. Perhaps it was snagged by the net of a powerful trawler. The bend occurs in the vicinity of the windlass. The hull is contiguous despite this twist to starboard.

The propulsion machinery dominates the middle of the wreck. The triple expansion reciprocating steam engine stood upright in the 1990's, but now it lies on its starboard side with the top of the cylinder heads broken off and lying adjacent to the block. Forward of the engine, two boilers lie side by side on their bedplates. Each boiler is twelve feet across. Close outboard of the starboard boiler, three copper pots appear to be fused together and pinned under wreckage. Forward of the two boilers is a donkey boiler, which lies diagonally with respect to the centerline. To the starboard of the engine, and beyond the perimeter of the hull, lies the wreckage of the wheel house.

A small section of shaft alley exists immediately abaft the engine. The shaft is exposed all the way to the iron propeller. Only one blade remains on the propeller hub. The rudder post lies immediately abaft of this blade.

Pete Manchee recovered a piece of machinery with a flange on which was stamped "Goteborg," which is a city in Sweden. This evidence suggests a vessel of Scandinavian origin. Despite this evidence, Manchee believes that this may be the wreck of the *F.J. Luckenbach* (q.v.).

Bottle Wreck

Location: Approximately 35 miles east southeast of Georgetown
No hull, nearly no relief   Depth: 100 feet

This site consists of a pile of solidified masses of cement that must have been cargo that was carried in barrels, as each mass has retained the shape of its container. The diameter of this oval-shaped debris field is about twenty feet by thirty feet. In the middle of the pile, the barrel-shaped cement units rise to height of about three above the surrounding seabed. A few timbers are exposed at the edge of the pile that appears to be the after end. The surrounding seabed is pure white sand which exhibits no relief.

Blue-green bottles have been found around and under the cement barrels. These bottles stand six and one-half inches tall. They are reminiscent of soda water bottles, and appear to have been manufactured circa 1890's. On one side they are embossed "JOHN WEDDING JACKSONVILLE FLA"; on the other side they are embossed "THIS BOTTLE NOT TO BE SOLD".

When first discovered, the pile of cement stood at least eight feet above the surrounding seabed. Since then, the sand appears to have built up around the base of the pile, thus covering the lower portion. Ironically, while the main pile has become partially sanded in, two distant sections

of the wreck have become exposed. In October 2002, a section that lay some seventy-five feet forward of the main pile made itself evident. At the time of observation, this section extended about six feet by eight feet, and consisted of a windlass, a pi-shaped piece of metal, and what appeared to be a brass pump that was four feet by six feet in size. Another section that lay some sixty feet aft of the main pile consisted of a ten-foot section of wooden hull and what appeared to be an iron pump with brass ends. Neither of these sections exhibits any relief; rather, the sand appears to have been brushed off of them.

Bud's Wreck

Location: Approximately 30 miles southeast of Georgetown
Wooden hull, low relief   Depth: 100 feet

In October 2002, while conducting final surveys for this book aboard the *Safari IV*, Captain Buddy Dennis took me to a hang that he had obtained from a fishing friend. The site turned out to be the wreck of a wooden-hulled sailing vessel. I approximated its length at between 150 and 175 feet. The rise above the bottom was no more than two to three feet. The exposed timbers were badly worm eaten, and in many places the calcareous tubes of teredoes (not worms, but wood-boring mollusks) lay free on the seabed because the wood in which they had been bored had long since disappeared. In a few places the rotted wood was undercut.

The bow was distinguished by a capstan that lay on its side, with the coverless top pointing to starboard. A windlass stood abaft and to the port side of the capstan, with anchor chain still wound around its portside drum head. A donkey boiler, with half its copper tubing exposed, lay close to the stern on the port side. The planks at the stern came to a point, giving the impression that this is the vessel's stem. What appears to be the stem is in actuality the lower portion of the stern hull, where the frame flares out to form an arch for the rudder. A length of exposed chain at that point may have been the safety chain for the rudder.

I named the wreck in honor of the captain.

Composite Wreck (alias Unknown Schooner)

Loran 45177.7 / 59713.6   GPS 32-54.694 / 78-19.693
Composite hull, medium relief (see *Percy Thompson*)   Depth: 130 feet

Governor (alias Civil War Wreck)

Loran 45333.6 / 59483.4   GPS 33-29.510 / 78-24.624
Wooden hull, medium relief (see *Suwanee*)   Depth: 75 feet

Ore Freighter (alias 18 Fathom Wreck)

Loran 45138.6 / 59398.2   GPS 33-12.120 / 77-47.545
Metal hull, high relief (see *Runa*)   Depth: 120 feet

Pipe Wreck

Loran 45301.1 / 59628.6   GPS 33-15.627 / 78-30.165
Wooden hull, medium relief   Depth: 90 feet

The encrusted conglomerate of the propelling machinery is practically the only part of this wreck that is exposed. That it is the remains of a side wheel steamer is made evident by the shafts that extend to either side of the central pile of machinery. The shaft hubs have six stubby arms that once were connected to paddles. This machinery pile is somewhat square and about twenty-five feet across. The machinery appears to predate the Civil War.

In 1990, Ed Dixon found a bronze ship's bell on the site. He and Danny Jones, Pete Manchee, and Elmer McCallum worked together to recover it. Embossed on the bell was "MENEELY'S WEST TROY N.Y. 1857." Manchee has speculated that this site may be the wreck of the *Governor* (q.v.). A vessel that was built in 1846 would not normally have been equipped with a bell that was dated eleven years later, unless the original bell was damaged or lost.

I have speculated that airlifting sand from the areas forward and aft of the machinery could yield valuable information, as well as an enormous supply of military accoutrements. My speculation, however, was preceded by actuality. Tuck Rion took a group to the site on his boat, and for three straight days, twenty-four hours a day, this group used a sand dredge to clear the bottom right down to the wooden hull. Rion thinks that the area they cleared was the starboard side forward - although on unidentified paddle wheelers it is often difficult to differentiate bow from stern unless a windlass or rudder is located. Nonetheless, this group excavated an area that extended some ten feet in width and some thirty to forty feet in length. They found nothing but six-inch bronze spikes.

Rosin Wreck

Loran 45170.2 / 59156.7   GPS 33-35.391 / 77-27.205

Metal hull, high relief   Depth: 115 feet

Geographically speaking, the Rosin Wreck lies closer to the coast of North Carolina than to the coast of South Carolina. I include it here because of the possibility that historical documentation might list the loss as one that occurred off South Carolina. It is called the Rosin Wreck because of the vast amount of rosin that is found in the cargo holds. Some chunks of rosin are the size of shopping carts. This rosin is translucent and dark amber in color. The rosin appears to have

been stowed in barrels; the wooden sides of the barrels have rotted away, leaving the rosin in the original shape of its container.

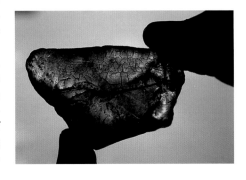

Rosin is a resin derived from the sap of various pine trees. It is used "to increase sliding friction on the bows of certain stringed instruments," and "in a wide variety of manufactured products including varnishes, inks, linoleum, and soldering compounds."

This large freighter is between 250 and 300 feet long, and rises some thirty feet above the seabed at its highest point: visually dramatic in its length and breadth. It lies with a list to port of about 45°, with the starboard side uppermost. The hull is contiguous along the hard sandy bottom, but the high side is broken down to various degrees in different places.

The bow and forecastle are intact. Both the port and starboard anchors are snugged in their hawse pipes. A spare anchor is secured to the top deck of the forecastle, positioned between the working anchors. A windlass sits on the deck immediately abaft the spare anchor. A section of breakdown is located abaft the forecastle. A winch and the stub of a mast are situated in this breakdown area.

The next aftermost section consists of the wheel house deck, from which the planking is gone but across which the cross members or supporting beams remain, lending the overall appearance of the floor of a house which has yet to have plywood nailed to the joists. At the base of this section is a debris field that contains wreckage of the bridge. China shards and a toilet lie close to the hull. One can easily penetrate this section by slipping between the beams. Thick slabs of rosin are stowed in the bottom of the hold. This part of the wreck rises the highest.

Abaft of this the hull and deck are broken down. On the low side, adjacent to the sand, an iron helm stand lies just inside the wreck. This spot is the forward end of a corridor that runs aft and exits where the hull is again broken apart. Above this corridor, on the high side of the wreck, a boiler is exposed above the surrounding wreckage. The engine lies immediately abaft this boiler. The top of the engine has been displaced; it lies abaft the engine.

Between the engine and the fantail lies the aft cargo hold. A pile of loose rosin can be found on the low side at the level of the sand. The after mast lies diagonally across the hull, from upper fore to lower aft. After this the wreck is broken down to its lowest point, less than fifteen feet above the seabed. Then comes the intact stern section, which rises higher. Under the fantail is an iron propeller. Atop the fantail is the steering quadrant, with its arm extension pointing downward. Some divers have mistaken this arm for the barrel of a deck gun.

The position of this wreck was established by the Sixth Naval District during World War Two, but no identification was made. In a letter dated February 8, 1944, it was noted, "The wreck, which is lying on its side, has 84 feet of water over it at mean low water." Confusingly, on the same date, the Sixth Naval District reported another wreck less than half a mile away. This wreck was annotated, "Wk which is approx. 381 ft in length is lying on its side with a LD [least depth] of 60 ft." These reports have led to the belief that two wrecks exist where only one has ever been located.

The few items that have been recovered from the wreck have not led to its identity. One quarter was dated 1903. Bob Jeffers recovered a narrow, two-pound lead bar that was stamped "Glenbro Warranted." George Purifoy recovered silverware from the wheel house debris field that had Spanish or Portuguese writing on it.

The Rosin Wreck could possibly be the *Runa* (q.v.).

Sailing Yacht

Loran 45146.7 / 59685.6   GPS 32-52.909 / 78-13.031
Fiberglass hull, medium relief   Depth: 290 feet

Pete Manchee approached me with a set of coordinates for a wreck that he wanted to check out. He had already run over the site with a depth recorder, and verified its existence. He told me it was deep: in the neighborhood of 270 feet. In October 1999, we decided to make a dive on air to determine if the wreck was worth further examination. Instead of taking the chance of fouling the grapnel in the wreck, which was small, we dropped a marker. The surface was calm and the water was a delicious deep blue in color. It seemed as if I could see forever down the buoy line - and it seemed to take that long to reach the bottom.

When I finally settled onto the snow-white sand and looked at my depth gauge, I learned that the actual depth was 290 feet! And nowhere was there a wreck to be seen. That the weight had dragged across the bottom was made evident by the long track in the sand. I secured my safety reel to the shot weight, then proceeded upcurrent along the shallow trough, deploying line like Hansel and Gretel leaving breadcrumbs in the forest. Pete was right by my side. After traveling only about twenty-five feet we noticed a dark, amorphous silhouette in the distance. After another twenty-five feet the wreck came clearly into view. We saw a hull that rose eight feet off the seabed, but that extended only twenty feet or so in either direction. We met the wreck about midship.

I tossed my reel over the bulwark, then took my first hard look at the wreck. It required only a couple of seconds to recognize that the wreck was an intact sailboat or sailing yacht some forty feet in length. With ambient light visibility in excess of seventy-five feet, we could see the wreck in its entirety. In the cockpit I noticed a plastic cooler whose lid lay next to it. An errant thought passed through my mind: why had the cooler sunk instead of floating away? And why had the lid not floated off, too? The cabin door was open, but the doorway was far too small to permit my entry - even had I wanted to try.

When I looked up, I saw Pete hovering over the cabin. I swam toward him, then both of us dropped to the seabed on the starboard side and examined the side of the bow for a name. The glossy white hull was thinly encrusted with dime-sized barnacles and a splotchy veneer of algae. We could see lettering under the encrustation, but we were not able to read the name.

Already it was time to go. I retrieved my reel and began spooling in the one hundred feet of line. Pete charged ahead so when I arrived at the shot weight, he had already loosened the loop for the reel. I freed the reel by pushing it through the loop, attached the reel  to a D-ring on my tank, and began the long ascent to the surface. Our bottom time was thirteen minutes. Decompression time was forty minutes, breathing two different gases: nitrox-40 and pure oxygen. The water temperature on the seabed was 72°; above the thermocline it was 77°.

Pete and I exchanged grins and grimaces while we were decompressing. With my index finger I made concentric circles around my temple; this pantomime generally means "crazy," but I was indicating how narked I had felt at depth. On the bottom I had responded normally with respect to routines that were part of my training and long experience. I had felt no impairment of performance in checking my gauges and deploying a line reel. But my powers of observation had been seriously diminished. My memory of the appearance of the wreck was already blurring.

I returned to the boat before Pete. Eagerly I related to the people onboard what we had found. In describing the wreck, I stated my impression of the boat sporting a single mast, but my retention was fading even as I spoke. I became befuddled, and although I thought that I had seen a standing mast, I was no longer certain.

After Pete climbed aboard, I asked him if he had seen a mast. He exclaimed with a laugh, "I was holding onto it when you looked at me." Despite his assurance, I could not retrieve that particular image with any degree of certitude. At the same time, there were aspects of the wreck that I had observed that Pete could not remember. Obviously, we had both been somewhat debilitated by the effects of nitrogen narcosis. We vowed that we would return to the wreck, but breathing a mixture of helium instead of air. Two years later, we did. I was much more clear-headed breathing trimix-17/44 than I had been breathing air. By then the mast had fallen overboard. The cooler and its lid sat exactly where I had seen them before. Part of the hatch had either collapsed or been torn open. Pete used a wire brush to try to clean the encrustation off the name on the starboard bow, but the barnacles were so strongly attached to the fiberglass hull that he was unable to do so. The marine growth that fouled the hull in 2001 was much thicker than it had been two years earlier.

The Sailing Yacht remains unidentified. Voluminous correspondence with the Coast Guard - which was extremely cooperative in combing through its records - has failed to unearth any documentation of a recent casualty that fits the location and description of the wreck. This implies that the Coast Guard did not conduct either a search or a rescue operation in the vicinity, and that the Coast Guard did not receive any transmissions of distress that originated in the area. Could the Sailing Yacht be the physical remains of a vessel that was lost with all hands, and was therefore never reported to local authorities? Only continued research, both in the water and out, will solve the mystery.

ST-541

Loran 45185.5 / 59408.5   GPS 32-52.909 / 78-13.031
Steel hull, medium relief   Depth: 110 feet

Strictly speaking, the *ST-541* does not belong in this section because it has been identified. Steve Speros was not only the first person to dive the wreck, but he recovered the ship's bell, on which the name/number and boat builder were stamped. I have included the wreck here because I have no information about its history or its loss. Yet, I did not want to exclude the wreck altogether - it is an interesting dive site and a productive fishing spot.

The *ST-541* was a U.S. Army harbor tug built in 1944 by the Port Houston Iron Works in Houston, Texas. She was 86 feet in length, 23 feet abeam, and 10 feet in depth of hold. She was equipped with a 650 horsepower diesel engine.

The hull is intact with a list to starboard of about 30°. The port side rises about 8 feet above a white sandy bottom. No superstructure remains. The upper deck planks are gone but many of the steel crossthwart support beams are still in place, especially near the fantail. The bulwark extends above a pronounced rub rail. As one would expect of a tug, the mooring bitts are exceptionally large for a vessel of this size. The towing bitts in the stern distinguish the vessel's primary function. The engine takes up considerable space amidships - so much that one has to squirm in order to fit between the engine and the hull. One blade of the bronze propeller protrudes from the sand forward of the rudder.

Large schools of fish inhabit the wreck.

ARTIFICIAL REEF WRECKS

SOUTH CAROLINA

Barracuda Alley

Steel hull, high relief   Depth: 50 feet
Loran 45386.4 / 59415.5   GPS 33-41.963 / 78-26.798

This recent wreck is a beginner's delight! Working in cooperation with the Department of Natural Resources, Coastal Scuba's Cameron Sebastian took a rectangular barge that was 140 feet in length and 40 feet wide, and, with the addition of thirteen tons of angle iron and steel reinforcing rods, converted it to an underwater Jungle Gym or playground monkey bars. These beams and re-bars were welded together to create triangular A-frame swim-throughs that simulate wreck penetration, but which offer continuous means of escape. Also welded to the main deck are three cement mixers. These mixer barrels were butted end to end and welded together with a frame around it, creating a tunnel that is ideal for testing one's confidence in wreck penetration.

Vertical steel tubes have been emplaced through the deck to the bottom of the hull. A novice diver can descend into these "sewer pipes" and stir the mud on the bottom to simulate limited visibility and silt-out conditions. At the top of the A-frame is a platform where trainees can perch with their instructor and either observe the abundant fish life, or practice check-out skills that are needed for certification.

As if that were not enough, a rope from the end of the barge leads to a connected series of armored personnel carriers whose military usefulness has become obsolete. These APC's still have treads on the drive train. The hatches are open so that the interiors are accessible.

Betsy Ross Reef

Betsy Ross (441-foot Liberty ship), high relief   Depth: 90 feet
Loran 45504.1 / 61061.9   GPS 32-03.285 / 80-24.996

Like the *Vermillion*, this wreck is exciting to explore and cannot be seen completely on a single dive. It is *huge*.

Cutaway illustration of a Liberty ship. (Courtesy of the Naval Photographic Center.)

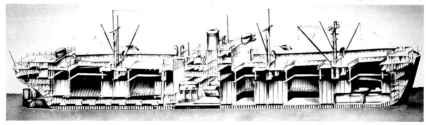

YO-224 (175-foot ship), high relief

Depth: 90 feet
GPS 32-03.142 / 80-25.132

Bill Perry Jr. Reef

65-foot tugboat, medium relief

Depth: 65 feet

Loran 45350.8 / 59580.4

GPS 33-25.652 / 78-33.293

BP-25

160-foot tanker, high relief
Depth: 95 feet
Loran 45306.0 / 59551.4
GPS 33-21.298 / 78-25.550

The propeller of the *BP-25*.

Cape Romain Reef

100-foot barge, medium relief
Depth: 65 feet
Loran 45463.2 / 59996.2
GPS 32-59.817 / 79-02.312

Dolphin (65-foot tugboat)
high relief

Depth: 65 feet
GPS 32-59.852 / 79-02.330

Capers Reef

90-foot tugboat, medium relief

Depth: 45 feet

Loran 45437.5 / 60368.6

GPS 32-44.539 / 79-34.345

100-foot barge, medium relief

Depth: 45 feet

Loran 45439.9 / 60367.2

GPS 32-44.405 / 79-34.507

150-foot barge, medium relief

Depth: 45 feet

Loran 45439.8 / 60366.9

GPS 32-44.965 / 79-34.484

120-foot barge, medium relief

Depth: 45 feet
GPS 32-45.087 / 79-34.486

Charleston 60-foot Reef

240-foot barge, medium relief

Depth: 60 feet
GPS 32-33.354 / 79-40.299

C.J. Davidson Jr. Reef

140-foot barge, medium relief

Depth: 53 feet

Loran 45381.4 / 59942.5

GPS 33-05.931 / 79-00.751

Comanche on site prior to scuttling. (Courtesy of the South Carolina Department of Natural Resources.)

Comanche

165-foot Coast Guard cutter, high relief
Loran 45295.1 / 60350.4

Depth: 105 feet
GPS 32-27.395 / 79-19.073

Eagle's Nest Reef

65-foot tugboat
Loran 45524.0 / 61121.3

Depth: 70 feet
GPS 32-01.298 / 80-30.421

Edisto 60-foot Reef

Page (330-foot ship), high relief
Loran 45485.0 / 60780.0

Depth: 65 feet
GPS 32-21.542 / 80-05.284

YDT-16 (264-foot ship), high relief

Depth: 65 feet
GPS 32-21.421 / 80-05.308

YDT-16 under tow to scuttling site. (Courtesy of the South Carolina Department of Natural Resources.)

Edisto Offshore Reef

Researcher (100-foot ship), medium relief
Loran 45382.7 / 60692.2

Depth: 80 feet
GPS 32-14.958 / 79-50.545

Fripp Island Reef

100-foot barge, medium relief
Loran 45546.1 / 60969.0

Depth: 35 feet
GPS 32-15.408 / 80-22.407

Hunting Island Reef

100-foot barge, medium relief
Loran 45524.0 / 60964.7

Depth: 50 feet
GPS 32-12.920 / 80-20.360

Georgetown Nearshore Reef

130-foot barge, medium relief

Depth: 30 feet
GPS 33-12.727 / 79-05.313

Georgetown Reef

100-foot ship, medium relief
Loran 45410.2 / 59882.2

Depth: 40 feet
GPS 33-14.237 / 79-00.025

Greenville Reef

140-foot barge, medium relief
Loran 45321.0 / 59955.3

Depth: 85 feet
GPS 32-56.818 / 78-54.643

YOG-78 (175-foot ship), high relief

Depth: 85 feet
GPS 32-56.906 / 78-54.848

175-foot Navy coastal tanker. (Courtesy of the South Carolina Department of Natural Resources.)

Hilton Head Reef

200-foot barge, medium relief

Depth: 50 feet
GPS 31-59.923 / 80-35.892

100-foot barge, medium relief

Depth: 50 feet
GPS 32-00.179 / 80-36.015

Kiawah Reef

Robison (437-foot Navy destroyer), medium relief

Depth: 40 feet
GPS 32-29.271 / 80-00.074

300-foot barge, medium relief
Loran 45495.4 / 60688.1

Depth 40 feet
GPS 32-29.531 / 80-00.200

A 115-foot LCU landing craft. (Courtesy of the South Carolina Department of Natural Resources.)

260-foot barge, medium relief   Depth: 40 feet
Loran 45494.9 / 60688.3   GPS 32-29.436 / 80-00.243

Drydock, medium relief   Depth: 40 feet
Loran 45493.2 / 60693.4   GPS 32-28.858 / 80-00.402

100-foot tugboat, medium relief   Depth: 40 feet
Loran 45493.5 / 60692.8   GPS 32-28.771 / 80-00.373
100-foot barge, medium relief   Depth: 40 feet
Loran 45491.2 / 60691.4   GPS 32-28.790 / 80-00.402

90-foot tugboat, medium relief   Depth: 40 feet
Loran 45492.6 / 60692.4   GPS 32-28.858 / 80-00.301

200-foot barge, medium relief   Depth: 40 feet
    GPS 32-28.749 / 80-00.104

110-foot and 120-foot barges, medium relief   Depth: 40 feet
    GPS 32-28.778 / 80-00.556

North Edisto Nearshore Reef

150-foot barge, medium relief   Depth: 30 feet
Loran 45529.8 / 60729.3   GPS 32-31.060 / 80-05.955

110-foot barge, medium relief   Depth: 30 feet
Loran 45530.6 / 60731.1   GPS 32-31.035 / 80-06.104

Ten Mile Reef

200-foot ship, medium relief   Depth: 45 feet
Loran 45427.4 / 59742.0   GPS 33-26.407 / 78-52.807

Will Goldfinch Reef

YO-225 (175-foot ship), high relief   Depth: 60 feet
GPS 33-17.005 / 78-45.372

Vermillion

460-foot Victory ship, high relief   Depth: 130 feet
Loran 45265.8 / 59835.5   GPS 32-57.553 / 78-40.044

The *Vermillion* is one of those wrecks that you just *have* to see! The wreck is an intact amphibious attack troop transport that was built to carry marines and landing craft to enemy beaches in the European theater in World War Two. She was completed too late to see action, and spent most of her career participating in convoy exercises. In 1988, she was prepared for a new peacetime career as an artificial reef. Only the masts and the top superstructure were razed. The lower superstructure, with its complex arrangement of passageways and compartments, remains for experienced wreck-divers to penetrate. Divers are cautioned that the interior is a maze of interconnecting corridors and large compartments. It is best to tie off a penetration line before exploring the vast and complicated interior.

Large rectangular holes were cut out of the hull above the waterline. These holes enable seawater to flow freely throughout the interior, while furnishing access to the holds for properly trained divers and for numerous species of fish. Outside the wreck, the empty gun tubs (two forward and two aft) give the *Vermillion* a distinctive warlike appearance.

The steel hull rises 50 feet from the white sandy bottom, looking like a sheer cliff face that is blanketed with colorful encrustation. The depth of the main deck is 80 feet; the top of the highest structure is 20 feet higher. The main deck is 63 feet in width, and visibility is generally good enough to see all the way across it.

The hull has created an interesting pocket in the seabed. I found the bottom on one side at 119 feet. I then entered the hold through a cut-out and discovered that the interior was three feet deeper. When I exited the hold through a cut-out on the opposite side, I found that the bottom had been scoured to a depth of 132 feet. It was as if a long trench had been excavated along the side of the wreck.

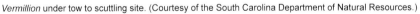
Vermillion under tow to scuttling site. (Courtesy of the South Carolina Department of Natural Resources.)

This disparity between depths was the work of a prevailing current that washed away sand from one side of the wreck and deposited sand on the other. Across the scour ditch and twenty feet from the hull there stood a vertical wall that rose twelve feet high, presenting a geological cross-section. A thin layer of granular sand

Inside the *Vermillion.*

capped the natural substrate of marl (a crumbly mixture of clays, calcium and magnesium carbonates, and remnants of shell).

You cannot see the entire wreck in a single dive - or even in a score of dives.

Y-73 Reef

| 180-foot tanker, high relief | Depth: 95 feet |
| Loran 45317.4 / 60316.1 | GPS 32-32.459 / 79-18.993 |

| *Helen* (90-foot tugboat), high relief | Depth: 95 feet |
| Loran 45319.1 / 60317.4 | GPS 32-32.589 / 79-19.244 |

| *T and A 9* (or *T & A #9*) (90-foot tugboat), high relief | Depth: 95 feet |
| Loran 45319.6 / 60318.5 | GPS 32-32.595 / 79-19.343 |

| Kimberly (90-foot tugboat), high relief | Depth: 95 feet |
| Loran 45320.3 / 60319.6 | GPS 32-32.636 / 79-19.504 |

GEORGIA

Addie Bagley Daniels, 441-foot Liberty ship, high relief   Depth: 55-75 feet
Loran 45497.8 / 61413.8   GPS 31-36.207 / 80-47.750

This is the main section of one of Georgia's two premier artificial reef wrecks. See *Edwin S. Nettleton* for a general description of Liberty ships and how these obsolete freighters came to be scuttled as artificial reefs. Both vessels were razed right down to the upper deck. Large holes were cut into the sides to permit water circulation and sunlight permeation. Unfortunately, these holes weakened the hull's structural stability. In 1979, Hurricane David not only tore the hull in two and caused considerable collapse, but dragged the after section some 200 to 300 yards away. All the king's horses and all the king's men, could not put the *Addie Bagley Daniels* together again. And so it remains.

Addie Bagley Daniels before the superstructure was razed. (Courtesy of the Georgia Department of Natural Resources.)

Loran 45497.5 / 61412.8   GPS 31-36.260 / 80-47.680
Addie Bagley Daniels (stern), Liberty ship, high relief   Depth: 55-75 feet

Deck barge, medium relief   Depth: 50-60 feet
Loran 45489.9 / 61324.6   GPS 31-42.039 / 80-41.241

Deck barge, medium relief   Depth: 30-40 feet
Loran 45585.5 / 61310.5   GPS 31-54.370 / 80-47.207

Deck barge with work boat, medium relief   Depth: 30-40 feet
Loran 45585.4 / 61311.1   GPS 31-54.299 / 80-47.229

Delta Diamond (tug), medium relief   Depth: 55-65 feet
Loran 45477.0 / 61265.8   GPS 31-44.948 / 80-36.405

Dump scow, medium relief   Depth: 150-170 feet
Loran 45102.2 / 61008.5   GPS 31-42.434 / 79-58.281

Elmira (tug), medium relief   Depth: 55-75 feet
Loran 45496.0 / 61413.0   GPS 31-36.082 / 80-47.673

Edwin S. Nettleton (441-foot Liberty ship), high relief   Depth: 70 feet
Loran 45349.6 / 61695.7   GPS 30-58.704 / 80-58.562

This is one of Georgia's two premier artificial reef wrecks (the other being the *Addie Bagley Daniels*, q.v.). Liberty ships were built during World War Two to a standard length of 441 feet. More than 2,700 of them were constructed. After the war, they found little employment in peacetime commerce. Many of them were subsequently laid up: forgotten relics were that slowly rusting away. The 1972 Liberty Ship Act released a great number of these obsolete freighters to the States for use as artificial reefs.

Since the *Edwin S. Nettleton* and the *Addie Bagley Daniels* were intended to be placed in shallow water, they were razed right down to the main deck. No superstructure was left standing. Scrappers removed everything of value as payment for their services in stripping the hulls for use as artificial reefs: copper cables, steel partitions, even the propulsion machinery. The superstructure was razed right down to the upper deck. Little was left except for the bare and practically hollow hull: compartments separated by bulkheads. Both vessels were scuttled in 1975.

The hatch covers were removed, and holes were cut through the upper deck and through the hull above the waterline - partly to increase the circulation of water through the interior, and partly to admit fish that could find protection from predators in the corners and cubbyholes inside. These cut-outs permit ample sunlight permeation, but they also weakened the hull's structural stability, resulting in the subsequent collapse of some of the large deck and side plates.

For the enterprising diver who is skilled in the art of wreck penetration, there is a great deal of these capacious hulls to explore. Entry is deceptively easy, so novices are warned to think twice about going inside, and are well advised to practice good penetration techniques: run a line, carry extra lights, and do not venture too far until you have learned progressively the myriad ways through the inner compartments and corridors. The wreck stands as high as 35 feet in depth, making this a wonderful and picturesque beginner dive.

Edwin S. Nettleton prior to scuttling. The superstructure has been razed. The *Addie Bagley Daniels* was similar in appearance when it was scuttled. (Courtesy of the Georgia Department of Natural Resources.)

Henry Bacon (dredge), medium relief
Loran 45480-0 / 61264.7

Depth: 55-65 feet
GPS 31-45.385 / 80-36.543

Honey barge, medium relief
Loran 45563.7 / 61321.1

Depth: 40-50 feet
GPS 31-50.944 / 80-46.290

Hopper barge, medium relief
Loran 45262.4 / 60953.1

Depth: 120-130 feet
GPS 31-42.878 / 79-58.577

Janet (ferry boat), medium relief — Depth: 55-75 feet
Loran 45497.1 / 61411.7 — GPS 31-36.298 / 80-47.575

John Bird, medium relief — Depth: 45-55 feet
Loran 45461.0 / 61608.9 — GPS 31-17.232 / 80-58.765

Jupiter (sailboat), medium relief — Depth: 40-50 feet
Loran 45560.4 / 61325.6 — GPS 31-50.211 / 80-46.343

Latex (barge), medium relief — Depth: 55-65 feet
Loran 45480.961266.1 — GPS 31-45.379 / 80-36.700

Mac Tide 21 (tug), medium relief — Depth: 55-75
Loran 45344.1 / 61681.0 — GPS 30-59.269 / 80-57.153

Matt Turecamo (tug), medium relief — Depth: 50-60 feet
Loran 45489.6 / 61308.8 — GPS 31-43.200 / 80-40.170

Motherlode barge, medium relief — Depth: 40-50
Loran 45563.9 / 61324.6 — GPS 31-50.699 / 80-46.533

Olympics barge, medium relief — Depth: 40-50 feet
Loran 45558.6 / 61326.6 — GPS 31-49.904 / 80-46.260

Recife (tug), medium relief — Depth: 55-75 feet
Loran 45345.9 / 61691.7 — GPS 30-58.617 / 80-58.034

Rio Apon (tug), medium relief — Depth: 55-75 feet
Loran 45517.1 / 61428.1 — GPS 31-36.180 / 80-49.364

Rio Caroni (tug), medium relief — Depth: 45-55 feet
Loran 45445.4 / 61598.0 — GPS 31-16.370 / 80-57.058

Sagebrush (165-foot Coast Guard buoy tender), high relief   Depth: 55-75 feet
Loran 45500.0 / 61412.0 — GPS 31-36.600 / 80-47.800

Semarca 40 (tug), medium relief — Depth: 120-130 feet
Loran 45258.5 / 60952.5 — GPS 31-42.434 / 79-58.281

Senasqua (tug), medium relief — Depth: 55-65 feet
Loran 45479.3 / 61268.3 — GPS 31-45.030 / 80-36.721

SMS Warehouse barge, medium relief — Depth: 50-60 feet
Loran 45492.4 / 61312.7 — GPS 31-43.220 / 80-40.638

SUGGESTED READING

Anonymous (2001) *Diving the Cooper River*, Blackwater Publishing, 410 Dubuise Road, Summerville, South Carolina 29483, (843) 832-3167.

Anonymous (2001) *Georgia's Offshore Artificial Reefs*, Georgia Department of Natural Resources, 1 Conservation Way, Suite 300, Brunswick, Georgia 31520-8687, (912) 264-7218.

Anonymous (2001) *South Carolina's Artificial Fishing Reefs and Wrecks*, Office of Fisheries Management, Marine Recreational Fisheries, P.O. Box 12559, Charleston, SC 29412.

Chance, Frank N. and Chance, Paul C. and Topper, David L (1985) *Tangled Machinery and Charred Relics: The Historical and Archaeological Investigation of the C.S.S. Nashville*, Sun Printing, Orangeburg, P.O. Box N, Orangeburg, South Carolina 29115.

Gentile, Gary (1995) *The Nautical Cyclopedia*, GGP, P.O. Box 57137, Philadelphia, PA 19111, $20.

----- (1989) *Track of the Gray Wolf*, Avon Books, New York City.

Herdendorf, Charles E. (1995 March) *The Ohio Journal of Science - Science on a Deep-Ocean Shipwreck*, The Ohio Academy of Science, 1500 West Third Avenue Suite 223, Columbus, Ohio 43212.

Klare, Normand (1992) *The Final Voyage of the Central America 1857*, Arthur H. Clark Company, Spokane, Washington.

McTeer, J.E. (1972) *Adventure in the Woods and Waters of the Low Country*, Beaufort Book Company, Beaufort, South Carolina.

Ragan, Mark K. (1995) *The Hunley: Submarines, Sacrifice, & Success in the Civil War*, Narwhal Press, 1629 Meeting Street, Charleston, South Carolina 29405.

Spence, E. Lee (1991) *Shipwreck Encyclopedia of the Civil War: South Carolina & Georgia, 1861-1865*, Shipwreck Press, P.O. Box 211, Sullivan's Island, South Carolina 29482.

----- (1995) *Shipwrecks, Pirates, & Privateers: Sunken Treasures of the Upper South Carolina Coast*, 1521-1865, Narwhal Press, 1629 Meeting Street, Charleston, South Carolina 29405.

----- (1995) *Treasures of the Confederate Coast: The "Real Rhett Butler" & Other Revelations*, Narwhal Press, P.O. Box 211, Sullivan's Island, South Carolina 29482.

LORAN / GPS NUMBERS - ALPHABETICAL

110-foot & 120-foot Barges (AR)			32-28.778	80-00.556
110-foot Barge (AR)	45530.6	60731.1	32-31.035	80-06.104
120-foot Barge (AR)			32-45.087	79-34.486
130-foot Barge (AR)			33-12.727	79-05.313
130-foot Barge (AR)	45321.0	59955.3	32-56.818	78-54.643
140-foot Barge (AR)	45381.4	59942.5	33-05.931	79-00.751
150-foot Barge (AR)	45529.8	60729.3	32-31.060	80-05.955
18 Fathom Wreck	45138.6	59398.2	33-12.120	77-47.545
200-foot Barge (AR)			32-28.749	80-00.104
200-foot ship (AR)	45427.4	59742.0	33-26.407	78-52.807
240-foot Barge (AR)			32-33.354	79-40.299
30-foot Barge (AR)			32-10.030	80-32.560
40-foot Barge (AR)			32-18.868	80-42.537
A-7 Airplane (AR)	45418.9	59737.6	33-55.387	78-51.605
Acteon	45520.7	60522.6		
Addie Bagley Daniels	45497.8	61413.8	31-36.207	80-47.750
(Liberty Ship, Main Section) AR				
Addie Bagley Daniels	45497.5	61412.8	31-36.260	80-47.680
(Liberty Ship, Stern Section) AR				
Ammo Dump	45115.0	60315.0		
Anchor Wreck	45314.6	60179.0	32-41.269	79-09.280
Arabian	45332.4	59046.0		
Aster	45329.7	59048.6		
Barge	45527.2	60518.7		
Barge	45611.3	61282.5		
Barge	45809.3	61365.7		
Barge (100 feet long) (AR)	45439.9	60367.2	32-44.405	79-34.507
Barge (100 feet long) (AR)	45491.2	60691.4	32-28.790	80-00.402
Barge (100 feet long) (AR)	45524.0	60964.7	32-12.920	80-20.360
Barge (150 feet long) (AR)	45439.8	60366.9	32-44.965	79-34.484
Barge (260 feet long) (AR)	45494.9	60688.3	32-29.436	80-00.243
Barge (300 feet long) (AR)	45495.4	60688.1	32-29.531	80-00.200
Barge (40 feet long) (AR)	45546.1	60969.0	32-15.600	80-22.440
Barge (62 feet long) (AR)	45411.8	59881.1	33-12.760	79-05.346
Barge (62 feet long) (AR)	45411.4	59881.5	33-12.730	79-05.205
Barge (62 feet long) (AR)	45493.6	60690.1	32-29.159	80-00.262
Barge (AR)	45418.7	59737.1	33-30.930	78-57.999
Barge (AR)	45463.7	59761.1	33-25.390	78-51.608
Barge (AR)	45464.8	59762.1		
Barge (AR)	45463.0	59763.0		
Barge (AR)	45425.3	59936.7		
Barge (AR)	45426.0	59937.7		
Barge (AR)	45426.1	59937.8		
Barge (AR)	45378.7	60026.5		
Barge (AR)	45480.6	60479.5		
Barge (AR)	45481.6	60480.2		
Barge (AR)	45492.9	60693.9		
Barge (AR)	45493.7	60695.3		
Barge (AR)	45545.4	61176.7	31-59.923	80-35.892
Barge (AR)	45547.7	61177.8	32-00.179	80-36.015
Barge (AR)	45613.8	61241.0	32-03.060	80-45.020
Barge (AR)	45613.2	61242.1		
Barge Wreckage (AR)	45613.2	61555.1	31-38.536	81-04.885
Barges (AR)	45379.8	60027.3		

Barges (AR)	45481.2	60479.4		
Barnstable	45520.5	61320.4		
Barracuda Alley (AR)	45386.4	59415.5	33-41.963	78-26.798
Beatrice (200 feet long)	45518.1	60514.7		
Betsy Ross (430-foot Liberty ship) AR	45504.3	61062.8	32-03.285	80-24.996
Big Rock	45138.0	59975.0		
Boat (AR)	45549.5	61177.8	32-00.152	80-36.006
Boiler Wreck	45609.8	61200.9		
BP-25 (160-foot tanker) AR	45306.0	59551.4	33-21.298	78-25.550
Brick Wreck	45252.7	59202.7	33-38.260	77-51.774
Caisson Wreck (Drydock) AR	45437.9	60371.0		
Camel	45426.8	59741.3		
Carolina Sea Channel	45115.0	60315.0		
Celt (160 feet long)	45518.9	60513.6		
Chris's Wreck	45224.8	59353.8		
City of Houston	45170.6	59281.6	33-24.305	77-42.731
City of Richmond	45343.8	59925.6	33-01.900	78-55.423
City of St. Helens	44890.8	59761.5		
Civil War Wreck	45333.6	59483.4	33-29.510	78-24.624
Comanche (160-foot CG Cutter) AR	45295.1	60350.4	32-27.395	79-19.073
Composite Wreck	45177.7	59713.6	32-54.694	78-19.693
Condor	45332.0	59048.6		
Constance	45499.4	60458.4		
D. Howard Spear	44931.9	59336.3		
Daventry (false)	45496.4	60517.9		
Deck Barge (AR)	45585.5	61310.5	31-54.370	80-47.207
Deck Barge (AR)	45495.3	61317.8	31-43.180	80-41.166
Deck Barge (AR)	45561.2	61319.6	31-50.775	80-46.015
Deck Barge (AR)	45489.9	61324.6	31-42.039	80-41.241
Deck Barge w/Work Boat (AR)	45585.4	61311.1	31-54.299	80-47.229
Deckhouse (AR)	45381.6	60690.5	32-14.925	79-50.355
Dee	45581.8	60871.2		
Delia Maria	45609.8	61200.8		
Delta Diamond (Tug) AR	45477.0	61265.8	31-44.948	80-36.405
Dirfys	45247.0	59211.9	33-37.026	77-51.502
Dolphin (65-foot tugboat) (AR)			32-59.852	79-02.330
Doris Kellogg	44954.2	59566.8		
Dredge Barge (AR)	45463.2	59996.2		
Drydock (AR)	45493.2	60693.4	32-28.858	80-00.402
Dump Scow (AR)	45102.2	61008.5	31-21.525	79-50.403
Dump Scow (AR)	45562.8	61325.5	31-50.502	80-46.507
Edwin S. Nettleton (Liberty Ship) AR	45349.6	61685.7	30-58.704	80-58.562
Elmira (Tug) AR	45496.0	61413.0	31-36.082	80-47.673
Esparta	45375.3	61832.2	30-50.850	81-10.155
Etiwan	45529.1	60531.6		
F.J. Luckenbach	45314.6	60179.0		
Feather	45330.3	59051.6		
Flamingo	45510.8	60507.8		
Flora (200 feet long)	45515.2	60514.0		
Frances Canady	45003.4	60246.3		
Fred W. Chase	45499.8	60563.2		
Frederick W. Day	45427.7	60471.7	32-36.025	79-40.141
Fripp Drydock (100 feet long)	45566.6	60981.3	32-15.408	80-22.407
Gaskin Wreck	45609.8	61200.9		
General Gordon	45580.1	61096.0	32-10.107	80-33.212
General Sherman	45413.3	59455.7	33-43.710	78-32.495

George MacDonald	44996.5	59851.5		
George Weems	45216.1	59190.9	33-35.868	77-43.271
Georgetown Rock	45136.0	59968.0		
Georgia (Ram)	45724.3	61391.2		
Georgiana	45498.3	60454.1		
Golden Liner	45481.8	59792.2		
Governor (possibly)	45301.1	59628.6	33-15.627	78-30.165
Gypsy Queen (65 feet long)	45659.3	61277.6		
Haban (Tugboat) AR	45380.2	60699.0		
Hang	45181.9	59236.9		
Hang	45470.4	60501.0		
Hang	45468.3	60535.2		
Hebe	45237.4	59612.7	33-08.451	78-20.421
Hector	45380.3	60027.1	32-59.984	79-06.108
Henry Bacon (Dredge) AR	45480.0	61264.7	31-45.385	80-36.543
Honey (Barge) AR	45563.7	61321.1	31-50.944	80-46.290
Hopper Barge (AR)	45262.4	60953.1	31-42.878	79-58.577
Houston	45170.6	59281.6	33-24.305	77-42.731
Janet (Ferry Boat) AR	45497.1	61411.7	31-36.298	80-47.575
John Bird (AR)	45461.0	61608.9	31-17.232	80-58.765
John Randolph	45525.5	60517.9		
John Rose	44994.4	59269.2		
Juan Casiano	44892.6	59806.4		
Jupiter (Sailboat) AR	45560.4	61325.6	31-50.211	80-46.343
Karsnaes (Schooner)	45500.9	60503.4		
Keokuk	45507.6	60542.2		
Lady Margaret	45224.8	59353.8		
Landing Craft (AR)	45385.9	59414.0		
Landing Craft (AR)	45386.9	59417.4		
Landing Craft (AR)	45386.5	59418.5	33-41.987	78-26.620
Landing Craft (AR)	45350.0	59581.7	33-25.550	78-33.381
Landing Craft (AR)	45350.6	59581.9	33-25.651	78-33.554
Landing Craft (AR)	45351.9	59582.6	33-25.462	78-33.275
Landing Craft (AR)	45350.5	59583.5	33-25.417	78-33.471
Landing Craft (AR)	45426.5	59742.6		
Landing Craft (AR)	45464.1	59763.2		
Landing Craft (AR)	45457.0	59814.0		
Landing Craft (AR)	45457.3	59814.6	33-26.082	79-00.686
Landing Craft (AR)	45456.9	59814.7	33-26.100	79-00.749
Landing Craft (AR)	45456.9	59814.7		
Landing Craft (AR)	45411.3	59883.0		
Landing Craft (AR)	45363.4	59996.0		
Landing Craft (AR)	45379.3	60026.2		
Landing Craft (AR)	45438.2	60369.0		
Landing Craft (AR)	45438.1	60369.7		
Landing Craft (AR)	45438.2	60370.0		
Landing Craft (AR)	45438.3	60370.5		
Landing Craft (AR)	45493.5	60694.0		
Landing Craft (AR)	45525.4	60964.6	32-13.120	80-20.497
Landing Craft (AR)	45525.6	60965.1		
Landing Craft (AR)	45524.2	61122.8	32-01.174	80-30.494
Landing Craft (AR)	45524.7	61123.1	32-01.424	80-30.578
Landing Craft (AR)	45551.0	61179.8		
Landing Craft (AR)	45548.6	61181.1		
Landing Craft (AR)	45481.7	61782.7	31-05.939	81-12.255
Landing Craft (AR)	45483.0	61784.6	31-05.926	81-12.483

Larch	45523.2	60634.1	
Lark (AR)	45437.7	60369.7	
Latex (Barge) AR	45480.9	61266.1	31-45.379	80-36.700
Life Boats (AR)	45491.1	60693.8	
Liverpool	45471.2	59933.1	
Louisiana	45331.6	59046.3	
Mac Tide 21 (Tug) AR	45344.1	61681.0	30-59.269	80-57.153
Mance Lassiter (tug) AR	45262.4	59433.4	
Marie Palmer	45261.2	59219.7	
Mary B. Baird	44653.4	59178.8	
Mary Barry	44830.2	59144.8	
Mary Bowers	45500.3	60456.0	
Mary Lou (crew boat) AR	45533.5	61695.7	31-18.422	81-09.180
Matt Turecamo (Tug) AR	45489.6	61308.8	31-43.200	80-40.170
Modena (Barge) AR	45545.3	61551.1	31-31.061	81-00.132
Modern Greece	45333.5	59042.3	
Moorefield	45331.1	59047.4	
Motherlode (Barge) AR	45563.9	61324.6	31-50.699	80-46.533
Mount Dirfys	45247.0	59211.9	33-37.026	77-51.502
Nellie	45510.2	60470.7	
Norseman	45505.5	60457.3	
North Carolina	45372.2	59650.6	33-24.185	78-40.557
Olympics (Barge) AR	45558.6	61326.6	31-49.904	80-46.260
Optimist (Landing Craft) AR	45381.1	61722.9	30-59.928	81-02.308
Ore Freighter	45138.6	59398.2	33-12.120	77-47.545
Page (300-foot Ship (AR)	45485.0	60780.0	32-21.542	80-05.284
Patapsco	45523.5	60521.9	
Pathfinder (90-foot Ship) AR	45437.5	60368.6	32-44.539	79-34.345
Percy Thomson	45177.7	59713.6	32-54.694	78-19.693
Peterhoff	45323.0	59075.9	
Petrel	45265.4	60253.9	
Pipe Wreck (Governor ?)	45301.1	59628.6	33-15.627	78-30.165
Presto	45518.1	60514.7	
Prince Albert	45516.0	60509.6	
Prince of Wales	45471.2	59933.1	
R/V Zapala (AR)	45457.5	61601.3	31-17.441	80-58.021
Raccoon	45512.2	60509.4	
Raritan	45248.2	59275.2	33-32.504	77-56.935
Rattlesnake	45510.7	60481.3	
Recife (Tug) AR	45345.9	61691.7	30-58.617	80-58.034
Researcher (100-foot ship) AR	45382.7	60692.2	32-14.958	79-50.545
Rio Apon (Tug) AR	45517.1	61428.1	31-36.180	80-49.364
Rio Caroni (Tug) AR	45445.4	61598.0	31-16.370	80-57.058
Robert B. Howlett	45496.8	60515.7	
Robison (437-foot-long destroyer) (AR)			32-29.271	80-00.074
Rose	45481.5	59899.4	
Rosin Wreck	45170.2	59156.7	33-35.391	77-27.205
Rover	45481.8	59792.2	
Ruby	45510.8	60557.2	
Runa	45138.6	59398.2	33-12.120	77-47.545
Sagebrush (Buoy Tender) AR	45500.0	61412.0	31-36.600	80-47.800
Sailing Yacht	45146.7	59685.6	32-52.909	78-13.031
Sayler (Barge) AR	45479.4	61266.1	31-45.200	80-36.596
Scalper (Landing Craft) AR	45380.6	61723.2	30-59.862	81-02.298
Screw Steamer	45314.6	60179.0	
Semarca 40 (Tug) AR	45258.5	60952.5	31-42.434	79-58.281

Senasqua (Tug) AR	45479.3	61268.3	31-45.030	80-36.721
Sherman	45413.3	59455.7	33-43.710	78-32.495
Shrimp Boat (AR)	45351.8	59582.5	33-25.673	78-33.577
SMS Warehouse Barge (AR)	45492.4	61312.7	31-43.220	80-40.638
ST-541	45185.5	59408.5	33-16.236	77-56.745
St. Cathan	45238.1	59616.6	33-08.303	78-20.789
Stonewall Jackson	44711.1	59322.1		
Stono	45518.5	60514.2		
Stormy Petrel	45330.0	59052.1		
Striker (Work Boat) AR	45348.1	61700.3	30-58.198	80-58.800
Suwanee	45333.6	59483.4	33-29.510	78-24.624
T.A. Ward	44844.9	59006.0		
T.J. Don	44567.9	59608.6		
Tampa (Tug) AR	45348.0	61700.3	30-58.203	80-58.804
Ten Mile Reef Wreck	45427.1	59741.3		
Thomas Watson	45518.3	60628.8		
Torungen (100-foot ship) AR	45410.2	59882.2		
Trawler	45490.5	60437.0		
Tropic	45490.1	60450.1		
Tug	45809.8	61364.9		
Tugboat (100 feet long) (AR)	45493.5	60692.8	32-28.790	80-00.373
Tugboat (65 feet long) (AR)	45524.0	61121.3	32-01.160	80-30.300
Tugboat (65 feet long) AR	45350.8	59580.4	33-25.652	78-33.293
Tugboat (90 feet long) (AR)	45319.1	60317.4	32-32.589	79-19.244
Tugboat (90 feet long) (AR)	45319.6	60318.5	32-32.595	79-19.343
Tugboat (90 feet long) (AR)	45320.3	60319.6	32-32.636	79-19.504
Tugboat (90 feet long) (AR)	45492.6	60692.4	32-28.858	80-00.301
Tugboat (AR)	45418.9	59737.7	33-25.389	78-51.609
Tugboat (AR)	45363.2	59996.7		
Tugboat (AR)	45363.3	59997.0		
Tugboat (AR)	45438.1	60370.0		
Tugboat (AR)	45492.5	60693.7		
Tugboat (AR)	45494.3	60694.4		
Tugboat (AR)	45545.7	61174.4		
Two Pair	45567.3	61140.2		
Unknown Schooner	45177.7	59713.6	32-54.694	78-19.693
Vermilion (460-foot Victory ship) AR	45265.8	59835.5	32-57.553	78-40.044
Virginius	45301.5	59205.0	33-43.473	78-00.872
Weehawken	45510.8	60528.1		
Whistling Wind	44487.5	59124.9		
William Lawrence	45596.8	61103.5	32-11.658	80-35.024
Wreck	45014.8	59111.0		
Wreck	44402.9	59140.4		
Wreck	44803.2	59273.1		
Wreck	44668.5	59292.8		
Wreck	44532.1	59362.5		
Wreck	45216.0	59419.0		
Wreck	45299.8	59733.5		
Wreck	45109.6	59967.8		
Wreck	44859.5	60003.1		
Wreck	45378.4	60044.8		
Wreck	45459.9	60115.6		
Wreck	45204.1	60483.4		
Wreck	45549.9	60522.2		
Wreck	45549.6	60523.5		
Wreck	45545.9	60528.0		

Wreck	45545.1	60531.1		
Wreck	45573.7	60965.6		
Wreck	45637.6	61301.0		
Wreck	45899.3	61361.6		
Wreck	45902.1	61363.1		
Wreck	45812.1	61365.8		
Wreck	45805.6	61368.7		
Wreck	46001.9	61405.0		
Wreck	45731.2	61405.2		
Wreck (165-feet long)	45201.8	59334.7		
Wreck (180-feet long)	45325.0	60325.0		
Y-73 (160-foot Ship) AR	45317.4	60316.1	32-32.459	79-18.993
YDS-68	45166.4	59369.4	33-17.925	77-47.888
YDT-16 (264-foot-long ship) (AR)			32-21.421	80-05.308
YO-224 (175-foot-long ship) (AR)			32-03.142	80-25.132
YO-225 (175-foot ship) (AR)			33-17.005	78-45.372
YOG-78 (175-foot ship) (AR)			32-56.906	78-54.849
YP-425	45614.0	61294.1		

LORAN / GPS NUMBERS - ASCENDING 5/6 LINE

T.A. Ward	44844.9	59006.0		
Modern Greece	45333.5	59042.3		
Arabian	45332.4	59046.0		
Louisiana	45331.6	59046.3		
Moorefield	45331.1	59047.4		
Aster	45329.7	59048.6		
Condor	45332.0	59048.6		
Feather	45330.3	59051.6		
Stormy Petrel	45330.0	59052.1		
Peterhoff	45323.0	59075.9		
Wreck	45014.8	59111.0		
Whistling Wind	44487.5	59124.9		
Wreck	44402.9	59140.4		
Mary Barry	44830.2	59144.8		
Rosin Wreck	45170.2	59156.7	33-35.391	77-27.205
Mary B. Baird	44653.4	59178.8		
George Weems	45216.1	59190.9	33-35.868	77-43.271
Brick Wreck	45252.7	59202.7	33-38.260	77-51.774
Virginius	45301.5	59205.0	33-43.473	78-00.872
Dirfys	45247.0	59211.9	33-37.026	77-51.502
Mount Dirfys	45247.0	59211.9	33-37.026	77-51.502
Marie Palmer	45261.2	59219.7		
Hang	45181.9	59236.9		
John Rose	44994.4	59269.2		
Wreck	44803.2	59273.1		
Raritan	45248.2	59275.2	33-32.504	77-56.935

City of Houston	45170.6	59281.6	33-24.305	77-42.731
Houston	45170.6	59281.6	33-24.305	77-42.731
Wreck	44668.5	59292.8		
Stonewall Jackson	44711.1	59322.1		
Wreck (165-feet long)	45201.8	59334.7		
D. Howard Spear	44931.9	59336.3		
Chris's Wreck	45224.8	59353.8		
Lady Margaret	45224.8	59353.8		
Wreck	44532.1	59362.5		
YDS-68	45166.4	59369.4	33-17.925	77-47.888
18 Fathom Wreck	45138.6	59398.2	33-12.120	77-47.545
Ore Freighter	45138.6	59398.2	33-12.120	77-47.545
Runa	45138.6	59398.2	33-12.120	77-47.545
ST-541	45185.5	59408.5	33-16.236	77-56.745
Landing Craft (AR)	45385.9	59414.0		
Barracuda Alley (AR)	45386.4	59415.5	33-41.963	78-26.798
Landing Craft (AR)	45386.9	59417.4		
Landing Craft (AR)	45386.5	59418.5	33-41.987	78-26.620
Wreck	45216.0	59419.0		
Mance Lassiter (tug) AR	45262.4	59433.4		
General Sherman	45413.3	59455.7	33-43.710	78-32.495
Sherman	45413.3	59455.7	33-43.710	78-32.495
Civil War Wreck	45333.6	59483.4	33-29.510	78-24.624
Suwanee	45333.6	59483.4	33-29.510	78-24.624
BP-25 (160-foot tanker) AR	45306.0	59551.4	33-21.298	78-25.550
Doris Kellogg	44954.2	59566.8		
Tugboat (65 feet long) AR	45350.8	59580.4	33-25.652	78-33.293
Landing Craft (AR)	45350.0	59581.7	33-25.550	78-33.381
Landing Craft (AR)	45350.6	59581.9	33-25.651	78-33.554
Shrimp Boat (AR)	45351.8	59582.5	33-25.673	78-33.577
Landing Craft (AR)	45351.9	59582.6	33-25.462	78-33.275
Landing Craft (AR)	45350.5	59583.5	33-25.417	78-33.471
T.J. Don	44567.9	59608.6		
Hebe	45237.4	59612.7	33-08.451	78-20.421
St. Cathan	45238.1	59616.6	33-08.303	78-20.789
Governor (possibly)	45301.1	59628.6	33-15.627	78-30.165
Pipe Wreck (Governor ?)	45301.1	59628.6	33-15.627	78-30.165
North Carolina	45372.2	59650.6	33-24.185	78-40.557
Sailing Yacht	45146.7	59685.6	32-52.909	78-13.031
Composite Wreck	45177.7	59713.6	32-54.694	78-19.693
Percy Thomson	45177.7	59713.6	32-54.694	78-19.693
Unknown Schooner	45177.7	59713.6	32-54.694	78-19.693
Wreck	45299.8	59733.5		
Barge (AR)	45418.7	59737.1	33-30.930	78-57.999
A-7 Airplane (AR)	45418.9	59737.6	33-55.387	78-51.605
Tugboat (AR)	45418.9	59737.7	33-25.389	78-51.609
Camel	45426.8	59741.3		
Ten Mile Reef Wreck	45427.1	59741.3		
200-foot ship (AR)	45427.4	59742.0	33-26.407	78-52.807
Landing Craft (AR)	45426.5	59742.6		
Barge (AR)	45463.7	59761.1	33-25.390	78-51.608
City of St. Helens	44890.8	59761.5		
Barge (AR)	45464.8	59762.1		
Barge (AR)	45463.0	59763.0		
Landing Craft (AR)	45464.1	59763.2		
Golden Liner	45481.8	59792.2		

Rover	45481.8	59792.2		
Juan Casiano	44892.6	59806.4		
Landing Craft (AR)	45457.0	59814.0		
Landing Craft (AR)	45457.3	59814.6	33-26.082	79-00.686
Landing Craft (AR)	45456.9	59814.7	33-26.100	79-00.749
Landing Craft (AR)	45456.9	59814.7		
Vermilion (460-foot Victory ship) AR	45265.8	59835.5	32-57.553	78-40.044
George MacDonald	44996.5	59851.5		
YO-225 (175-foot ship) (AR)			33-17.005	78-45.372
Barge (62 feet long) (AR)	45411.8	59881.1	33-12.760	79-05.346
Barge (62 feet long) (AR)	45411.4	59881.5	33-12.730	79-05.205
130-foot Barge (AR)			33-12.727	79-05.313
Torungen (100-foot ship) AR	45410.2	59882.2		
Landing Craft (AR)	45411.3	59883.0		
Rose	45481.5	59899.4		
City of Richmond	45343.8	59925.6	33-01.900	78-55.423
Liverpool	45471.2	59933.1		
Prince of Wales	45471.2	59933.1		
Barge (AR)	45425.3	59936.7		
Barge (AR)	45426.0	59937.7		
Barge (AR)	45426.1	59937.8		
140-foot Barge (AR)	45381.4	59942.5	33-05.931	79-00.751
130-foot Barge (AR)	45321.0	59955.3	32-56.818	78-54.643
YOG-78 (175-foot ship) (AR)			32-56.906	78-54.849
Wreck	45109.6	59967.8		
Georgetown Rock	45136.0	59968.0		
Big Rock	45138.0	59975.0		
Landing Craft (AR)	45363.4	59996.0		
Dredge Barge (AR)	45463.2	59996.2		
Tugboat (AR)	45363.2	59996.7		
Tugboat (AR)	45363.3	59997.0		
Wreck	44859.5	60003.1		
Landing Craft (AR)	45379.3	60026.2		
Barge (AR)	45378.7	60026.5		
Hector	45380.3	60027.1	32-59.984	79-06.108
Dolphin (65-foot tugboat) (AR)			32-59.852	79-02.330
Barges (AR)	45379.8	60027.3		
120-foot Barge (AR)			32-45.087	79-34.486
Wreck	45378.4	60044.8		
Wreck	45459.9	60115.6		
Anchor Wreck	45314.6	60179.0	32-41.269	79-09.280
F.J. Luckenbach	45314.6	60179.0		
Screw Steamer	45314.6	60179.0		
Frances Canady	45003.4	60246.3		
Petrel	45265.4	60253.9		
Ammo Dump	45115.0	60315.0		
Carolina Sea Channel	45115.0	60315.0		
240-foot Barge (AR)			32-33.354	79-40.299
Y-73 (160-foot Ship) AR	45317.4	60316.1	32-32.459	79-18.993
Tugboat (90 feet long) (AR)	45319.1	60317.4	32-32.589	79-19.244
Tugboat (90 feet long) (AR)	45319.6	60318.5	32-32.595	79-19.343
Tugboat (90 feet long) (AR)	45320.3	60319.6	32-32.636	79-19.504
Robison (437-foot-long destroyer) (AR)			32-29.271	80-00.074
110-foot & 120-foot Barges (AR)			32-28.778	80-00.556
Wreck (180-feet long)	45325.0	60325.0		
200-foot Barge (AR)			32-28.749	80-00.104

Comanche (160-foot CG Cutter) AR	45295.1	60350.4	32-27.395	79-19.073
Barge (150 feet long) (AR)	45439.8	60366.9	32-44.965	79-34.484
Barge (100 feet long) (AR)	45439.9	60367.2	32-44.405	79-34.507
Pathfinder (90-foot Ship) AR	45437.5	60368.6	32-44.539	79-34.345
YDT-16 (264-foot-long ship) (AR)			32-21.421	80-05.308
Landing Craft (AR)	45438.2	60369.0		
Landing Craft (AR)	45438.1	60369.7		
Lark (AR)	45437.7	60369.7		
Landing Craft (AR)	45438.2	60370.0		
Tugboat (AR)	45438.1	60370.0		
Landing Craft (AR)	45438.3	60370.5		
Caisson Wreck (Drydock) AR	45437.9	60371.0		
Trawler	45490.5	60437.0		
Tropic	45490.1	60450.1		
Georgiana	45498.3	60454.1		
Mary Bowers	45500.3	60456.0		
Norseman	45505.5	60457.3		
Constance	45499.4	60458.4		
Nellie	45510.2	60470.7		
Frederick W. Day	45427.7	60471.7	32-36.025	79-40.141
Barges (AR)	45481.2	60479.4		
Barge (AR)	45480.6	60479.5		
Barge (AR)	45481.6	60480.2		
Rattlesnake	45510.7	60481.3		
Wreck	45204.1	60483.4		
Hang	45470.4	60501.0		
Karsnaes (Schooner)	45500.9	60503.4		
Flamingo	45510.8	60507.8		
Raccoon	45512.2	60509.4		
Prince Albert	45516.0	60509.6		
Celt (160 feet long)	45518.9	60513.6		
Flora (200 feet long)	45515.2	60514.0		
Stono	45518.5	60514.2		
Beatrice (200 feet long)	45518.1	60514.7		
Presto	45518.1	60514.7		
Robert B. Howlett	45496.8	60515.7		
Daventry (false)	45496.4	60517.9		
John Randolph	45525.5	60517.9		
Barge	45527.2	60518.7		
Patapsco	45523.5	60521.9		
Wreck	45549.9	60522.2		
Acteon	45520.7	60522.6		
Wreck	45549.6	60523.5		
Wreck	45545.9	60528.0		
Weehawken	45510.8	60528.1		
Wreck	45545.1	60531.1		
Etiwan	45529.1	60531.6		
Hang	45468.3	60535.2		
Keokuk	45507.6	60542.2		
Ruby	45510.8	60557.2		
Fred W. Chase	45499.8	60563.2		
Thomas Watson	45518.3	60628.8		
Larch	45523.2	60634.1		
Barge (300 feet long) (AR)	45495.4	60688.1	32-29.531	80-00.200
Barge (260 feet long) (AR)	45494.9	60688.3	32-29.436	80-00.243
Barge (62 feet long) (AR)	45493.6	60690.1	32-29.159	80-00.262

Deckhouse (AR)	45381.6	60690.5	32-14.925	79-50.355
Barge (100 feet long) (AR)	45491.2	60691.4	32-28.790	80-00.402
Researcher (100-foot ship) AR	45382.7	60692.2	32-14.958	79-50.545
Tugboat (90 feet long) (AR)	45492.6	60692.4	32-28.858	80-00.301
Tugboat (100 feet long) (AR)	45493.5	60692.8	32-28.790	80-00.373
Drydock (AR)	45493.2	60693.4	32-28.858	80-00.402
Tugboat (AR)	45492.5	60693.7		
Life Boats (AR)	45491.1	60693.8		
Barge (AR)	45492.9	60693.9		
Landing Craft (AR)	45493.5	60694.0		
Tugboat (AR)	45494.3	60694.4		
Barge (AR)	45493.7	60695.3		
Haban (Tugboat) AR	45380.2	60699.0		
150-foot Barge (AR)	45529.8	60729.3	32-31.060	80-05.955
110-foot Barge (AR)	45530.6	60731.1	32-31.035	80-06.104
Page (300-foot Ship (AR)	45485.0	60780.0	32-21.542	80-05.284
Dee	45581.8	60871.2		
Semarca 40 (Tug) AR	45258.5	60952.5	31-42.434	79-58.281
Hopper Barge (AR)	45262.4	60953.1	31-42.878	79-58.577
Landing Craft (AR)	45525.4	60964.6	32-13.120	80-20.497
Barge (100 feet long) (AR)	45524.0	60964.7	32-12.920	80-20.360
Landing Craft (AR)	45525.6	60965.1		
40-foot Barge (AR)			32-18.868	80-42.537
Wreck	45573.7	60965.6		
Barge (40 feet long) (AR)	45546.1	60969.0	32-15.600	80-22.440
Fripp Drydock (100 feet long)	45566.6	60981.3	32-15.408	80-22.407
Dump Scow (AR)	45102.2	61008.5	31-21.525	79-50.403
Betsy Ross (430-foot Liberty ship) AR	45504.3	61062.8	32-03.285	80-24.996
General Gordon	45580.1	61096.0	32-10.107	80-33.212
William Lawrence	45596.8	61103.5	32-11.658	80-35.024
30-foot Barge (AR)			32-10.030	80-32.560
YO-224 (175-foot-long ship) (AR)			32-03.142	80-25.132
Tugboat (65 feet long) (AR)	45524.0	61121.3	32-01.160	80-30.300
Landing Craft (AR)	45524.2	61122.8	32-01.174	80-30.494
Landing Craft (AR)	45524.7	61123.1	32-01.424	80-30.578
Two Pair	45567.3	61140.2		
Tugboat (AR)	45545.7	61174.4		
Barge (AR)	45545.4	61176.7	31-59.923	80-35.892
Barge (AR)	45547.7	61177.8	32-00.179	80-36.015
Boat (AR)	45549.5	61177.8	32-00.152	80-36.006
Landing Craft (AR)	45551.0	61179.8		
Landing Craft (AR)	45548.6	61181.1		
Delia Maria	45609.8	61200.8		
Boiler Wreck	45609.8	61200.9		
Gaskin Wreck	45609.8	61200.9		
Barge (AR)	45613.8	61241.0	32-03.060	80-45.020
Barge (AR)	45613.2	61242.1		
Henry Bacon (Dredge) AR	45480.0	61264.7	31-45.385	80-36.543
Delta Diamond (Tug) AR	45477.0	61265.8	31-44.948	80-36.405
Latex (Barge) AR	45480.9	61266.1	31-45.379	80-36.700
Sayler (Barge) AR	45479.4	61266.1	31-45.200	80-36.596
Senasqua (Tug) AR	45479.3	61268.3	31-45.030	80-36.721
Gypsy Queen (65 feet long)	45659.3	61277.6		
Barge	45611.3	61282.5		
YP-425	45614.0	61294.1		
Wreck	45637.6	61301.0		

Matt Turecamo (Tug) AR	45489.6	61308.8	31-43.200	80-40.170
Deck Barge (AR)	45585.5	61310.5	31-54.370	80-47.207
Deck Barge w/Work Boat (AR)	45585.4	61311.1	31-54.299	80-47.229
SMS Warehouse Barge (AR)	45492.4	61312.7	31-43.220	80-40.638
Deck Barge (AR)	45495.3	61317.8	31-43.180	80-41.166
Deck Barge (AR)	45561.2	61319.6	31-50.775	80-46.015
Barnstable	45520.5	61320.4		
Honey (Barge) AR	45563.7	61321.1	31-50.944	80-46.290
Deck Barge (AR)	45489.9	61324.6	31-42.039	80-41.241
Motherlode (Barge) AR	45563.9	61324.6	31-50.699	80-46.533
Dump Scow (AR)	45562.8	61325.5	31-50.502	80-46.507
Jupiter (Sailboat) AR	45560.4	61325.6	31-50.211	80-46.343
Olympics (Barge) AR	45558.6	61326.6	31-49.904	80-46.260
Wreck	45899.3	61361.6		
Wreck	45902.1	61363.1		
Tug	45809.8	61364.9		
Barge	45809.3	61365.7		
Wreck	45812.1	61365.8		
Wreck	45805.6	61368.7		
Georgia (Ram)	45724.3	61391.2		
Wreck	46001.9	61405.0		
Wreck	45731.2	61405.2		
Janet (Ferry Boat) AR	45497.1	61411.7	31-36.298	80-47.575
Sagebrush (Buoy Tender) AR	45500.0	61412.0	31-36.600	80-47.800
Addie Bagley Daniels (Liberty Ship, Sterr Section) AR	45497.5	61412.8	31-36.260	80-47.680
Elmira (Tug) AR	45496.0	61413.0	31-36.082	80-47.673
Addie Bagley Daniels (Liberty Ship, Main Section) AR	45497.8	61413.8	31-36.207	80-47.750
Rio Apon (Tug) AR	45517.1	61428.1	31-36.180	80-49.364
Modena (Barge) AR	45545.3	61551.1	31-31.061	81-00.132
Barge Wreckage (AR)	45613.2	61555.1	31-38.536	81-04.885
Rio Caroni (Tug) AR	45445.4	61598.0	31-16.370	80-57.058
R/V Zapala (AR)	45457.5	61601.3	31-17.441	80-58.021
John Bird (AR)	45461.0	61608.9	31-17.232	80-58.765
Mac Tide 21 (Tug) AR	45344.1	61681.0	30-59.269	80-57.153
Edwin S. Nettleton (Liberty Ship) AR	45349.6	61685.7	30-58.704	80-58.562
Recife (Tug) AR	45345.9	61691.7	30-58.617	80-58.034
Mary Lou (crew boat) AR	45533.5	61695.7	31-18.422	81-09.180
Striker (Work Boat) AR	45348.1	61700.3	30-58.198	80-58.800
Tampa (Tug) AR	45348.0	61700.3	30-58.203	80-58.804
Optimist (Landing Craft) AR	45381.1	61722.9	30-59.928	81-02.308
Scalper (Landing Craft) AR	45380.6	61723.2	30-59.862	81-02.298
Landing Craft (AR)	45481.7	61782.7	31-05.939	81-12.255
Landing Craft (AR)	45483.0	61784.6	31-05.926	81-12.483
Esparta	45375.3	61832.2	30-50.850	81-10.155

Books by the Author
Fiction

Vietnam	Science Fiction
Lonely Conflict	*Entropy*
	Return to Mars
Action/Adventure	*Silent Autumn*
Memory Lane	The Time Dragons Trilogy
Mind Set	*A Time for Dragons*
Supernatural	*Dragons Past*
The Lurking	*No Future for Dragons*

Nonfiction

Advanced Wreck Diving Guide	*Track of the Gray Wolf*
Ultimate Wreck Diving Guide	*Shipwrecks of New Jersey*
Shipwrecks of Delaware and Maryland (1990)	*Wilderness Canoeing*

Order the following titles directly from: GARY GENTILE PRODUCTIONS
Shipping: $3 per order (not per book)   P.O. Box 57137
Nonfiction
Philadelphia, PA 19111

- $25 *Andrea Doria: Dive to an Era* (hard cover)
- $20 *The Nautical Cyclopedia*
- $20 *USS San Diego: the Last Armored Cruiser*
- $20 *Wreck Diving Adventures*
- $20 *Primary Wreck Diving Guide*
- $30 *The Technical Diving Handbook*
- $30 *Great Lakes Shipwrecks: a Photographic Odyssey*

Civil War ironclad *Monitor*
- $25 Book (hard cover) *Ironclad Legacy: Battles of the USS Monitor*
- $25 Videotape (NTSC/VHS): *The Battle for the USS Monitor*

The *Lusitania* Controversies (hard covers)
(These two volumes cover the evolution of wreck-diving from 1955 to 1995)
- $25 Book One: *Atrocity of War and a Wreck-Diving History*
- $25 Book Two: *Dangerous Descents into Shipwrecks and Law*

The Popular Dive Guide Series
- $20 *Shipwrecks of New York*
- $20 *Shipwrecks of New Jersey: North*
- $20 *Shipwrecks of New Jersey: Central*
- $20 *Shipwrecks of New Jersey: South*
- $20 *Shipwrecks of Delaware and Maryland* (2002 Edition)
- $20 *Shipwrecks of Virginia*
- $20 *Shipwrecks of North Carolina: from the Diamond Shoals North*
- $20 *Shipwrecks of North Carolina: from Hatteras Inlet South*
- $20 *Shipwrecks of South Carolina and Georgia*

Wreck Diving Adventure Novel
- $20 *The Peking Papers* (hard cover)

Website: http://www.ggentile.com